THE ROMAN SHORE FORTS

COASTAL DEFENCES OF SOUTHERN BRITAIN

ANDREW PEARSON

TEMPUS

First published 2002

PUBLISHED IN THE UNITED KINGDOM BY:

Tempus Publishing Ltd
The Mill, Brimscombe Port
Stroud, Gloucestershire GL5 2QG
www.tempus-publishing.com

PUBLISHED IN THE UNITED STATES OF AMERICA BY:

Tempus Publishing Inc.
2 Cumberland Street
Charleston, SC 29401
1-888-313-2665
www.tempuspublishing.com

British Library Cataloguing in Publication Data.
A catalogue record for this book is available from the British Library.

ISBN 0 7524 1949 8

Typesetting and origination by Tempus Publishing.
PRINTED AND BOUND IN GREAT BRITAIN

Contents

Acknowledgements

In the writing of this book, I owe an enormous debt of thanks to numerous people. The present work was born out of a PhD thesis written at Reading University between 1996 and 1999. Although what is contained within these pages amounts to a far more general discussion of the Shore Forts, significant elements of the thesis have been incorporated, notably within Chapters 4 and 5. Foremost my thanks go to Mike Fulford and John Allen, whose advice and encouragement from the outset of my studies has been invaluable, and without whom neither the PhD nor this book could ever have been completed. Many other staff and students, at Reading and elsewhere, as well as individuals within the professional and amateur branches of archaeology, have also given unsparingly of their time and expertise. In particular I would like to thank the following: Martin Bell, Cheryl Bishop, Barry Cunliffe, Janet DeLaine, David Gurney, Maria Medlycott, John Potter, Stephen Rippon, Bruce Sellwood, Ruth Shaffrey and Matthew Woodman. Thanks also to the members of the Hertfordshire Archaeological Trust, for providing a scholarly and stimulating working environment during my time with them.

Early drafts of the book were kindly read by Mike Fulford and Sue Pearson, and their comments have been much appreciated. Any remaining errors of fact or interpretation are, of course, my own. The illustrations benefited greatly from the use of Casella Science and Environment's computing facilities. My thanks also go to Nick and Carol King for their hospitality during the writing of this book, and to my partner Iona for her support throughout. Above all, I wish to acknowledge my parents; without their unfailing encouragement and assistance over many years the present study could never have been accomplished. It is to them that this book is dedicated.

Cardiff
September 2001

List of illustrations and tables

Text figures

Colour plates

1   The church of St Mary the Virgin, Brancaster
2   The site of the Brancaster Shore Fort
3   The south wall, Burgh Castle
4   Fallen bastion and wall, Burgh Castle
5   St Peter's chapel, Bradwell
6   Reused Roman stone in the Saxon chapel of St Peter, Bradwell
7   The east wall, Reculver
8   Facing stones in the south wall, Reculver
9   The south gate, Reculver
10 The west wall, Richborough
11 The north wall, Richborough
12 Romney Marsh and the ruins of the Roman fort at Lympne
13 Bastion on the north wall, Lympne
14 The west wall, Pevensey
15 Tower on the west wall, Pevensey
16 Roman facing on the north wall, Portchester
17 The Roman lighthouse, Dover
18 Detail of the west wall, Richborough
19 Interval bastion on the east wall, Burgh Castle
20 Lincolnshire Limestone, St Peter's chapel, Bradwell
21 Kentish ragstone, Lympne
22 The west gate, Richborough
23 The church of St Mary, Reculver
24 The church of St John the Baptist, Reedham
25 The medieval castle, Pevensey

Tables

A   Summary of transport requirements for the building of the Shore Forts
B   Estimated labour for the building of the Shore Forts
C   Average labour forces for the building of the forts at Dover and Pevensey
D   Average labour forces for the building of the later Shore Forts

Introduction

During the third century AD, the Romans built a series of stone forts on the East Anglian and southern coasts of Britain. These installations were to form a vital component of the coastal network throughout the late Roman period; listed clockwise, they are Brancaster, Caister-on-Sea, Burgh Castle, Walton Castle, Bradwell, Reculver, Richborough, Dover, Lympne, Pevensey and Portchester (**1**). During the last years of the fourth century, or the first years of the fifth, nine of these eleven monuments came to be listed in the document known as the *Notitia Dignitatum*, where they were recorded under the command of the 'count of the Saxon Shore'. Both the title and the monuments themselves have proved remarkably enduring. Today the 'Saxon Shore Forts' survive within the modern landscape as some of the finest, and certainly some of the most substantial, Roman remains in Britain.

Many authors on Roman Britain find themselves compelled to justify the need for yet another book on their particular subject. This, I would contend, is not necessary in the case of the Shore Forts. In the post-war years there have been only two single-author works on the monuments, namely Donald White's *Litus Saxonicum* (1961) and Stephen Johnson's *The Roman Forts of the Saxon Shore* (1976). Two edited volumes on the subject have been produced more recently, in 1977 and 1989, both titled *The Saxon Shore*. During the two and a half decades since the publication of Johnson's work the subject has moved on significantly. Archaeological investigations have brought – and continue to bring – new information to light about many of the sites. The writing up of old, previously unpublished investigations, notably those of Charles Green at Burgh Castle and Caister, has also added greatly to our understanding. The report on the latter site has succeeded in adding an eleventh 'Shore Fort' to our list, when previously there was considered to have been only ten.

The present book is, at least in part, concerned with the same basic questions as Johnson, and indeed most scholars before him who wrote on the Shore Forts. Who built the monuments, when, and why? How did they operate, who garrisoned them, and for how long? For Johnson, the answer – at least to that of function – was relatively obvious. Barbarian piracy was rife, he argued, and his study set out to elucidate the nature of the threat, and to explain how the 'Saxon Shore' was created and operated to counter that danger. Johnson's views remain dominant in the literature, but perceptions are beginning to change. The notion of the Shore Forts as an anti-pirate scheme now seems less satisfactory, particularly because there is actually little evidence for any large-scale maritime threat to Britain. The *raison d'être* for the Shore Forts is, therefore, perhaps far less clear-cut than has commonly been supposed. In recent years a number of scholars have taken a different view of the military situation in late Roman Britain, and have offered alternative reasons for the existence of the Shore Forts. While I do find the new arguments to be persuasive, particularly the theory that the sites served as ports rather than a defensive system, it is not yet possible to reach a final conclusion on the subject. Nor are the supposedly conflicting roles necessarily mutually exclusive. For this reason I have chosen not to nail my colours to any particular mast, and have merely set out the debate as it presently stands.

I have, however, placed much greater emphasis on what might be termed the economic and social aspects of the monuments. The Saxons, if they came at all to the coast of Roman Britain, were probably only a nagging, intermittent threat, rather than an ever-present danger. By contrast, the occupation of the forts was a day-to-day reality which extended over a period of two centuries in some cases. For this reason I have devoted considerable space in Chapter 7 to the character of the habitation, both within the forts, and beyond them in their extra-mural areas. I have gone no further 'beyond the walls' of the installations, although the relationship between the forts and their hinterlands is one which is worthy of future investigation.

In the discussion of these subjects it is sometimes difficult to avoid the impression that our understanding of the forts is vastly outweighed by the gaps in our knowledge. This is not the case, but it is certainly true that significant questions still remain. The potential for archaeology to provide new answers about the Shore Forts in the future is very considerable, but I suspect that we are many years – perhaps generations – away from possessing a satisfactory data set. The partial destruction of the monuments must also lead to some pessimism as to how far the excavated data will be able to take us. Partly because of this situation I have turned to other sources of data, for these have the potential to enhance our understanding of the traditional issues of date, function and operation. Crucially, they also enable us to broaden our outlook on the monuments, and to ask new questions. One example is Chapter 4, which draws extensively from the fields of quantity surveying and geology in order to examine the construction of the Shore Forts. Here we can look beyond the reasons why the installations might have been built, to understand how these monuments were actually created. Similarly, the following chapter addresses the ancient landscape of the installations, a study that once again relies on geological data as well as archaeological information. Overall, I hope that this inter-disciplinary approach, combining science with more traditional archaeological and historical methods, has enabled a truer and more complete understanding of what the installations were like, and how they operated within the Roman world.

Turning to technical matters, the title and the scope of this book require some justification. I have not employed the term 'Saxon Shore Forts', either as part of the book title or within the text itself. The name is derived from the *Notitia Dignitatum*, a document compiled at a late, but somewhat uncertain date, for an unknown reason, and which does not always accurately reflect the true situation on the ground. I have severe misgivings as to whether, during their operational lifetime, the installations ever had much to do with the Saxons, and suspect that they had even less connection with the *Notitia*. Thus, while Johnson afforded the *Notitia* a central place in his argument, I have confined it to where I feel it best belongs, which is to say in discussions of the late fourth or early fifth century. Despite this, the term 'Saxon Shore' is, as Peter Salway has commented, 'a thoroughly unsatisfactory title, but one that is completely entrenched'. I have, nevertheless, omitted the prefix 'Saxon' wherever possible.

The main geographical focus of the work is confined – as many writings on the Shore Forts have been – to military monuments ranged along the coast between the Wash and the Solent. I recognise that this scope is rather restricted, and once again I would repeat my doubts that the command described by the *Notitia* was accurately represented by anything in reality. In outlining the context of the Shore Forts in Chapter 3, I hope to dispel the idea that the installations were in any way isolated, promoting instead the notion that they were part of a far wider, coherent coastal system that extended around the shores of Britain and north Gaul. Nevertheless, this book is intended to be a 'monument-based' study, and as such there are more than sufficient data from the eleven 'Shore Forts' to occupy the available space. I would argue that the omission of the installations on the Gallic 'Saxon Shore' from the main discussion is excusable on the grounds that, militarily, they may have had far less to do with the British forts than many scholars have previously supposed. For this reason, therefore, they can probably be safely disengaged from their British 'counterparts'.

There is a vast amount that could be said about the Shore Forts, and the scope of this book is necessarily limited. Others would doubtless have placed emphasis on different aspects from those that I have chosen, and I envisage that some of the ideas I have put across will meet with disagreement. I would hope, however, that this book encourages a necessary, broad-based approach to the Shore Forts in the future.

1   The monuments

The purpose of this initial chapter is to describe the Shore Forts, as they were during the Roman period – at least insofar as the surviving remains and the archaeology of each site makes this possible – and as they are in the modern day. In so doing, many themes are encountered to which later chapters will return, particularly the dates of construction, the architecture, the internal arrangements, and the history of activity both within the fort, and in the areas beyond the defences. Previous works on the subject have normally addressed only ten monuments ranged along Britain's south and East Anglian coasts. Here, however, an eleventh site at Caister-on-Sea is also considered, due to the fact that the character of this site gives it equal claim to having been an integral part of the military coastal network.

Brancaster

The site of the fort lies on the picturesque north Norfolk coast, between the villages of Brancaster and Brancaster Staithe. Robbing of the fort walls for building stone had already begun by the medieval period, evidence for which can be seen in the nearby Brancaster parish church, where ashlar blocks (probably facing stones taken from the perimeter defences) were used in the south wall of the twelfth-century chancel (**colour plate 1**).[1] Despite this, the Roman masonry is known to have remained substantially intact well into the Early Modern period, Spelman's *Icenia* (written *c*.1600) recording that the walls stood to a height of 3.6m (12ft). For the modern visitor, however, there are now virtually no visible remains of the fort. The pace of demolition quickened from the mid-eighteenth century onwards, and much stone was taken for the construction of a great malthouse at Brancaster Staithe, itself later demolished. Writing in 1775, Blomefield commented that the fort still stood, but soon this was no longer so; in 1788 another visitor to the site recorded that 'the walls were all erased'.[2]

No masonry is now visible above ground, though Roman building stone and tile fragments lie scattered across the fort site and in neighbouring fields. The destruction has in fact been so thorough that Lee-Warner, the first excavator of the site in 1846, had to devote most of his efforts to re-discovering the plan of the defences, which he achieved by tracing the line of the perimeter ditch. Where Lee-Warner actually excavated the wall, mostly on the north and east sides of the fort, he rarely found it standing above the level of the foundations and in places it had been totally destroyed.[3] Later investigations in 1935, concentrating on the western parts of the fort, and in particular on the west wall itself, encountered a similar situation. The

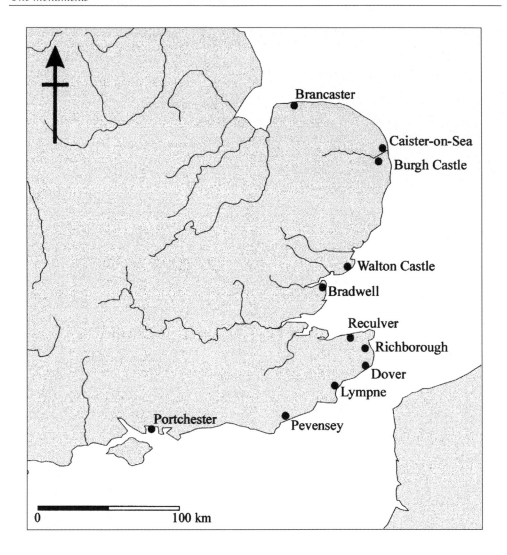

1   The Saxon Shore Forts

excavator, St Joseph, concluded that the northern half of the west wall had been entirely destroyed; his attempts to locate masonry on the south wall also met with failure.[4] Although Lee-Warner had noted stonework *in situ* on either side of the west gate, here St Joseph found only the robbed foundation trench. Lee-Warner claimed that his barn at Thorplands (near Fakenham, Norfolk) was built with blocks from the *porta decumana*, and ironically it may have been he that was responsible for the final demolition of the west gate.

At ground level only the eastern ditch of the fort is now easily recognisable, preserved as a distinct roll in the ground (**colour plate 2**). However, the fort appears clearly on aerial photographs, which also show it to have been associated with a sizeable extra-mural settlement or *vicus* (**2, 70**).[5] The Shore Fort seems to adhere to

2   *Aerial photograph of the Roman site at Brancaster, looking east. The square plan of the fort defences can be seen in the lower part of the photograph, whilst beyond them, at a slightly different orientation, are the ditches and trackways of the extra-mural settlement.*
Photo by Derek A. Edwards. Copyright Norfolk Museums and Archaeology Service

the traditional design apparent in most Roman forts of the second and early third centuries in Britain, for example those on Hadrian's Wall. The defences are virtually square in plan, with rounded corners, internal angle towers and with a substantial earth rampart against the inside of the perimeter wall (**3**). The wall, 2.9m wide and enclosing an area of 2.56ha (6.3 acres), was considered by St Joseph to have risen to its full height without any internal offsets, but in truth the lack of surviving masonry to any great height prevents judgement on this issue. Projecting bastions and other

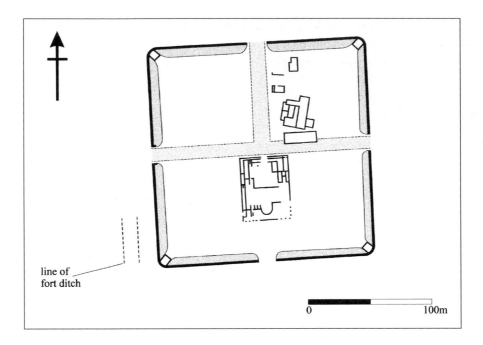

line of
fort ditch

0   100m

3   The fort at Brancaster. The internal buildings show as cropmarks on aerial photographs

design features such as bonding courses (horizontal courses of brick, or occasionally stone, built at vertical intervals up the wall in order to tie the shallow facing into the mass of the core) are noticeably lacking at Brancaster. Such features are very prominent in many of the Shore Forts built after *c*.260, and their absence at Brancaster is commonly used as an argument for the fort having been built during the early third century. In Chapter 3, however, we shall see that the archaeological evidence for its construction is rather more ambiguous. Building could have taken place as late as the 260s, though an earlier date remains most probable. Inside the defences, aerial photographs show the *principia* (headquarters building) situated in traditional fashion within the central range, while in the northern half of the fort several other structures show as cropmarks. During his excavations St Joseph encountered traces of other structures in the south-west quarter of the fort; these consisted of two phases of floors and stone foundations, now dated to the late fourth century.

There is good evidence to suggest that there was a military installation at Brancaster prior to the establishment of the Shore Fort. Investigation of the extra-mural settlement shows that activity there began during the second century,[6] and the fact that the field systems and roads of the *vicus* have a slightly different orientation from that of the Shore Fort defences also emphasises their separate origin. The site of any earlier fort has not been proven, but aerial photographs show a large building within the area now encompassed by the Shore Fort, considered likely to have been the *praetorium* (commander's residence). This structure is not aligned with the Shore Fort defences but with the extra-mural settlement, and may well relate to a previous installation on the same site. A round-cornered, double-ditched rectilinear enclosure to the north, now partially enveloped by salt marsh, has also been proposed as an earlier fort, but is perhaps more likely to have simply been a large field.

Caister-on-Sea

Unobtrusively tucked away in the midst of a modern housing estate are the remains of the Roman fort at Caister-on-Sea (hereafter referred to as Caister). This site had for many years been considered to be a small civil settlement, perhaps a port to which goods destined for the major town of *Venta Icenorum* (Caistor-by-Norwich) would have been offloaded. However, recent work by Darling and Gurney has led to a reassessment of this view.[7] They point out that the morphology of the Caister defences compares well to that of the broadly contemporary Shore Forts at Brancaster and Reculver, and emphasise the general unsuitability of this isolated site for a civilian settlement. As discussed in Chapter 7 the archaeological finds from Caister, though not overwhelmingly 'military' in character, do not differ in any crucial respect from the assemblages yielded by the other Shore Forts. The present impression, therefore, is of a military installation rather than a walled town, and as such the site now has equal claim to the Roman name of *Gariannonum*, previously attributed to nearby Burgh Castle.

The stone defences of the fort survived into the seventeenth century, but appear to have been demolished by the 1720s. The site was completely levelled, and even the ditches were deliberately filled to make way for agriculture. Ploughing has doubtless obliterated much evidence of the Roman occupation; particularly vulnerable will have been those layers at a shallow depth relating to the final years of the fort. During the last century farmland gave way to building development, and much of the fort (including the central range where administrative buildings such as the *principia* were probably located) now lies under housing.

There is evidence of very limited Roman occupation prior to the construction of the Shore Fort, but the vast majority of activity relates to the third and fourth centuries. Building of the perimeter wall took place not earlier than the late second century, and more probably during the first years of the third century. There have been suggestions that defences of earth and timber were built very shortly before the erection of the stone perimeter, but the evidence for such a palisade is not completely convincing. As with Brancaster, the stone defences are of typical second- to early third-century style (4). The slightly off-square perimeter has rounded corners, the narrow, rectangular-profiled wall being backed by an earth rampart.[8] The defences, 2.9m wide, were constructed from local flint cobbles and other beach stone; bonding courses were not present, although a little brick was used in the south gatehouse. A square internal tower was found in the south-east corner, but corresponding towers are not thought to be present at the north-east or north-west angles. Two ditches surrounded the fort, the outer one of which was substantially widened at some stage, probably during the early fourth century. In the present day only parts of the south-

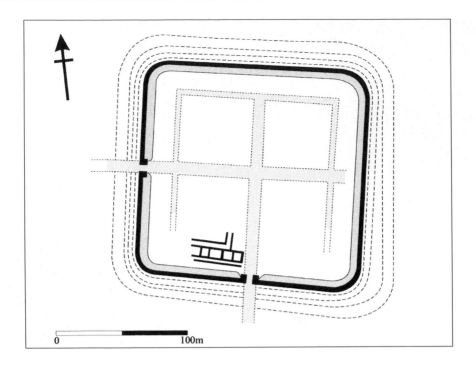

4   *The fort at Caister*

west quarter of the fort are exposed to view. A short section of the south wall and the south gatehouse are visible, though in the most westerly portion of the defences only the foundations remain. The stub of a wall that was built to retain the tail of the earth rampart also survives (**5**).

The interior of the fort was some 2.8ha (6.9 acres) in area, and excavations suggest regularly-planned internal arrangements. A series of metalled streets has been proven, and in the south-west quarter of the fort several stone buildings have been found, including the south wing of a large structure, which may have been a courtyard building. In existence by the late third century, originally as a luxurious domestic residence, this structure was to undergo significant modifications during its lifetime. It continued in use into the fourth century, and the evidence suggests that it was finally converted to serve in some industrial capacity, quite possibly for butchery and tanning. The existence, arrangement and history of buildings elsewhere within the fort has yet to be established, though the find of a heating flue close to the east defences suggests the presence of at least one more substantial structure. Beyond the defences there is evidence for significant activity, most of which was contemporary with the Shore Fort. A road leading from the south gate probably linked the fort to its harbour or beaching place, and it is in this area to the south of the defences that most activity appears to have been concentrated, although there may also have been limited habitation to the west.

5   *The southern wall of the defences at Caister. In the foreground is the gatehouse of the south gate*

Burgh Castle

Situated on a raised tongue of land on the edge of the Norfolk Broads, Burgh Castle overlooks the much-diminished 'Great Estuary', upon whose shores it once stood. Three sides of the defences now remain, including the entire east wall (**6, 7, colour plates 3 & 4**).[9] The south wall has survived particularly well, albeit leaning at a rather precarious angle in places. The facing of split flints set in pink *opus signinum* mortar is excellently preserved in places on the exterior face, but the interior of the defences has been badly robbed. The west wall once stood at the top of a gentle scarp, but has now tumbled down into the marshes below, where masonry fragments can still be seen in winter. Looking north-east through the gap created by its fall, the modern water tower at Caister-on-Sea is just visible across the Broads.

The construction of the fort, though imprecisely understood, dates to the period after 260. The fact that this installation was built somewhat later than the first group of Shore Forts (Caister, Reculver, and probably Brancaster) is reflected in the architecture of the defences. Burgh Castle exhibits a number of features that are clearly related to advances in Roman defensive technology which reached Britain from the continent during the later third century, of which more will be said in Chapter 4. In place of a regular shape, the fort has a trapezoidal quadrilateral plan, encompassing an area of 2.4ha (5.9 acres). Projecting bastions were

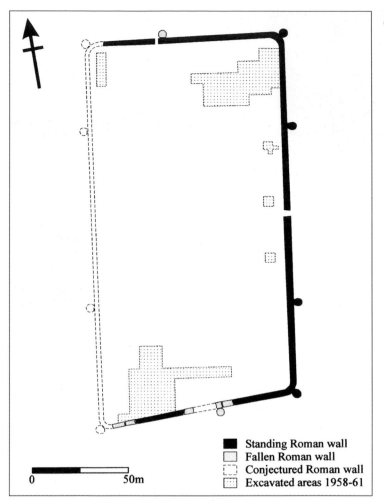

6   *The fort at*
     Burgh Castle

Standing Roman wall
Fallen Roman wall
Conjectured Roman wall
Excavated areas 1958-61

0   50m

present, of which there were probably originally ten, though only six now remain. The bastions are joined to the fort wall only in the higher levels, suggesting that they may have been an addition to the original structure, or that the builders were uncertain as to how this new design feature was to be incorporated. The corner bastions were imperfectly designed, as they did not project far enough beyond the line of the walls to provide an adequate field of fire. There have been suggestions of an internal tower in the north-east angle, and of an interval tower on the south wall, but the evidence for both of these structures is inconclusive. A major gate was centrally placed in the east wall and a postern can be found on the north wall. No other gates have been located.

The flint-faced and predominantly flint-cored wall still stands to heights above 4m. The inner face is not vertical, but is stepped in or tapered as it rises. This innovation allowed the wall to be free-standing, and unlike other Shore Forts such as Dover and Caister, an earth rampart was unnecessary. Triple bonding courses of brick were employed at close vertical intervals on the exterior face, and to a lesser extent

7   *The east wall, Burgh Castle*

on the interior, tying the shallow flint facing more securely to the core. The width of the wall varied around the circuit. Those parts close to the scarp (the west wall and western portions of the north and south walls) were 2.2m thick: the heavier east wall, built on more level ground, was 3.2m wide.

The interior of the fort has fared badly, having been quarried for clay and gravel up until the nineteenth century. The motte of a Norman castle, built against the fort's south wall, has been completely levelled by this practice. The site passed into state guardianship in 1926 but continued to be ploughed into the 1950s. Little is known of the Roman occupation of the interior, in part because of this destruction but also because of the limited amount of excavation within the defences. Traces of buildings have nevertheless been discovered in the north-east, north-west and south-west corners of the fort. The most recent investigations of the site have concentrated on the extra-mural area, and have revealed evidence for substantial activity outside the defences to the north, east and south.

Walton Castle

The Roman fort at Walton Castle, which stood on land a little to the north of modern Felixstowe, has been entirely destroyed by coastal erosion. However, although the last fragments of masonry were washed into the sea during the eighteenth century, a drawing and plan executed at about that time, supplemented by antiquarian descriptions, prove the existence of a late Roman fort on the site.[10]

19

The written observations date almost exclusively to the early eighteenth century, by which time a large part of the fort had already collapsed down the face of the eroding cliff. In 1722 a certain Dr Knight wrote to the Society of Antiquaries of London, describing a Roman monument to the east of Walton in the following terms:

> … tis 100 Yards long, five foot high above ground, 12 broad at each end turnd with an Angle. its composed of Pepple and Roman bricks in three courses. all around footsteps [?foundations] of buildings, & severall larg pieces of wall cast down upon the strand by the seas underming ye Cliff, all which have the Roman brick. at low water mark very much of the like is visible at some distance in the sea. There are two Entire Pillars with Balls, the Cliff is 100 foot high.[11]

John Kirby's *Suffolk Traveller*, published in 1735, made note of 'the Ruins of a Quadrangular Castle advantageously situated' in Felixstowe. A more detailed account was published in the second edition of Kirby's work (written in 1754), describing the monument as 187 yards long (170m) and 9ft thick (2.7m). This latter account went on to state that 'there can be no doubt but *Walton* Castle was a *Roman* Fortification, as appears from the great Variety of *Roman* Urns, Rings, Coins &c. that have been found there.'[12]

One drawing exists of the fort before its destruction (**8**). This drawing, thought probably to be an early eighteenth-century copy of an original dating to 1623, shows a rectangular structure that is superficially comparable to Burgh Castle. Round bastions are present at the corners of the defensive wall, which appears to have been substantially robbed, particularly close to ground level. These, it may be supposed, were the 'pillars with balls' described by Dr Knight. Brick bonding courses are also depicted, once again corresponding to Knight's description of the fort as being 'composed of Pepple [pebbles/cobbles] and Roman bricks in three courses'. A plan accompanying the drawing shows a rectangular structure, much longer on its east-west axis than on its north-south axis. The 'ruins' drawn in the corner of the fort probably relate to the rebel earl Hugh Bigod's twelfth-century castle, built within the Roman perimeter and destroyed by Henry II around 1176. The tumbled remains of the Shore Fort, littering the beach below the cliff on which it had once stood, are shown on a further drawing made *c.*1700.

At extreme low tide rocks are visible at a distance from the beach beneath the modern cliff line at Walton. Some are natural outcrops of septaria, but others have proved to be the remants of the Roman defences. In 1937 it was reported that 'a visit by boat … showed it to be composed of lumps of stone (septaria), Roman bricks, etc. held strongly together with cement or mortar'[13]. Still more recently, in 1969, a dive by the Ipswich branch of the British Sub-Aqua Club confirmed the presence of very large pieces of Roman masonry, including what is probably one of the corner bastions.[14] These modern investigations support the antiquarian descriptions of a late Roman fort, the defences of which were built of flint and septaria, with bonding courses of brick, and incorporating bastions. The presence of bastions is good evidence for a construction date after *c.*260, confirming that this installation is a

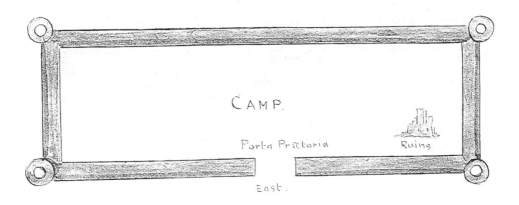

8   *Drawing and plan of Walton Castle*

contemporary of other Shore Forts such as Burgh Castle and Bradwell. Stray Roman finds from the locality of the fort are of second- to fourth-century date, but in themselves they shed little light on the history of Walton Castle.[15]

Beyond this, it is difficult to say a great deal more about the site. The differing measurements given by Knight and Kirby, combined with the fact that much of the fort had already been lost at the time of their writing, make reconstruction of the fort little more than guesswork. Knight's figure of 90m for the length of the west wall is quite plausible, as is Kirby's figure of 170m, though the round numbers quoted by Knight suggest estimation of the dimensions rather than actual measurement. Kirby's figures pretend to a greater precision and are perhaps more likely to be correct, though this impression of accuracy may be deceptive. A length of 170m would certainly be comparable with Burgh Castle's east wall. One recent reconstruction tentatively envisages the fort as roughly square, and of similar dimensions as the Shore Fort at Bradwell. Bastions are present at the angles, but interval bastions are shown, somewhat inexplicably, only on the south wall.[16] In reality, however, the accuracy of this or any other reconstruction is unlikely ever to be proved or disproved.

Bradwell

Situated on the edge of the Dengie Marshes, in Essex, the remote site of the Roman fort at Bradwell is now marked only by the seventh-century Saxon chapel of St Peter. The chapel, at the place named *Ythancaester* in the writings of Bede, was built in approximately 654 by the missionary St Cedd following his conversion of the East Saxons to Christianity (**9, colour plate 5**). Somewhat curiously, it occupies the location of the Roman west gate rather than being actually inside the fort; at the time of its construction it is likely to have been bracketed by the very substantial ruins of the west wall of the defences. The chapel was restored during the early twentieth century, and is spectacular as much for its location as it is for its preservation. By contrast only a very short and extremely unimpressive portion of the actual Roman defences at Bradwell remains exposed above ground, and even this is now obscured by heavy overgrowth. However, much Roman material is evident in the chapel, which is predominantly built of reused brick and ashlar, although the central sections of the north and south walls were repaired in the last century using newly imported stone. Particularly notable is the reuse of large blocks of limestone, employed as quoins

9   The seventh-century chapel of St Peter, Bradwell. View from the west

on the west wall of the chapel, which exhibit lewis holes (small rectangular slots cut into the block for the insertion of lifting gear) of presumably Roman date. These blocks were probably robbed from the monumental gate of the fort (**colour plate 6**).

As well as being plundered for the building of St Peter's chapel, stone was also quarried from the Roman walls for other churches on the Dengie peninsula, and was doubtless taken for secular structures.[17] Nevertheless, the defences survived to Early Modern times, and were described as a 'huge ruin' by Philemon Holland in his 1637 translation of Camden's *Britannia*.[18] The subsequent demolition must have been quite rapid, as by the early eighteenth century the site had been completely lost. The fort was only rediscovered during soil removal for the embankment of the Essex marshes during the later nineteenth century.[19] The resulting excavations, published in 1867, established once again the trapezoidal plan of the Roman defences, where they had survived on the north, south and western sides (**10**).[20] No gates were discovered, the gaps in the perimeter relating only to the robbing of the walls. Fragments of masonry were excavated on all three sides, the best preserved being a 20m stretch of the south wall. The surviving walls enclose 2ha (4.9 acres) and the whole fort was doubtless rather larger, but the position of the eroded east wall is unknown. A projecting bastion was found on the north-west angle, and also an interval bastion between this corner and St Peter's chapel. A third bastion was suggested at the south-west angle, but its existence was not proven. The presence of these bastions indicates a construction date after *c*.260, while the rather scanty coin series recovered from the nineteenth-century excavations suggests that building may have taken place a little later in the third century.

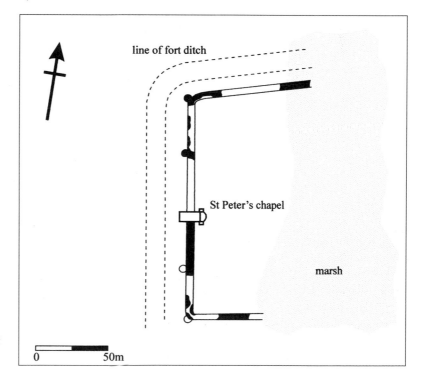

line of fort ditch

St Peter's chapel

marsh

10   The fort at Bradwell

0   50m

Where the wall has been investigated, it has been shown to be built of local septarian cementstones, used for both the core and the facing. On the exterior of the wall, triple courses of brick provided bonding at regular vertical intervals. A section cut across the line of the south wall in 1947 showed it to be 4.2m thick (as wide as for the fort at Pevensey), indicating a tall, substantial superstructure.[21] A triple offset of tiles was extant at ground level on the external face. Because of the extensive destruction of the site, the presence of a rampart behind the wall has not been conclusively proved. However, a roll in the ground and a mass of yellow clay behind the north and west walls would seem to indicate its existence. A ditch surrounding the defences is known, although sections cut across it failed to establish its profile.

Apart from a few isolated stubs of masonry, of which little sense has been made, few remains of internal buildings have been encountered. However, given the extent of destruction (even the perimeter defences have proved difficult to locate in places), traces of any such buildings may have been entirely removed. The acidic character of the soil is also hardly likely to have aided preservation. Furthermore, given the date (and also the quality) of the excavations of the interior, it is quite plausible that much evidence for timber-framed structures was at that time entirely overlooked. Recent geophysical survey of the site does indeed suggest that this was the case; a long rectangular building – perhaps a barrack block – has been located in the north-west corner of the fort, and further structures have been detected against the internal perimeter.[22] Finds from the site provide more evidence for occupation; writing on the fort in 1867, Thomas Lewin drew attention to the many artefacts of Roman date recovered during the excavations. Beyond the fort, very recent work has begun to produce evidence for extra-mural settlement, particularly in the areas to the west and south of the defences.

Reculver

Besieged on two sides by caravan parks and on the third side by the sea, the fort at Reculver is now dominated by the ruins of the twin-towered church of St Mary, built within the Roman perimeter (**11**). The site of *Raculf* was given by Egbert, king of Kent, to Bassa for the foundation of a minster in 669. The present church retains something of the plan of the original seventh-century church, though it was much extended during the thirteenth century, and the distinctive towers are of late twelfth-century date. Almost half of the site has been destroyed by coastal erosion, and the church, which once stood in the centre of the fort, is now situated perilously close to the cliff-edge. Only with the creation of sea-defences in the nineteenth century has the retreat of the coast finally been arrested.

The defences of the Roman fort are of 'traditional' style, as befits the construction date of the fort in the early third century. The relatively narrow wall, 3m wide at the base and reduced by two internal offsets to 2.4m, was backed by a substantial earth rampart. A single angle tower has been proved in the south-west corner. Two

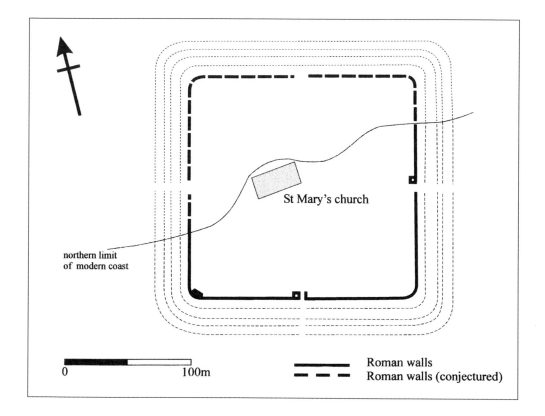

11 The fort at Reculver

V-profiled ditches surrounded the walls: these had begun to silt up quite early in the fort's lifetime, and today no trace can be seen. The defences originally enclosed an area of approximately 3.1ha (7.5 acres). Little now remains of the wall, which has been substantially reduced by stone robbing, much of it for the building of St Mary's church. Above ground level most of the Kentish ragstone facing has been removed, and all that remains is the flint–rubble core, standing about 2m high on the south side of the fort, and in part on the east and west (**12, colour plates 7 & 8**). The single most impressive architectural feature still open to view is the south gate: here, three monumental blocks which once formed the arched entrance to the fort can be seen (**colour plate 9**). Successive remetalling of the roadway through the gate had raised the level of the road by over 1m during the fort's lifetime. The east gate also remains, but this is a less impressive affair. It was never as important an entrance as that on the south side, and was blocked during the late third or fourth century. Excavations within the fort have provided evidence of a regular layout of roads and buildings during the initial period of occupation, while some traces of activity have been discovered in the area beyond the defences.[23]

12   *The east wall, Reculver*

Richborough

First dug in 1792, Richborough was probably the first of the Shore Forts to be subjected to archaeological investigation. The site was also the focus of several nineteenth-century excavations, before being very extensively dug in a series of campaigns between 1922 and 1938. The resulting reports provide a wealth of information about the site and its history, which complements the high level of preservation of the perimeter walls.[24]

Richborough has a complex history of Roman occupation, all of which is reflected in the archaeology, and in the visible remains, of the site (**13**). Activity probably began in AD 43, when the site is thought to have been the bridgehead for the invasion of the province. Two parallel ditches dating to this period have been detected, running for a distance of over 600m and cutting off the end of the Richborough promontory from the mainland. These were presumably for the protection of the invasion force.

By the later first century the invasion base and subsequent stores depot had given way to the thriving civilian port and settlement of *Rutupiae*. In AD 80-90 a large monumental arch was built across the east–west street of the town, probably to mark the completed conquest of Britain under the governor Agricola. The so-called 'Great Monument' was a symbolic gateway to the province: standing perhaps 25m high, encased by white marble imported from northern Italy and adorned by bronze statuary, it must have been truly impressive. Civilian occupation continued throughout the second century. A substantial masonry shop development was present on the road front immediately adjacent to the Great Monument, and nearby was a *mansio* ('hotel'), originally built of timber but converted to stone later in the century. Traces of other wooden buildings have been detected in the vicinity of the arch, and the town is thought to have been extensive, with settlement spreading a considerable distance westward along the Canterbury road. Masonry buildings have been discov-

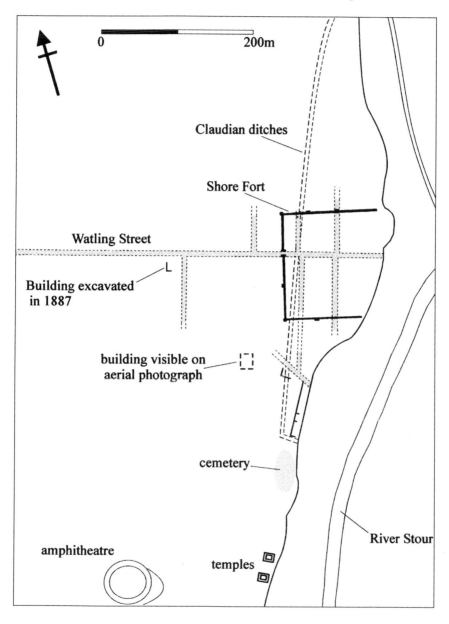

13   *General plan of the site at Richborough.* After Cunliffe (1968, Fig. 25). Courtesy B. Cunliffe and The Society of Antiquaries of London

ered 150m from the west wall of the Shore Fort, and an amphitheatre survives as a slight hollow 400m distant. A cemetery and two small Romano-Celtic temples are also known. The find of a 'triangular' brick structure during the nineteenth century has also led to suggestions of there having been a 'landing place' to the north of the fort, but the physical remains of any harbour have not yet been located by modern excavations. The date of all of these features, and therefore whether they predate the Shore Fort or were contemporary with the installation, remains to be established.

By the third century times were changing, and probably around the middle or later part of the century the army reoccupied Richborough. Most of the central buildings of the town were levelled and the monumental arch (by then in a serious state of disrepair) was converted into a watchtower surrounded by a rampart and triple ditch. The lifetime of this fortlet was probably brief, however, and soon the ditches were filled in and the remnant of the Great Monument finally demolished, in order to make way for a much larger stone-built installation that was the Shore Fort. The new defences were initially intended as a square, but the original foundations for the east wall were abandoned and left unused in favour of others 20m further east. In addition to the abortive east wall foundation, other surveying or constructional errors are also apparent, where the two halves of both the north and west walls on either side of their respective gateways are not quite correctly aligned.

The perimeter now survives on three sides, the east wall and eastern sections of the north and south walls having collapsed into the River Stour, which is gradually eroding the Richborough peninsula. Although a little smaller in area than the neighbouring fort at Reculver (2.5ha/6 acres), the Richborough defences seem to have been significantly more substantial, and were certainly more architecturally advanced (**14, colour plate 10**). The walls, 3.3m wide at the base, still survive to heights above 8m. They were built predominantly of flint, with a variety of other, mostly local, materials employed in the facing. The north wall was built in large part using stone from the demolished Great Monument: in its facing can be seen a deliberate attempt at decoration of the defences through the use of stone blocks of differing colours (**colour plate 11**). Double bonding courses of brick (and a little reused tile) are present at vertical intervals of around 1m. The walls were protected by bastions, which at the corners were round, and in the intervals between the corners and gates were rectangular. The defences were augmented by two ditches; a stretch of the inner ditch of the west wall was originally dug in the wrong place and had subsequently to be recut.[25]

Despite the intensive excavation of the interior, the fort's internal layout has not been satisfactorily established. The *principia* is thought to have been placed centrally within the defences, standing on the foundation platform of the monumental arch. A small bath block occupied the position of the former *mansio* and two further stone structures are known, one adjacent to the *principia* and the other just within the west gate, but the function of these latter buildings is uncertain. It must be assumed that any other structures within the Shore Fort were of timber, but none has been specifically identified. That the fort was densely occupied is attested by the very large volume of finds recovered from the interior.

14 *Richborough. In the foreground are the excavated ditches of the third-century earth fortlet that surrounded the remains of the Great Monument. Beyond are the south and west walls of the Saxon Shore Fort*

Dover

Although scholars had long suspected the existence of a late Roman military installation at Dover, it was not until rescue excavations in 1970 that the first remains of Roman defences were positively identified.[26] Subsequent rescue excavations lasting until 1977 revealed the existence of not one, but three forts under the modern town. The first of these (dated to *c.*120) was never completed, but was superseded by a second fort, built on the same site and on the same orientation in approximately 130-40. Both these early installations are strongly associated with the Roman navy in Britain, the *classis Britannica* (**15**). Overlying the demolished north-east corner of the second *classis Britannica* fort was the defensive wall of the Shore Fort, built during the later third century. Further to the north and east this new fort had been superimposed over elements of a former (presumably civilian) settlement of the second and third centuries, including a bathhouse and the prestigious dwelling known as the 'Painted House', so-called because of the painted wall plaster used in its fine decoration.[27] More of the Shore Fort defences have since come to light during work between 1988 and 1991.[28]

Only small sections of the defensive wall have been excavated, all of which are fragments of the south-western portion of the fort. The plan of the whole is

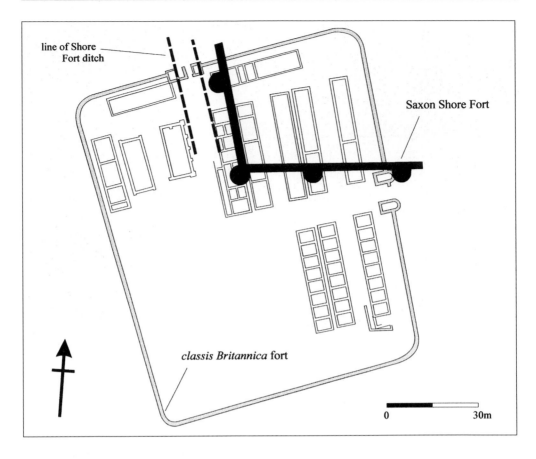

line of Shore
Fort ditch

Saxon Shore Fort

classis Britannica fort

0   30m

15   *The Roman forts at Dover. The second-century defences and buildings of the* classis
      Britannica *fort are overlain by the south-west corner of the Saxon Shore Fort*

therefore uncertain, although a completely regular rectangular shape is ruled out
because the south and west walls meet at an angle greater than 90°. Where
excavated, the wall itself has been found in very good condition (**16**). It was mainly
built of chalk and tufa (much probably reused from the *classis Britannica* fort) and
was found to be between 2.3m and 2.6m thick. It has survived to heights of 4.5m
and, apart from a slight step-in at ground level on the exterior face, appears to have
risen to its full height without offsets. An earth rampart was present behind the
wall. In total six bastions have been excavated, spaced at slightly irregular intervals
of between 23m and 30m. Two bastion types have been encountered, some built
as an integral part of the wall, and others added later (though quite possibly still
during the main construction phase of the fort). The building materials also differ
between these two types: the integral bastions are constructed from chalk and tufa,
while the added bastions have a flint facing that employs brick bonding courses.
Beyond the defences was a substantial ditch, which has been traced for a distance
alongside the west wall.

16 *The Roman forts at Dover. In this exposed section, the wall and bastion of the Shore Fort can be seen cutting across the east gate of the* classis Britannica *installation*

A significant number of regularly-planned stone barracks and store buildings were present within the second of the *classis Britannica* forts. However, the nature of any buildings within the Shore Fort has not been so clearly established, due in large part to the extensive disturbance caused by medieval and later occupation on the site. Traces of several timber buildings and huts of late Roman date have been discovered within the area of the Shore Fort, but no substantial structures to compare with those of the *classis Britannica* installation have yet come to light.

Lympne (Stutfall Castle)

The remnants of the Roman fort at Lympne lie scattered on the slopes of an ancient degraded sea cliff, overlooking the lowland region of Romney Marsh, in Kent (**17, colour plate 12**). Extensive land-slipping, which perhaps began as early as the fourth century, has gradually torn the fort apart. This process, combined with a great amount of stone robbing, has left only isolated fragments of the defences intact. The site has been described as being akin to a true Victorian 'romantic ruin', and so it is: overgrown sections of masonry, upright, tilted or tumbled, can be found scattered across a wide area of the picturesque, tree-dotted slope (**18, colour plate 13**).

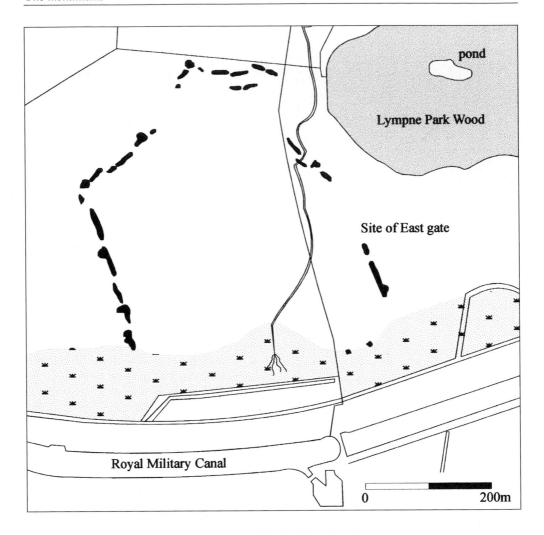

17   Stutfall Castle, Lympne. After Cunliffe (1980a, Fig. 2)

The destruction of the fort has led to considerable confusion as to its original plan. Probably none of the remaining masonry is in its original position, and the complete loss of the south wall above ground had even cast doubts on its existence until it was proved by excavation in the late nineteenth century.[29] A square plan has been suggested at times, but the most recent reconstruction, based on a geotechnical examination of the slope, envisages the fort as an irregular pentagon, with an angle mid-way along the north wall (**19**).[30] Such a fort would have been 3.4ha (8.4 acres) in area. The surviving portions of the northern, western and eastern walls are suffi-cient to show that the defences were very substantial, and also of advanced design. In places they still stand 6m tall and 3.9m thick at Roman ground level, flanked by semi-circular bastions, of which originally there were probably around 14. Only the east gate to the fort, also flanked by bastions, has been located.

18   *A section of the ruined north wall, Lympne.* Photo by J. Potter

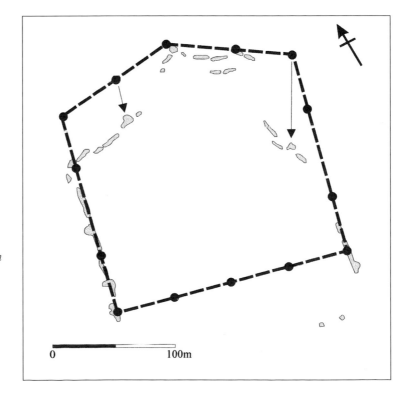

19   *Reconstruction of the fort at Lympne.* After Hutchinson *et al.* (1985, Fig. 12)

0   100m

There is a very considerable quantity of reused material in the walls of the Shore Fort. Many *tegulae* and some *imbrex* roof tiles can be observed in the bonding courses, and the large stone slabs in the foundation of the east gate bastion were also recycled. Significantly, two altars have been found in reused contexts, including one that was set up by a certain Aufidius Pantera, prefect of the *classis Britannica*, dated to *c.*135/45. This altar was encrusted with barnacles, indicating that it had lain underwater or on a foreshore for some while before it was salvaged for use as building material in the Shore Fort's east gate (*see* **27**). A number of stamped second-century tiles of the British fleet have been recovered during excavations of the fort interior, along with a small assemblage of early pottery and a coin of Antoninus Pius (AD 138-61). All this strongly hints at an earlier occupation on or near the site, quite possibly of military character. However, as yet no structures or features have been found that might relate to any such second-century base, and certainly it seems not to lie underneath the Shore Fort. It may be that the earlier installation was located at the base of the slope immediately below the Shore Fort, and has since been entirely lost. An alternative is that it lay a few hundred metres to the south-east at West Hythe, where a quantity of Roman tile fragments (one stamped) and some pottery sherds have been found, incorporated within storm beach deposits; these are clearly derived from a Roman structure, quite plausibly a second-century fort.[31]

Pevensey

The fort at Pevensey, East Sussex, remains to this day an impressive monument. The irregular oval plan of the defences, atypical of Roman military construction as a whole, and in marked contrast to forts such as Richborough and Portchester, can be explained by the need to fit the installation to the end of the peninsula on which it was built (**20, colour plate 14**). Occupying an area of nearly 4ha (10 acres), this is the largest of the Shore Forts. The south-east corner of the Roman perimeter is now occupied by the medieval castle, first established during the Norman period.

Built in AD 293 or shortly after, approximately two-thirds of the original perimeter of 760m has survived to the present day. A large portion of the south wall has been lost between the west gate and the medieval keep, while a section of approximately 50m has also fallen on the north wall, probably deliberately demolished during or immediately after sieges in the twelfth or thirteenth centuries. The defences still stand over 8m high, are 4.2m in width at the base, and are thinned by a series of internal offsets to 2.4m. The uppermost courses of the wall are missing, the crenellations of neatly coursed flint on the north-west quarter of the circuit being a post-Roman addition. The original facing was composed of sandstone blocks, with bonding courses of brick and sandstone slabs. The core was comprised mainly of flint. A small rampart was present, extending a short distance up the inner face of the wall.

The walls were flanked by at least 13 solid, semi-circular bastions, placed at irregular intervals around the perimeter. The tower on the north side, projecting well

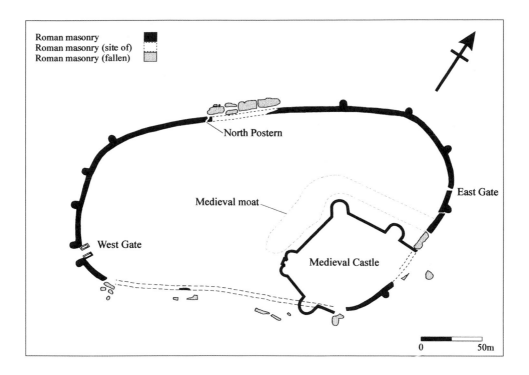

Roman masonry
Roman masonry (site of)
Roman masonry (fallen)

North Postern

East Gate

Medieval moat

West Gate

Medieval Castle

0   50m

20   Pevensey Castle

above the level of the wall-walk, is often said to be Roman, but the upper storey is in fact more probably of medieval age (**colour plate 15**). Three gateways are known: a heavily defended west gate, a less elaborate east gate and a narrow north postern. The existence of at least one more entrance, somewhere along the southern wall, seems probable. Stone robbing is evident at all parts of the circuit, but in many places the preservation is superb. This is particularly true of the north wall, where the majority of the external facing above 1.5m remains *in situ* (**21**). Where excavated on the northern wall, the buried inner face of the wall was also found to be in pristine condition. The scale and appearance of the Pevensey defences provides a good impression of how less well preserved (but originally probably equally imposing) Shore Forts such as Bradwell and Lympne would have looked.

Within the fort, much of the Roman ground surface is obscured by upcast material from the ditch of the medieval castle. Investigation of the interior has been limited. Excavations early in the last century, concentrating on the north-west quarter of the fort, encountered a series of hearths, but the probable timber-framed buildings to which they related were so insubstantial as to leave no recognisable trace. A timber-framed well was also found. Further excavations between the 1930s and 1960s recovered large amounts of pottery and other material from the initial occupation layers, and once again identified a few possible traces of structures within the perimeter, though nothing substantial.[32]

21 The north wall of the Roman fort, Pevensey. In the foreground, the vertical break in the wall shows the defences at this point to have been built in two distinct sections, each probably the responsibility of an individual working party. Beneath the tree, a narrow horizontal aperture cut into the fallen Roman masonry betrays the presence of a Second World War pillbox

Portchester

Portchester Castle, at the head of Portsmouth Harbour, has the longest and most continuous post-Roman history of occupation of any of the Shore Forts (**22**). There was extensive use of the site during Saxon, medieval and Post Medieval times, and it only finally ceased to function as a military installation during the early nineteenth century. This fact is reflected in the modern monument's fabric, which exhibits numerous repairs, alterations and additions spanning the Saxon period to the present day. Particularly prominent within the Roman perimeter are the medieval castle inserted in the north-west corner, and the church in the south-east quarter. Tidal erosion of the promontory on which the fort was built has brought the sea within a few metres of the walls. A gravel build-up against the east wall showed that the water once lapped against the defences.

The Roman fort, probably built in the 280s, took the form of a regularly planned square enclosing 3.43ha (8.48 acres), surrounded by a double ditch (**23**). There were 20 hollow, semi-circular bastions originally present: 14 now remain, two having been demolished to make way for the medieval castle, while the others – certainly the three on the east wall — have been destroyed by the sea. Four centrally placed gates were extant in Roman times, those on the east and west walls (the Landgate and Watergate) being protected by substantial inset gatehouses. Both these entrances, and the posterns on the north and south walls, have been extensively modified in the post-Roman period. As at Pevensey, whose defences it resembles, the walls at Portchester were substantial. 3.8m wide at the base, Roman masonry survives to around 6m and was probably originally rather higher. The Roman core of the wall remains largely intact, albeit significantly reduced on the inner face during the medieval period, when stone was robbed for the building of the bailey. The original flint facing can only be seen above modern ground level on a short exterior length of the northern defences, where medieval overburden that built up against the wall has been cleared in recent times (**colour plate 16**). Elsewhere the facing exhibits a patchwork of post-Roman repairs of many dates. Original Roman bonding courses of stone, set deep into the wall, can be observed at numerous parts of the circuit: double brick courses were also employed, although less extensively. Roman brick is most in evidence on the west and south walls but much is not in its original position, having been reinstated during later repair work.

Some parts of the interior were investigated under the auspices of the Ministry of Works after the castle passed into state guardianship in 1926. By far the most extensive and significant excavations, however, were those of Cunliffe between 1961 and 1972.[33] Cunliffe's investigations included an open excavation of a substantial area to the south of the medieval bailey (covering roughly one-eighth of the total of the fort interior), which revealed a large number of Roman features. These consisted of

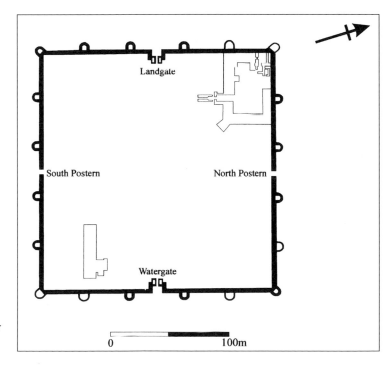

*22 Portchester
     Castle*

0   100m

23   The east wall of Portchester Castle at low tide. On the extreme right of the photograph can be seen the Portsdown Heights, from which many of the raw materials used to build the fort were quarried

a grid of gravel-surfaced 'roads', wells and rubbish- and cess-pits. Little convincing evidence for contemporary structures was found, however, though shallow-lying traces of timber buildings may well have been destroyed by activity during later periods, which included ploughing. Alternatively, buildings may have only been present in parts of the fort not yet excavated; the find of building materials, albeit not *in situ*, indicates that they were not entirely absent. Late Roman activity within the fort certainly appears to have been extensive, and Cunliffe's analysis of the features and finds led to the suggestion of three main phases of occupation during the late third and early fourth centuries: noticeable breaks in activity occur between these episodes. Although coin finds attest to a continued presence through to the late fourth century, the character of the occupation appears to have become rather less orderly after *c*.365.

2 The Roman Empire in the third century

The Roman Empire ended the third century in some senses much as it had begun: territorially united, with secure frontiers, and under strong, authoritarian leadership. This situation, however, belied the massive upheavals experienced during the course of the century, and in the context of which the Shore Forts and many other coastal installations in Britain, and also in Gaul, had developed.

The Severan dynasty

In AD 196 the defeat of the imperial claimant Clodius Albinus, formerly governor of Britain, by the army of Septimius Severus at the battle of Lyons, brought to an end the civil war that had gripped the Empire since the murder of the emperor Pertinax four years previously. Frontier concerns occupied the first years of the new Severan regime and victory in the civil war was followed almost immediately by campaigns against Rome's ancient enemy, Persia. Between 197 and 199 significant gains were made in Arabia, Syria and Mesopotamia, extending the frontier further east than at any time previously. The campaigns culminated in the sacking of the Persian capital at Ctesiphon. On a number of inscriptions throughout the Empire Severus is hailed as *propagator imperii* – extender of Empire – and his campaigns both in Persia, and subsequently against the desert peoples in the African province of Tripolitania, demonstrate his aggressive expansionist policies.[1]

After several years spent in Rome, Severus turned his attention to Britain. The state of the province at the time is not altogether clear, but the northern frontier does not appear to have been entirely secure during the early years of the Severan dynasty. The historian Dio Cassius records that the threat from the Maeatae tribe was bought off during the late 190s by the then governor Virius Lupus,[2] while the dispatch to Britain in 205 of L. Alfenius Senecio, the eminent and highly experienced former governor of Syria, is further evidence of the seriousness of the situation. Campaigns by Alfenius Senecio in 205-7 were followed by a major military expedition, one that was led personally by the ageing Severus, who was accompanied by his two teenage sons Caracalla and Geta. A huge army was assembled, gathered from several continental legions, and the invasion of Scotland began in earnest in 209. The chronology and course of the campaign is not precisely understood, but Roman forces are known to have penetrated almost to the northern limits of Britain. Initial Roman successes rapidly forced the barbarians to seek peace terms, but large-scale rebellions north of Hadrian's Wall were still occupying

Severus at the time of his death at York in 211. Severus' death effectively marked the end of the campaigns, and of the last attempt to bring the whole of Britain under direct Roman rule. Peace treaties were agreed with the Maeatae and Caledonians, while Caracalla and Geta, each manoeuvring for the imperial succession, departed for Rome.

Caracalla (sole emperor from 211-17 after his murder of Geta) never returned to Britain, being initially concerned with internal politics, and later with troubles in Germany and with a planned expedition to conquer the Parthian East. Caracalla's German campaigns were conducted against a loose confederation of tribes known as the Alemanni, who are first recorded at this time as enemies of Rome. His victories of 214 in the area of the junction between the upper Rhine and upper Danube, followed by a policy of pacification through subsidies, were to stave off the German peril for the next two decades. Caracalla was assassinated in 217, and after a brief interlude which saw the praetorian prefect Macrinus as emperor, the imperial title passed back to the Severans, first to Elagabalus (218-22) and then to Severus Alexander (222-35). History records neither as being particularly effective rulers: Elagabalus' religious fanaticism was matched only by his hedonistic lifestyle, while Severus Alexander, a minor when he assumed power, appears never to have been an authoritative figure.

Crisis and recovery

The dynastic succession of ineffectual rulers such as Elagabalus and Severus Alexander could be tolerated as long as the Empire faced no great difficulties, either within its frontiers, or beyond them. However, as the third century progressed, problems that had been developing for many decades, combined with others that had been inherent in the political framework of the Empire since its very inception, came increasingly to the fore. By the 230s these difficulties could no longer be ignored or avoided, and events were shortly to plunge the Empire into a half-century of turmoil.

The so-called third-century 'crisis' was composed of many interwoven strands, in which internal political and economic problems were combined with, and exacerbated by, a variety of external threats and invasions from beyond the frontiers. The murder of Severus Alexander in 235 and his replacement by the German legions with their commander Maximinus (235-8) marks a turning point in the fortunes of the third-century Empire. In itself the violent usurpation of power, and the creation of emperors by the army at the frontiers rather than in Rome, was nothing new. The first-century emperors Caligula, Claudius and Nero, amongst others, had all been murdered, and following the demise of the Julio-Claudian dynasty in AD 68, Vespasian emerged as the victor of a civil war that had seen the different legions of the Empire proclaiming (and fighting for) rival candidates. The second century can in fact be seen as rather exceptional in that the succession passed comparatively smoothly from one individual to the next. Although the inherent problems with the succession resurfaced after the assassination of Commodus in 192, victory in the civil war brought another stable period under the Severans.

The killing of Severus Alexander, however, ushered in an unparalleled era of political chaos. The ending of the Severan dynasty left no clear successor, and there was not (nor had there ever been) an established mechanism by which a new emperor was to be selected. This institutional weakness was to be mercilessly exposed over the following five decades, during which time over 60 individuals would lay claim to the imperial title. One usurper followed the next, and only one emperor died of natural causes (Claudius II, of plague); all other incumbents met a violent end.[3] Competent or otherwise, each of the many mid-third-century emperors struggled, mostly unsuccessfully, with the problem of governing a polity of the immense size of the Roman Empire. With mounting threats on many frontiers, and military insurrections within the Empire, it was impossible for the emperor to be everywhere he was required. In an era when few imperial regimes had a strong power-base, and where still fewer could claim any form of legitimacy, a vicious cycle developed. A victorious general on the frontier would find himself proclaimed emperor by his troops, and would thereupon march with his army to confront his imperial rival: in so doing the frontier was denuded of troops, and was once again made vulnerable to attack.

The quiescence of Rome's neighbours during most of the first and second centuries meant that the occasional political instability and civil war had not threatened the stability of the Empire as a whole. However, in the changed circumstances of the third century the effect was disastrous. The external threats to the Roman Empire during the third century were numerous (**24**), but probably the single most concerted danger was on the eastern frontier. Ironically the success of the Severan campaigns at the close of the second century had fatally destabilised the Parthian regime, and from the 230s the Romans found themselves facing a renewed Persian threat under the militaristic Sassanid dynasty. Between 244 and 260 the Persians made major inroads into Roman territory, defeating three Roman emperors in the field and reaching as far as Antioch – third largest city in the Empire – which was sacked. The Persian invasion was finally halted by the forces of the allied city of Palmyra, which then assumed independent control of Syria and Mesopotamia, and eventually of Egypt. The separatist Palmyrene

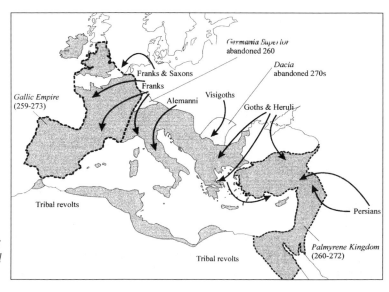

24   Threats to the Roman Empire during the third century AD

kingdom endured from 259 to 271, its existence a *fait accompli* only tacitly accepted by Roman emperors who for the moment had other, more pressing, concerns.

The troubles in the east coincided with pressures on the European frontier, stretching from the Black Sea to the English Channel. The redeployment of troops from the western and central parts of the Empire for the wars against Persia heightened the difficulties on the Rhine and Danube. In 248/9 there was a major incursion by Goths (a tribe newly arrived in southern Ukraine), Vandals and other allied tribes into the Balkans, and in 256 and 257 Gothic naval forces attacked Roman cities in the eastern Black Sea region. In 267 a fleet of Goths and Heruls forced a passage into the Aegean, raiding Greece, the west coast of Asia Minor, and the islands of Cyprus and Crete. Campaigns by Gallienus (253-68) and his successors Claudius II (268-70) and Aurelian (270-5) eventually drove the Goths back from the Balkans and across the Danube, although raids across the frontier continued into the late 270s.

Germanic pressure on the Rhine frontier, subdued since Maximinus' campaign of 235, intensified once again from the 250s. In 258 the Alemanni breached the frontier, sweeping through the undefended towns of Gaul and into Italy before they were turned back by Gallienus. Troubles with the Goths in Pannonia (modern Hungary) called Gallienus away shortly afterwards, leaving his teenage son Saloninus in Cologne to act as regent. Saloninus, however, was murdered shortly afterwards by one of the military commanders in Gaul, Cassius Latinius Postumus, who was then proclaimed emperor by his troops. Postumus gained the support of the armies and provinces of Germany, Gaul, Britain and Spain, and an abortive attempt in 263 by Gallienus to recover these north-western provinces met with failure. The polity known by historians as the 'Gallic Empire' outlived Postumus himself (d. 269), enduring as an independent but fully Roman state under Victorinus (269-71) and Tetricus (271-4). The Gallic emperors had to contend, above all, with the Germanic threat. In this they initially failed, because the Rhine frontier was completely overrun again in 260, the Alemanni once more penetrating deep into Gaul, this time possibly reaching Spain. In the long term, however, the Gallic Empire can probably be judged a reasonable success, signified by the fact that the historians of the period do not record any more major incursions by barbarians during its lifetime. Nevertheless, a need to rationalise the frontier led to the abandonment of the province of Germania Superior, which lay between the Rhine and the Danube. The garrison was withdrawn around 260 and the province was never reoccupied.

Warfare and political chaos within the Empire were accompanied by economic problems. The constant frontier wars sapped the Empire's financial and human resources, while the rising tide of civil war exacerbated the situation, causing losses of manpower that could be ill afforded. The conflicts were still more damaging because (in contrast to virtually all previous wars) they took place mostly within the imperial frontiers, causing collateral damage both to Roman urban centres and to the countryside. Plague, first brought back from the east by the army in the 160s, caused further losses within both the civilian and military populations. The endemic warfare also became more costly, and as the financial resources of the State became ever more stretched, successive emperors turned to debasement of the currency as a means of raising money. The debasements created a hyper-inflationary spiral, which required yet more coins (and therefore increasing debasements) to meet ever-rising prices. The main victim was the government itself, which was compelled to combat relentless military pressures not only with inadequate manpower, but also with insufficient financial resources.

From the 270s, however, the crisis appears to have turned a corner, although the cycle of regicide and military insurrections continued apace. The reign of Aurelian (270-5) saw the restoration of the territorial unity of the Empire. The separatist Palmyrene kingdom was destroyed in two campaigns in 271 and 272, and the military power of the Gallic Empire was broken in 274 at the battle of Châlons. The last Gallic emperor, Tetricus, surrendered to Aurelian and the north-west provinces were peacefully reintegrated into the Empire. Foreign dangers also started to abate. The eastern threat, largely coincident with the reign of the Persian king Shapur I (241-72), began to recede, and it is notable that from this period the Roman Empire was able to carry the war into enemy territory. In 282 the Persian capital Ctesiphon was once more sacked by Roman forces, this time commanded by the short-lived emperor Carus. Barbarian pressure on the Danube and Rhine frontiers continued to manifest itself, however. Despite the successful Roman campaigns from the 250s onwards, Aurelian's eventual successor Probus (276-82) had to contend with an invasion of the eastern Goths that penetrated as far as Ankara in central Anatolia. Further rationalisation of the frontier occurred during this period, with the giving up of the north-eastern border province of Dacia. The north-western provinces also remained under threat. A major incursion occurred in 276, when the Alemanni and other tribes ravaged central and southern Gaul, Switzerland (*Maxima Sequanorum*) and Bavaria (*Raetia*). Further to the north the Franks, a new confederation occupying the lower Rhine region, also breached the frontier to raid the coastal province of *Belgica Secunda*. This tribe, together with the Saxons, may also have posed a maritime threat to Gaul and Britain over the longer term. This is a central issue in the discussion of the Shore Forts, to which Chapter 6 will return.

Much of Probus' reign appears to have been devoted to the north-western provinces, during which time the Rhine frontier was significantly strengthened. Probus also continued work which had commenced under the Gallic emperors to restore the Gallic towns – many having been very badly damaged by the barbarian raids of the past decades – and to provide them with defensive walls. The walls of Rome, begun by Aurelian, were also completed during his reign.

The Tetrarchy

In outlining the woes of the third century, it is necessary not to overstate the case. Certain areas of the Empire remained relatively isolated from the troubles. Barbarian raids, for example, touched only a few parts of Spain. Egypt – 'granary of the Empire' – suffered no external threats, nor did many parts of Asia Minor. Most pertinently to the present study, Britain appears to have been comparatively tranquil: the Severan campaigns pacified the northern frontier for nearly a century, and the English Channel insulated southern Britain from similar Germanic incursions, despite neighbouring Gaul suffering repeated barbarian invasions. There are a few hints that some military campaigning in Britain may have occurred from time to time, though the evidence is ambiguous. Inscriptions on certain coins of Postumus reading *Neptuno Comiti* and *Neptuno Reduci* perhaps suggest naval operations carried out in the North Sea. Similarly, the assumption of the title 'Britannicus' by Carinus (283-5) together with a rather vague historical reference to his campaigns '*sub arcto*' – a poetic reference to the Pole Star often used as a literary device to describe the 'far north'– may indicate similar operations.[4]

With the accession of Diocletian in 284 the Roman world is often seen by historians as emerging successfully from its crisis, although as we have already seen the military fortunes of the Empire were already significantly improved by this date. Diocletian's achievement lay in his solutions to the political instability and economic problems that had bedevilled the Roman state for much of the century. The reforms initiated by Diocletian were wide-ranging. The Army, together with provincial boundaries and administration, was reorganised, while the economic crisis was met by a series of currency reforms and price edicts. The solutions adopted were not entirely novel – many were prefigured in the reigns of his immediate predecessors – nor in many cases did they prove to be enduring. Nevertheless, the years 284-305 were of markedly greater stability than the preceding period.

Diocletian's solution to both the problem of the succession, and the need for the emperor to be in many places at once, was to appoint another senior military commander, Maximian, as co-ruler, initially with the junior rank of Caesar, and from 286 as Augustus, making him an equal colleague. Maximian assumed responsibility for the western parts of the Empire, while Diocletian ruled in the east. The system was further extended in 293 with the nomination of two Caesars, Constantius and Galerius, subordinate to the two Augusti and with responsibilities in the west and east respectively. The establishment of the system known to modern scholars as the Tetrarchy did not eliminate the possibility of military revolt, but as long as the partners worked in concert it limited the extent to which an uprising could destabilise the imperial regime. The survival of the Tetrarchy in the face of several insurrections (in Egypt, Syria, Italy, and as we shall see, in Britain) is testament to its effectiveness.

Carausius and Allectus

The most serious and long-lived rebellion with which the Tetrarchy – and more specifically the western emperors Maximian and Constantius – had to contend, was that of Carausius and Allectus in Britain and northern Gaul. This episode assumes a central place in the discussions that follow regarding the development of coastal installations in both Britain and Gaul, in particular with the inception of the system later to be known as the 'Saxon Shore Forts'.[5]

The background to the revolt is somewhat opaque. The only contemporary historical sources consist of panegyrics, that is, speeches given in honour of Maximian and Constantius, dating between 289 and 310.[6] The bias of these documents is clear. More dispassionate accounts can be found in the late fourth-century histories of Eutropius and Sextus Aurelius Victor,[7] but the relevant passages are brief and written at a considerable distance in time from the actual events. The basic course of the early events, as described by Eutropius, is worth quoting in full:

> At this period, Carausius, although a man of the lowest birth, had achieved great distinction through military service since he had accepted the commission at Boulogne to pacify the sea, which the Franks and Saxons were infesting throughout the regions of *Belgica* and *Amorica*. Although he caught many barbarians, he did not give their spoils back intact either to the provincials or to the imperial treasury, and when he began to be suspected of allowing the barbarians in so that he could intercept them sailing past with their spoils and thus become rich, under sentence of death under Maximian, he assumed the imperial power and seized Britain.

The date and duration of the revolt are not precisely understood, though Eutropius and the other historical sources are all in agreement about the fact that Carausius had been appointed to a naval command by Maximian, probably in 286. The rebellion followed shortly after, either in 286 or, at the latest, in 287. Carausius' original appointment seems to represent an attempt to deal with piracy in the English Channel, and if so it was part of Maximian's wider efforts to stabilise the situation in Gaul. The latter's campaigns dealt initially with internal disturbances of *bagaudae* (an ill-understood term which probably relates to bands of deserters and peasants in revolt, terrorising both town and country alike), before reaching beyond the frontiers to subdue the German tribes. The threat to the coastal zone of Gaul was evidently sufficient to warrant a significant Roman response. However, as we shall see in Chapter 6, the actual seriousness of this danger – particularly during the third century – is very much open to question. It is equally unclear whether piracy ever extended to British shores. That Carausius genuinely allowed the barbarians to land and raid in order to capture them and their spoils on the return journey is also rather dubious. As has already been shown, in the third century the step from successful military commander to imperial pretender was a small one, and it is perhaps more plausible for these to have been false charges engineered by Maximian in order to remove a potentially dangerous rival. In the context of the unstable times such pre-emptive action is understandable, even if it was not necessarily justified.

The military command to which Carausius was originally appointed encompassed the Gallic coast, and may have included the southern British seaboard. Certainly, once the rebellion began, the breakaway regime rapidly assumed control in both northern Gaul and southern Britain. However, the absence of references to *Legio VI Victrix* on Carausian coins of the period may be an indication that the army of *Britannia Inferior* may not have supported the usurpation as quickly, or as wholeheartedly, as the units in southern Britain and north Gaul.[8] The extent of Carausius' continental territory is unclear, but is known to have included the major maritime towns of Boulogne and Calais, both of which were the locations of mints producing Carausian coins. An initial attempt by Maximian to oust Carausius from the continent in 288-9 seems to have failed, possibly with the destruction of the western emperor's invasion fleet,

25 *Carausian diplomacy. A coin minted by Carausius attempts to portray the British usurper as an equal colleague of the emperors Diocletian and Maximian. The legend reads 'Carausius et fratres sui' – 'Carausius and his brothers'.* Courtesy N. Faulkner

either by enemy action or because of storms. The attempt does not appear to have been repeated in the years immediately following, probably because Maximian had more pressing concerns securing the Rhine frontier against the Alemanni, Heruli and Chamavi, as well as with the Franks in the lower Rhine region. The late 280s and early 290s witnessed diplomacy on the part of Carausius to gain legitimacy for his position. Carausian coin issues attest this, presenting him as an equal colleague of Diocletian and Maximian, and which also show his honorific adoption of the Maximian's names, becoming 'Marcus Aurelius Mausaeus Carausius' (**25**). Such diplomacy does not appear to have been reciprocated, however, and any possibility of a constitutional resolution was ended with the establishment of the Tetrarchy.

The campaign against Carausian Gaul resumed in 293 under the command of the new Caesar Constantius, this time meeting with greater success. Boulogne was captured by siege in this year, and although it is possible that other continental lands took rather longer to subdue, these events ultimately proved fatal for Carausius himself. At around this time he was assassinated by his finance minister Allectus, who then assumed control over the administration's remaining possessions. The Allectan regime endured for a further three years, until brought to an end by invasion. In 296 a fleet sailed for Britain from the continent. One part, under the command of the praetorian prefect Julius Asclepidotus, sailed from the mouth of the Seine and landed somewhere on the south coast, having managed to evade the waiting Allectan fleet thanks to a sea fog. Poor weather appears to have hampered the progress of the second contingent of the fleet, which departed from Boulogne under Constantius himself, and played little part in the subsequent events. Having burnt his boats, Asclepidotus marched inland, and, at some unknown location in the south of England, he engaged the forces of Allectus. The Allectan army, which, if the contemporary historical sources are to be believed, consisted mainly of Germanic mercenaries, was soundly defeated. Allectus himself was killed during the fighting. Constantius' much-delayed army arrived in London, apparently just in time to save it from sack at the hands of the surviving German troops. Ten years after it had begun, the last separatist regime of the third century had finally been brought to an end.

3 The development of a coastal system

It is against the historical backcloth laid out in the previous chapter that we must view the development of the Shore Forts. The coastal network was constantly in flux; at any one period some sites were being abandoned, while others were reoccupied or were newly constructed. Here an attempt is made to outline the history of the development of military installations on the shores of Britain, with particular reference to those on the south and south-east coasts. Although it is recognised that coastal towns may well have contributed in a significant way to the maritime network (including acting as fleet bases or in a defensive role), the emphasis is here laid on strictly military sites. The third century does not stand alone, and the Shore Forts grew up and operated within a network of existing coastal sites, many of which were long established. Similarly, the region considered as the 'Saxon Shore' did not develop in isolation, and for this reason the discussion has been broadened to take in a wider geographical area.

The nature of the evidence

The historical framework described in Chapter 2 is principally derived from written Roman sources, but when we come to examine the detailed history of the Romano-British coast it is archaeology that provides by far the greatest volume of data. Contemporary sources (largely confined to histories, maps and itineraries) are of only limited use, and in particular shed little light on the development and character of individual sites. It is necessary, therefore, to understand the nature of the archaeological record and in particular its shortcomings.

Lost sites
One of the greatest difficulties lies in the fact that the picture we have of Roman coastal sites is doubtless incomplete. As described in Chapter 5, erosion has destroyed large tracts of the British coast, particularly on the east and south. Roman coastal installations that were built at a safe distance inland now hang precariously on cliff-edges, while other monuments have long since fallen into the sea. We are aware of some of these lost sites because of their presence in Roman documents. One such is *Sitomago*, a walled town on the East Anglian coast which is listed in the Antonine Itinerary, a document describing the major routes of the Empire and

probably compiled around the reign of Caracalla. The same town (commonly associated with the lost medieval settlement of Dunwich, Suffolk) also features as *Sinomagi* on the Peutinger Table, a thirteenth-century copy of a fourth-century Roman road map.[1]

Some forts or settlements which have been lost within the last few centuries also feature in antiquarian or historical records. Examples of these include the Shore Fort at Walton Castle, the documentation of which has already been discussed, and another probable Roman site at Skegness. However, the data we possess about such sites is inevitably scant: the antiquarian records are often rather vague and not infrequently contradictory, and in general terms the longer ago a site was lost, the lower the quality of information. In most cases we are left to guess at the character of a site, and have little or no data about the history of occupation.

The number of destroyed sites beg a further question: how many other forts and civilian settlements in the coastal zone have vanished without trace? It is probably true that we are aware of most of the major Roman sites on Britain's south-east and southern coasts, due in part to the fact that this region features in several historical documents, from Ptolemy's *Geography* in the second century to the *Notitia Dignitatum* in the late fourth or early fifth century. Other areas of Britain are less well covered by such sources, and here we can be less certain. This is particularly true where the fourth century is concerned: the surviving part of the Peutinger Table covers only the south-east, while the Welsh section of the *Notitia Dignitatum* is also missing or perhaps was never compiled. The picture is most likely to be incomplete in terms of minor sites – installations too small to have attracted the attention of the historians, geographers and bureaucrats of the central Empire. One such class of site is the signal station, groups of which remain on the Yorkshire and Cumbrian coasts. However, the find of an isolated example at Shadwell (inner Thames) and the possibility of other similar sites, for example at Thornham (Norfolk), Corton (Suffolk) and Hadleigh (Essex), suggests that there may once have been a far more extensive chain of such sites, knowledge of which is now to a large extent lost.[2]

Surviving monuments

For those forts that remain, either as standing monuments or as excavated sites, there continue to be many uncertainties. Over the centuries all have been damaged to a greater or lesser amount by the actions of man and nature: the data we have about each site is determined by the degree of that destruction, and by the extent and quality of the archaeological investigations. Modern urban sites tend to present particular difficulties, as here the archaeological investigations tend to be both piecemeal and small-scale. For this reason we have only fragmentary information about Roman occupation at Dover, for example, and the same situation applies to most of the sites on the continental coast.

Establishing a chronology for individual sites, and for the coastal system as a whole, remains a major concern. In early antiquarian scholarship the dating of many monuments was only understood in the vaguest terms, and theories often varied wildly. The Shore Forts are a case in point: during the sixteenth and seventeenth centuries they tended to be assigned to the very last phases of Roman Britain, while in the eighteenth century the forts were commonly attributed to Diocletian.[3] Only since the advent of excavation in the 1800s has more reliable chronological data become available about their inception and occupation. Our knowledge, however, remains incomplete and some monuments are better understood than others. The construction dates of forts such as Caister, Richborough and Portchester are now reasonably well established, certainly within a range of ten years or thereabouts. Only rarely does the evidence allow greater precision to be achieved, as at Pevensey for example. By contrast, forts such as Burgh Castle and Bradwell have yielded little by way of conclusive dating evidence (either for their construction or occupation),and can only be placed within a broad period of roughly half a century. It goes without saying that it is virtually impossible to establish a history for those sites lost to coastal erosion, such as Walton Castle, Skegness and *Sitomago-*?Dunwich.

The first and second centuries

There had been a fleet operating in British waters since the Claudian invasion of the province in AD 43. The *classis Britannica* ('British Fleet') was probably initially established to serve the invasion army, although the actual name is not known to have been used before the Flavian period.[4] As with other provincial fleets created for a particular campaign (for example the *classes Pannonica* and *Germanica*, formed in 25 BC and 12 BC respectively), the British fleet continued in operation long after its original purpose was fulfilled.[5]

From Claudian or Neronian times the headquarters of the fleet was probably at Boulogne. Here, excavations in the modern upper town have revealed the presence of a large fort constructed at the beginning of the second century AD.[6] Although the first-century base has yet to be located, there is strong circumstantial evidence to suggest its existence. The earliest British base of the fleet was probably at Richborough, the beachhead for the Claudian invasion. Other contemporary (though almost certainly short-lived) sites are also suspected; a Claudian ditch at nearby Reculver suggests the presence there of an early depot or fortlet, and supply bases have also been proposed at Fingringhoe (Essex), Fishbourne (Sussex) and Hamworthy (Dorset).[7]

During the early second century a new British headquarters was established at Dover, where a fort was built in approximately 130-40, overlying the foundations of an unfinished defensive wall that was begun and abandoned *c.*120.[8] This site, perhaps the *Novus Portus* ('new harbour') in Ptolemy's *Geography*,[9] appears to have eclipsed the original British base at Richborough, which had become a civilian port by the later first century. Boulogne continued as the main base, however: this fact is immediately apparent from the size of the fort there (12ha/29 acres), as opposed to the much smaller installation at Dover (1.05ha/3 acres). Lighthouses were present at both ports, and one of the probable pair at Dover still survives within the walls of the medieval castle (**colour plate 17**).

At its inception, the main task of the *classis Britannica* was troop transport and logistical support. Throughout the first century the fleet continued to support military operations, activities that were well documented by Tacitus during Agricola's campaigns in the north and in Scotland during the 70s and 80s. There may also have been an element of anti-piracy in the fleet's role. However, as J.C. Mann has observed, it is probable that 'piracy did not exist in the English Channel or the North Sea during the Principate [the period encompassing the reigns of Augustus to Severus Alexander] precisely because the *classis Britannica* did exist'.[10]

In addition to its military roles, the fleet was also engaged in industry. This is most apparent in the eastern parts of the Weald of Kent, where the *classis Britannica* was directly involved in the large-scale manufacture of iron.[11] Industrial sites here developed very rapidly after the Roman conquest, and it has been suggested that the eastern Weald may have been under the direct control of the State, which commonly took charge of mineral extraction.[12] The fact that production fell, at least in part, under the auspices of the *classis Britannica* is attested by the abundant tiles stamped with the fleet's CLBR monogram at some of the largest sites (Beauport Park, Bardown and Cranbrook). The presence of a standard-pattern barrack block at Bardown also suggests direct military involvement, as does the find of CLBR tiles at the estuarine port of Bodiam (Sussex), from which the iron was presumably exported.[13]

Tile production was itself a major enterprise and is generally presumed to have been carried out in order to supply the fleet's building projects.[14] Very large numbers of stamped tiles were used at Boulogne and Dover, and their presence elsewhere indicates other sites that may well have been associated with the fleet (**26**). Their use

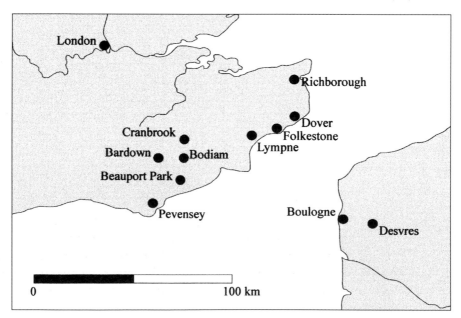

26 Classis Britannica *tile find sites*

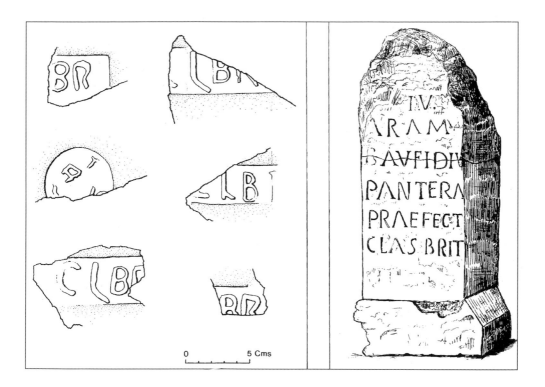

27 *Early Roman finds from Lympne; the altar of Aufidius Pantera and stamped tiles of the* classis Britannica. Courtesy B. Cunliffe

at the Folkestone villa, for example, has led to proposals that this house was the residence of the prefect commanding the *classis Britannica*.[15] In excess of 30 CLBR tiles have also been discovered at Lympne, which strongly suggest the existence of a second-century fort or supply depot on or near the site of the later Shore Fort (**27**) Although no such installation has yet been identified, the amounts of reused building materials in the Shore Fort defences, combined with a limited number of other finds from the site hint at second-century activity. The extent of any occupation, and whether military or civilian in character, remains to be established.

At Reculver, at least 40 Roman tiles made from a clay indistinguishable from that used by the *classis Britannica* ('Fabric 2') were later incorporated into St Mary's church. Some others remain in their original position, built into the east gate of the Shore Fort.[16] None is positively known to have been stamped, but only the sides of the tiles in the church are exposed; the flat top and bottom surfaces (where any stamps would be found) therefore cannot be examined. Whether the presence of tiles from the Weald amounts to evidence for a second-century installation on the site is, however, rather dubious.[17] The *classis Britannica* was still in existence at the time of Reculver's construction in the early third century, and so the tiles were probably imported to the site for the building of the Shore Fort (mostly, it is to be suspected, for the roofs of internal structures). Other isolated examples of the fleet's stamped tiles have also been discovered at Richborough and Pevensey, but here, as at Reculver, there is no supporting evidence for second-century military facilities. If any did exist it must be assumed that they were short-lived: of the three sites only Richborough has so far yielded evidence for substantial occupation during the second century, and that was of a civilian nature.

The wider development of coastal installations around Britain can also be observed during the first and second centuries, most notably during the Hadrianic period. A large number of camps and forts was established during the conquest of Wales in the latter parts of the first century. Military sites on the coast, or situated within easy reach of the sea, included the legionary fortresses at Caerleon and Chester, and smaller sites at Cardiff, Neath, Carmarthen, Pennal, Caernarvon and Caerhun.[18] The Roman presence in Wales as a whole was scaled down during the course of the second century, however, such that by *c.*190 only Caerleon, Cardiff, Caernarvon, Caerhun and Chester remained occupied. Another new military base on the north-west coast was built not later than 160 at Lancaster (replacing a late first-century fort on the same site), while at approximately the same date a series of forts, milefortlets and signal stations was established on the Cumbrian coast. These stations formed a southward extension of Hadrian's Wall, and were intended to guard against any enemy crossing of the Solway Firth. Despite being reconstructed during the Antonine period, these had largely fallen out of commission by AD 200, although some were to be resurrected for use in the fourth century.

At the eastern end of Hadrian's Wall was the outpost fort at South Shields on the River Tyne, probably occupied from the late first century and rebuilt in stone in 163. However, despite the undoubted involvement of the *classis Britannica* in the campaigns in northern England and Scotland during the later first and second centuries, this is one of a very few military sites of this period known on England's east coast. No stamped CLBR tiles have been found at any coastal site north of the Thames, but this is not to say that there were never any fleet bases. The likelihood of occupation at Brancaster prior to the building of the Shore Fort certainly raises the question of whether there was an earlier base on the same site, perhaps in existence from the mid-second century onwards.

It is also possible that large, formal forts were not thought necessary, and indeed there are various precedents from the Roman world for squadrons, flotillas or even entire fleets based in civilian ports: Ravenna, headquarters of the Adriatic fleet, is one very prominent example of a civilian port that was also a Roman naval base. Another location that has been suggested as a naval station of the period is Brough-on-Humber, where the early defensive circuit was extended and remodelled during the Hadrianic period.[19] The nature of this site is problematic: much doubt remains as to whether it was exclusively a civilian settlement (perhaps even the capital of the *Parisi* tribe) or a military base. The absence of public buildings and the lack of a regular street pattern, together with the provision of defences at an unusually early date, tend (amongst other factors) to argue for the idea that Brough-on-Humber was a military installation from the outset.[20] However, the possibility of it being a small town that shared its defensive enclosure with naval units cannot yet be ruled out.

The Severan period

The very last years of the second century and the first decades of the third witnessed significant reorganisation of the south and east coast military forts of Britain (**28**). The Severan campaigns themselves involved the construction of several military installations in Scotland, including two within easy reach of the eastern coast, the vexillation fortress at Carpow on the Tay and a more southerly fort at Cramond on the Forth. Probably about the same time (although the archaeological evidence only suggests a date early in the third century) the fort at South Shields was also substantially remodelled. The barrack blocks were demolished, and in their place 20 new granaries were built, adding to the four already in existence, thus creating a major supply depot for the expeditionary army in Scotland.[21] In the event, the ending of the Severan campaigns in 211 and the subsequent re-adoption of Hadrian's Wall as the northern frontier meant that neither Carpow nor Cramond was to become a long-term element of the Roman coastal network. South Shields, by contrast, continued in use until at least the mid-fourth century, presumably forming the northern terminus of Roman shipping routes on the east coast.

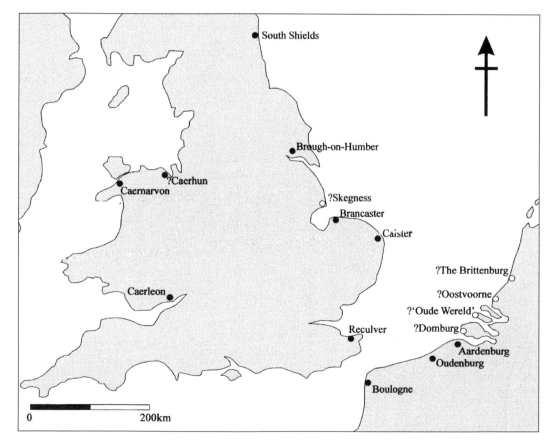

28   *Early third-century coastal installations*

During broadly the same period other military installations on the eastern coast of England were also created or remodelled. Once again the dating evidence from individual sites is not particularly precise, but the developments are broadly coincident with the reign of the Severan dynasty, although some projects may have stretched into the 240s. This series of forts includes the first group of new installations south of the Wash that would later form part of the Saxon Shore defences, at Caister, Reculver and with a possible contemporary site at Brancaster.

The fort at Caister, situated on the Great Estuary near the east Norfolk coast, was built on unoccupied ground at some point around the early third century. It has been suggested (on the basis of the find of a 'palisade trench') that defences of earth and timber were constructed very shortly before the erection of the stone perimeter, but this hypothesis lacks conclusive proof.[22] Pottery in the fill of the supposed palisade trench dates the stone defences to *not earlier* than the late second century, and more probably to the early third century. Pottery in a rubbish deposit dumped onto the rampart is of early to mid-third-century character, and so provides a *terminus ante quem* for the completion of construction. On the north Kentish coast, and broadly contemporary with Caister, is the fort of Reculver. A building inscription celebrating the construction of the headquarters building (*principia*) was originally thought to date to the Severan, or immediately post-Severan period, but this interpretation has since been revised and it is now only possible to suggest a late second to late third-century date.[23] However, the evidence provided by coins and pottery recovered during excavations of the rampart bank appears to confirm an early third-century date for construction.[24]

Another important site, generally assumed to have been built in the first decades of the third century, is the fort at Brancaster. The assumption of an early third-century date for Brancaster rests solely on the supposedly early style of the architecture, as the defences themselves have not actually been dated by archaeological evidence. A rubbish deposit overlying the rampart contained a coin of Tetricus (271-4), demonstrating that the rampart was not built after *c.*270, while pottery in the same deposit is also of late third-century character. The lowest occupation levels within the fort relate to the mid- and late third century,[25] corresponding with the general coin evidence from the site, which suggests that the most intense phase of occupation was during the latter parts of the third century. Carausian coins form by far the largest group, but issues of Tetricus are also reasonably represented.[26] Some caution is therefore required in assigning an early third-century date for the fort. If the installation was indeed built during the early third century then its construction seems to have pre-dated the first period of its intensive use by several decades.

These forts may have been intended to operate in conjunction with other defended sites on the east coast of Britain. One of these sites was Brough-on-Humber (already proposed as a mid-second-century fleet base of the *classis Britannica*), where the Hadrianic defences were rebuilt, and a new earth and timber rampart was constructed around the built-up area in *c.*200.[27] Between Brough-on-Humber and Brancaster lies another possible fort at Skegness. The site was lost to erosion during the fifteenth or sixteenth centuries, but the small amount of evidence that exists does support the idea that a Roman fort or walled town once stood there.[28] Its date, and whether it is military or civilian in character, is unlikely to be established with certainty, but it is plausible that this defended site was intended to operate in tandem with Brancaster, which it faced across the Wash. To these east-coast sites might be added one other, namely the civilian town of Rochester on the outer Thames estuary. Here, the earth rampart of the late second century was fronted with a stone wall: the construction of this wall is poorly dated, but it is thought to have built at the beginning of the third century.[29]

In contrast to the developments in eastern Britain, there is practically no evidence for renewed military activity – and certainly not for new installations – on the south coast. Indeed, the picture is in fact one of decline, rather than of renewed growth. The *classis Britannica* was doubtless heavily involved in support of the Severan campaigns, and its probable redeployment to the north has been linked to the abandonment of the fort at Dover, which occurred at about this time. This fort had been occupied throughout most of the second century (albeit with occasional periods of disuse, probably relating to the fleet's absence on campaign), but was demolished and abandoned between 200 and 210.[30] The complete abandonment of the fleet base at Dover is a rather curious event, as it coincided with an episode when the military operations in the north must have greatly increased the volume of maritime traffic between Britain and the continent.

The occupation of Lympne is known to have continued during the early third century, as evinced by the name *Lemanis* featuring in the Antonine Itinerary. The inclusion of Lympne is reasonable evidence for some form of activity there, though whether there was a fort or only a civilian port is not known. The limited early material evidence from the site of the Shore Fort itself, however, is from the second century. There is nothing to indicate early third-century occupation and therefore it would appear that if Lympne had been an active base, then as with Dover, it had fallen out of use during the early 200s.

Some fortification of the Gallic coastline can be observed during this period, insofar as the sparse dating evidence from the various sites allows. The only developments appear to be on the coastline to the north of Boulogne, the area closest to the Rhine frontier that fell within *Belgica Secunda* (see **28**). Evidence from the fort at Boulogne shows it to have remained in use around 200, but there was a partial closing down of the base during the course of the third century, perhaps leading to a complete (albeit probably brief) abandonment by 270. Towards the end of the second century or the beginning of the third, a defensive earthen rampart was constructed around the civilian settlement of Oudenburg. Urban defences were also built around the town of Aardenburg, although in this case the date range for construction spans the period *c.*200-50. Other contemporary forts have been postulated further to the north at Domburg, 'Oude Wereld' (off the island of Goeree), Oostvoorne and the Brittenburg, although the evidence for early third-century military installations is rather scant in all of these cases.

The later third century

The second half of the third century – the eye of the Roman Empire's political and military storm – witnessed significant developments around the British coast (**29**). New military installations were built in East Anglia and Kent, augmenting those forts constructed during the earlier parts of the century. Significantly too, new defences were erected on the south coast from Dover to the Solent, as well as in Wales. The growth of defended maritime strongholds around Britain was also matched by the building of new coastal fortifications in Gaul.

Extensive town wall building in both Britain and Gaul is also apparent. By the late second century many towns and some smaller settlements in Britain had been provided with linear defences, normally in the form of earthworks. The conversion of some of these defences to stone appears to have begun early in the third century, and although the dating evidence is poor, the process probably continued throughout the course of the century. Gaul presents a rather different picture, in that virtually all towns were undefended at the time of the barbarian invasions of the 260s and 270s. Only after this date were the urban centres of Gaul fortified, often utilising the rubble of the ruined towns. Many sites were provided with walls during the later parts of

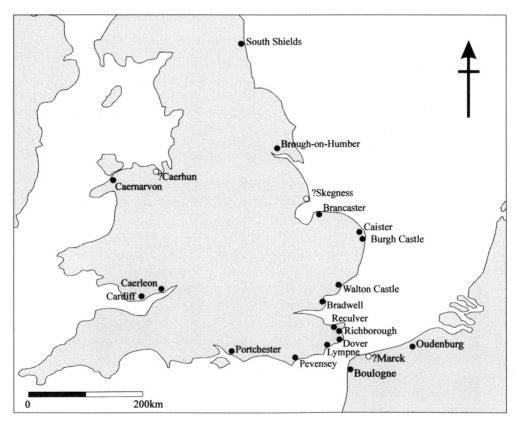

29 British coastal installations c.AD 300

the third century, although there is evidence to show that certain others remained undefended until after the mid-fourth century. This subject is not pursued further here, but is one which is revisited in the following chapter, when the context of the Shore Forts' construction is considered.

The presence of new forts on the British coast attests to a continued naval presence, and indeed it is the navy that we might expect to have been responsible for the building of these installations. At this time, however, the *classis Britannica* disappears from the archaeological record. The last epigraphic evidence of the fleet comes from Arles, where a dedication set up during the reign of Philip I (244-9) recorded the commander of the *classis Britannica Philipiana*.[31] The lack of evidence from this date onwards does not in itself amount to definitive proof that the fleet was disbanded, and indeed it seems highly likely that a naval presence was maintained in British waters throughout the period of the late Empire. The hints of naval campaigns conducted by Postumus and Carinus adds weight to this view. Nevertheless from the mid-point of the third century the fleet is not directly apparent in the archaeological record. This is nowhere more evident than in the Weald where iron production, which had reached its peak during the mid-second century, had been scaled down to almost nothing by the mid-third. Until the time of the *Notitia Dignitatum* well over a century later we have no direct knowledge of how the Roman navy in Britain was organised.

New defences between the Solent and the Wash

In the main, discussions of late third-century coastal defences have tended to concentrate on the monuments traditionally associated with the Saxon Shore, as defined by the *Notitia Dignitatum* (see **62**). Listed clockwise they are Burgh Castle, Walton Castle, Bradwell, Richborough, Dover, Lympne, Pevensey and Portchester. The archaeological evidence is sufficient to demonstrate that the construction of these defences is detached in time from those built during the Severan period or shortly after. Moreover, the architectural style of these new forts sets them apart from sites such as Caister and Reculver, and indeed most other British forts of the first, second and early third centuries. The perimeter walls of many of these new forts were built on an altogether more massive scale, and incorporated the latest defensive architectural innovation in the form of projecting bastions. Beyond this general observation, however, the precise chronology of these later forts' development remains to be established.

The evidence for the date of Burgh Castle is insubstantial, and there is nothing that relates directly to the perimeter defences. Excavation of a small section of the interior between 1958 and 1961 produced no evidence of occupation prior to the reign of Constantius in Britain (296-305/6), and demolished structures adjacent to the perimeter wall have been dated to the second quarter of the fourth century. The placing of buildings against perimeter defences is a characteristic of fourth- rather than third-century military planning, however, and therefore these structures may post-date the erection of the perimeter.[32] Surface finds from the site suggest that it was indeed occupied during the later third century, but allow no more precise an interpretation concerning the nature of activity at that time.[33]

The complete destruction by the sea of Walton Castle means that the date of its construction will almost certainly never be known. The few depictions of the site show a fort superficially similar to Burgh Castle, and the portrayal of bastions is at least good evidence for a date post-260. Field walking on the nearby settlement, 500m from the site of the fort, has found pottery spanning the second to the fourth century, but how this relates to the Shore Fort is unknown.[34] The dating of the fort at Bradwell is also poorly established, relying entirely on the interpretation of the very limited coin series unearthed during excavations in the nineteenth century.[35] The third-century coins are mostly those of the Gallic Empire, and of Carausius and Allectus, but they are few in number and none has an archaeological context. The series is reminiscent of that of Portchester, thought to be a Carausian project (as discussed below), but this association alone cannot confirm a similar date for the construction of Bradwell.

At Richborough, a military presence on the site was re-established after an interval of perhaps two centuries, when growing military concerns led to the civilian settlement at Richborough undergoing a drastic conversion. The developments at Richborough during the second half of the third century can be divided into two distinct phases. First, the Great Monument was ringed with a triple ditch and an earth rampart, the arch becoming a watch- or signal-tower (**30**). The history of this fortlet is imprecisely understood, but is generally considered to have been relatively short-lived, the ditches of the defences being backfilled at some point after *c*.273.[36] This latter event was part of site-clearance operations making way for a much larger and more substantial fort, this time built of stone (**31**). The evidence of the finds from the site suggests that construction work began immediately after the demolition of the earth fortlet, or after only a very brief interlude. Neither the backfilled fortlet ditches nor a nearby pit (the latter filled in with building rubble, so probably relating to the tidying up of the site after building work was complete) contained Carausian coins, with one exception, of uncertain stratification.[37] The earliest occupation layers of the new 'Shore Fort', by contrast, contained many Carausian issues, so as a whole the evidence supports a date for construction between 273 and the very earliest stages of Carausius' rule, before his coins became common.

The south coast was also re-fortified, a programme that included the reoccupation of the site of the *classis Britannica* fort at Dover after an interval of at least 50 years. Here, soil accumulation over the rubble of the demolished second-century fort was found to contain coins which indicated that construction of the new installation did not begin earlier than 253.[38] On balance, however, it seems likely that building began at a slightly later date: a clay layer, interpreted as the tail of the rampart of the south wall, contained coins of 260-80, and tip layers forming the west wall rampart yielded finds dating from 275 to the early fourth century. Unless there was a pause of several years between the building of the south and west walls – perhaps a rather unlikely possibility – it seems that building work began after 275-80.[39]

As at Dover, a new fort was constructed at Lympne, utilising a substantial quantity of reused building materials. As noted above, it is only from the Shore Fort period that there is definite evidence of Roman occupation and it is therefore reasonable to suppose that the building of the new installation took place after a lengthy abandon-

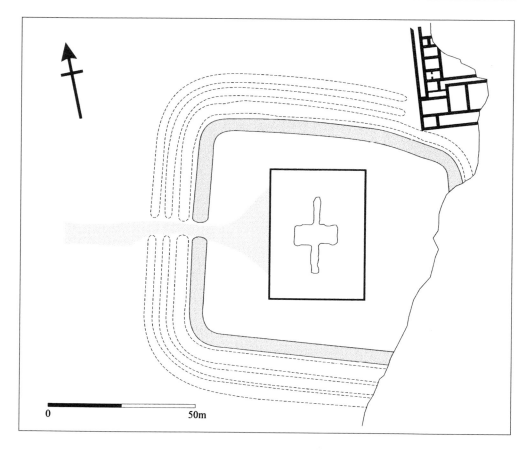

30   The third-century earth fortlet at Richborough

ment of the site. The date of the Shore Fort's construction is mainly based on coin evidence, the bulk of which comes from Roach Smith's excavations of the 1850s and which have no context.[40] With one exception the coins are issues of 259 and later. While occupation of the site in the 260s could be supported by the evidence, a date during the 270s is more likely. A Carausian building date is also plausible, although the coin series as a whole perhaps points to a slightly earlier date.

Some 40km (25 miles) to the west a new large fort was established at Pevensey, East Sussex. Until recently the dating of this monument rested on the find of a single coin of Constantine of 330-5. This coin was found in a cavity 0.9-1.2m beneath one of the bastions on the north wall: the circumstances of its find, published in 1932, were never made clear, and it may perhaps be intrusive.[41] The evidence of the coin was at variance with the results of excavations of the fort's interior in 1936-9, which showed that the initial occupation layers contained large amounts of late third-century pottery and Carausian coins.[42] Recent investigations of the site have shed considerable new light on the matter. Excavations on the line of the fallen south wall uncovered a series of oak piles from the foundations, which

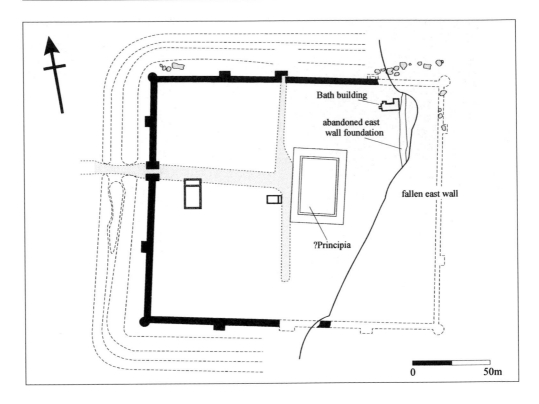

31   The Shore Fort at Richborough

dendrochronology shows to have been felled between 280 and 300 (**32**). Two associated coins, one of Carausius and the other of Allectus, refine this date further, giving an unequivocal *terminus post quem* of 293.[43] The Constantinian coin still requires explanation, however. It may indeed be intrusive, but if not then it must point towards a more complex history of construction, with building or repair work on the north wall continuing well into the fourth century. Similarly the occupation evidence from the fort interior remains to be explained, as it seems to pre-date the building of the south wall. The existence of an immediately pre-Shore Fort phase on the site is plausible, but awaits conclusive proof.

A similarly massive fort to that at Pevensey was established at Portchester, situated in modern day Portsmouth harbour. The dating evidence from this site is rather better than it is for many of the other Shore Forts. Coins of Tetricus in the early construction phases of the defensive perimeter and internal roads show the fort to have been built after 260-8, while the recovery of Tetrican and Carausian coins from the very earliest occupation levels suggests a slightly later date for the first use of the installation. The excavator preferred a Carausian date for the fort's construction,[44] although this interpretation has yet to be proved beyond doubt.

Various other sites within the geographical limits of the British Saxon Shore also require attention. In a triangular area of land formed by a bend in the River Itchen,

32 *Foundation piles under the south wall of the Roman defences, Pevensey.*
Dendrochronological analysis of the timber suggested a felling date of 280-300, whilst
coins of Carausius and Allectus, found in association with the piles, refined the construc-
tion date of the fort to 293 or shortly after. Photo courtesy M. Fulford & S. Rippon

close to Southampton Water, is the defended site at Bitterne (*Clausentum*). During
the early Roman period *Clausentum* is thought to have been a town, originally
occupying some 11ha (27 acres), though by around AD 150 the settlement had
contracted significantly and was sheltered behind a wooden stockade.[45] Second-
century buildings of timber and later of stone have been identified, some of which
continued to be used into the earlier third century. At this point activity appears to
have ceased for a time, before the site was reoccupied and provided with stone

defences. The gap in habitation was once thought to have lasted until the period 350–70, but the reassessment of a coin from the site has led to a revision of this view. It would now seem that the defences were built rather earlier than was previously supposed, most probably during the latter stages of the third century, bringing this site broadly into line with the other south-coast forts at Portchester, Pevensey, Lympne and Dover.[46] The defences at Bitterne, which no longer survive above ground and which at present have been located on only two sides of the settlement, were substantial. Whether *Clausentum* was a fort or a militarised town, however, has yet to be clearly established.

A still more enigmatic site is that at Carisbrooke on the Isle of Wight, where a rectilinear enclosure has been detected under the motte of the Norman castle. In plan this enclosure exhibits superficially Roman characteristics – a 'playing card shape' (i.e. a rectangle with rounded corners), inturned gate entrances and slight traces of semi-circular bastions. It was once proposed (albeit with some reservations) that the site was indeed Roman, and perhaps was an early installation of the Shore Fort series.[47] This idea now tends to be dismissed. The excavations of the site yielded practically no Roman pottery, and the suggested alternative – that this site is in fact a Saxon *burh* – seems at present the more plausible.[48]

The walled town of Chichester is a more likely candidate for a site that supplemented the military network of the south coast, probably mirroring the role played by Rochester in Kent. It has been suggested that the walls of Chichester dated to the first decades of the third century, by implication arguing that the town played a role in the defence of the south coast from an early stage. In reality, however, the defences are extremely poorly dated and could in fact have been built at any point during the century.[49]

One further site remains to be considered within the 'Saxon Shore', and that is the signal station or watchtower at Shadwell, on the inner Thames. Excavated in 1974 in London's then derelict Docklands area, only the foundations had survived.[50] Nevertheless, these remains were sufficient to demonstrate that the structure was some 8m square, and with walls 2m thick a tall superstructure must have been present. Immediately to the east, traces of clay floors, sill-beam foundations and burnt wattle and daub walls attested to timber buildings that were probably associated with the tower. A double ditch was also discovered, presumably a defence on the river side of the site. The tower, presumably intended to give advanced warning of enemies approaching London, was built at some point in the later third century. Of the several hundred coins recovered from the site, those of Carausius and Allectus predominate, suggesting either construction, or an intensification of activity on the site during this episode.

Defences in Wales, northern Britain and Gaul

Beyond the restricted geographical area between the Solent and the Wash there was relatively little new military building on the British coast during the later third century. The focus of activity appears to have shifted in large part to the south and East Anglian coasts, and we can only assume that elsewhere the existing installations were judged adequate for their task.

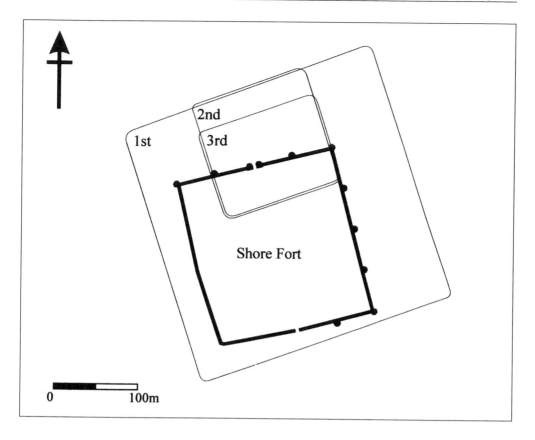

33   The Roman forts at Cardiff. After Webster (1981, Fig. 2)

Two sites in particular deserve attention, however. The first is Brough-on-Humber, where the existing perimeter wall was augmented by the addition of projecting bastions, bringing the defences into line with the later Shore Forts. These towers date to the late third or, at the very latest, the early fourth century: they provide compelling evidence for sites north of the Wash having been intrinsically connected with the Saxon Shore. In Wales, and in contrast to the general dearth of military building in the region, a large stone fort was built at Cardiff.[51] This fort, the fourth on the site, was very similar in design to Portchester (**33**, **47**). The defences were virtually square in plan, with projecting five-sided bastions flanking the walls at regular intervals. Similar bastions also defended the gates. Archaeology dates the building of the site to post-260, but the architectural similarities with Lympne and Portchester might suggest a slightly later third-century inception. It is also reasonable to see the construction of the Cardiff fort as contemporary with, rather than earlier than, the development of defences on the south coast of England.

On the continental coast there was a significant programme of fortification between the Rhine frontier and the River Loire (**34**). Some of the sites were

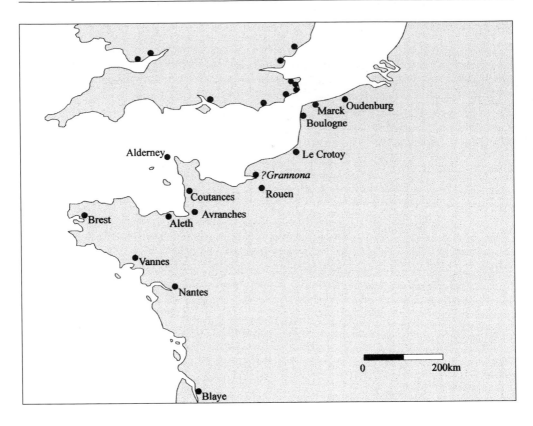

34   Continental coastal installations c.AD 300

defended towns (e.g. Nantes, Rouen, Avranches, Coutances) while others were
dedicated military complexes (e.g. Oudenburg, and also the fortlet on the Channel
Island of Alderney). Whether certain sites were essentially military or urban, such as
Brest and Aardenburg, remains a matter of dispute. The size of the sites was also
extremely varied, from the fortlet at Alderney (40m square) to the extensive defences
of towns such as Nantes, which had a perimeter of some 1,665m enclosing some
16ha (40 acres).[52] The archaeological evidence for these sites is variable in quality.
Some sites listed in the *Notitia Dignitatum* have only been proposed on the basis of
place-names, but in other cases the defences have been located and investigated. The
evidence for construction dates is often rather scant, but is sufficient to show that
most of the sites were built during the late third or early fourth centuries. Certain
defences, such as those of Boulogne and Rouen, have been linked (largely on historical grounds) with the Carausian revolt (*c.*286-93), but in general the evidence is not
sufficiently precise to show how the development of the continental coastal defences
related to the new forts on the British side of the English Channel. The analogy of
the Gallic town defences as a whole, to the sites on the continental Atlantic coast,
would perhaps suggest that construction took place over a fairly lengthy period,
probably from the time of Probus (276-82).[53]

The fourth century

By AD 300 the coastal network around Britain had largely been established in the form that would remain until the end of the Roman occupation of the province. The only major additions to the network were in the north of England. At Lancaster a fort with massive stone walls and at least one bastion was built; a slightly worn coin of *c*.326 in the construction layer suggests a date of *c*.330/350 for the defences. This installation was the last of a series on the site, and was presumably built as part of the attempt to protect the west coast against raiding from Scotland and Ireland, as described in Chapter 6. Some of the chain of Cumbrian coastal stations to the south of Hadrian's Wall, abandoned throughout the third and early fourth centuries, were also refurbished, probably as a component of the same scheme. In the closing years of the Roman occupation (probably *c*.380) an entirely new series of defended signal towers was built along the Yorkshire coast. Five are known, at Huntcliff, Goldsborough, Ravenscar, Scarborough and Filey (see **64**). Others may have existed, later to be destroyed by coastal erosion. The towers within the defences at these sites may have stood over 25m high, and would have served as look-out and signal posts, designed to give early warning of impending attack from the sea.

For the most part, however, understanding the Roman coast in the fourth century is not a question of plotting new installations, but of appreciating when existing sites fell out of use. The operation of the Shore Forts within the context of their contemporary installations, and their eventual abandonment, are topics that will be addressed in the final two chapters of this study.

Conclusions: the construction dates of the Shore Forts

The preceding discussion shows the Shore Forts to have been but one part of a far wider, and long-established coastal network in Britain and Gaul. The archaeological evidence points a fairly clear (if perhaps rather basic) pattern for the development of these 11 installations, which in the late fourth century we have come to associate with the Saxon Shore (**35**). The forts at Caister and Reculver can be placed with reasonable confidence in the early decades of the third century, while Brancaster is perhaps of a similar date, although it could equally have been built up to 50 years later. Into this first phase can be placed several installations north of the Wash, at Brough-on-Humber, South Shields, and, for a brief period, Cramond and Carpow. The remainder of the forts were built at some point from the 260s onwards, with work on at least one site (Pevensey) taking place during the 290s. In this second phase we can also observe the construction or improvement of defended sites over a wider geographical area, for example at Bitterne, Cardiff, Brough-on-Humber, and which continued into the fourth century at sites such as Lancaster.

Archaeology only informs us up to a certain point, however, and for this reason scholars have turned to the turbulent history of the third century as a means of explaining the role of these military coastal sites. This issue will be addressed in

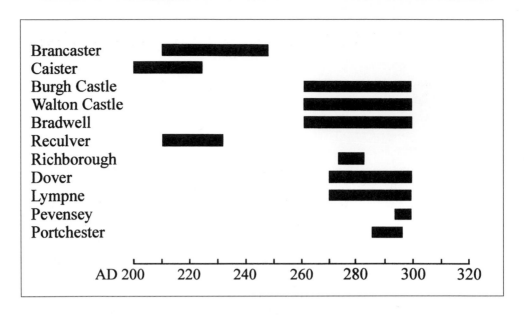

35   *The construction dates of the Shore Forts. Each bar represents the range of time over which the archaeological evidence suggests each fort was built. At precisely what point within this range construction actually took place is not known, nor is the duration of each building project. An arbitrary cut-off date for construction is taken as AD 300*

detail in Chapter 6, and as will be seen, some of the theories used to explain the building of the Shore Forts posit specific dates, periods or timescales for their construction. It is not the intention of this book to argue for any particular one of these theories, and nor do I feel it is yet possible to argue for precise construction dates (i.e. within five years or so) for any but a very few of the Shore Forts. Nevertheless, even without a precise understanding of the dates involved, investigation of the building of the monuments remains a possible, valid exercise, and it is to this that we now proceed.

4 Building the Shore Forts

Each of the Shore Forts was the product of a generating process of considerable complexity. Although the intricacies of this process cannot be fully grasped at this distance in time, it is nevertheless possible to describe – at least in basic terms – the manner in which these imposing monuments came to be created. As we have seen in the previous chapter the building of the installations may have spanned nearly a century, from Caister in *c*.200 to Pevensey in 293 or shortly after. As such it is perhaps erroneous to consider them as a single 'project', though the later group of forts may have constituted a more coherent, planned programme of building.

Gaining an insight into engineering in the ancient world is an end in itself, but we can go further. In the following pages an attempt is made to quantify the process of construction: how much raw material was required and where was it being procured? By what means were those materials moved, and how great was the scale of the transport demand? How much manpower was needed and from where was the labour force gathered? By calculating the demands of the project in this way and considering how those needs could have been met, we are able to more fully appreciate the *materiel* and effort required to build the Shore Fort series. Other ancient building programmes have been analysed in a similar fashion, and therefore we can also compare the relative size of the Shore Fort programme, both with the great buildings of the Roman Empire, and with provincial military undertakings such as Hadrian's Wall. In the final parts of this chapter the place of the forts within the broader context of large-scale construction in third-century Britain and Gaul is considered. Here we find that the installations were only a single element within a wider phenomenon of building work during this period, both of a military and civilian character. We begin our study at the outset with one of the very first stages of the generating process, that of design.

Design and architecture

Construction methods

The mode of constructing the Shore Fort defences was, in all cases, broadly similar. The building process began with the excavation of a roughly vertical-sided, flat-bottomed trench, ranging in depth from 0.7m to 1.5m between sites. The main constituents of the foundations were 'dry' materials, such as flint, chalk, or other locally available stones, and occasionally clay. Thin spreads of concrete were employed at Brancaster and Pevensey, respectively as the lowest and highest components of the foundations. Where the subsoil was felt to be unstable, particularly when the fort wall stood on a slope, timber piles were driven into the base of the trench to provide additional underpinning. This is the case at Lympne, Pevensey and Richborough, and piles are also known to have been employed in other sizeable Romano-British structures, including the London town wall.

The complexity of the foundations varied significantly. Some were very simple, for example those at Reculver, which consisted of a trench that was filled entirely with small flint cobbles. By contrast, those at Pevensey were far more elaborate. Here, above piles driven into the trench base, successive layers of flint and chalk were laid down and rammed. Resting on the highest chalk layer, just below the Roman ground level, was a lattice of large timber baulks. Chalk was packed in the spaces between the timbers and a layer of mortar spread over the top, sealing the foundations and ensuring a level platform for the superstructure. Similar timber foundation frames were also employed at Richborough and Portchester, though in no case have the actual baulks survived, only the cavities left behind after their decomposition. The Roman builders clearly had a sound appreciation of ground conditions, and foundations could vary even within a single site, a fact most apparent at Burgh Castle. The western parts of the defences, built close to the top of a scarp, were far less substantial than those on the east side, and the foundations differed accordingly. The wider east wall rested on a trench some 0.6m deep, and was filled entirely with concrete, while the foundations for the slighter western walls were far less substantial, comprising a shallow trench only a 'few inches deep'. Closer to the scarp, at the north-west angle of the fort, the foundation trench deepened sharply to allow for the weight of the corner bastion, and for the potential instability of the sloping ground to the west.[1]

Construction of the superstructure began at, or a little below, the contemporary ground surface. The lowest component was normally a plinth of large blocks, wider than the masonry above, and stepped out on one or both faces. Above the plinth the outer face was vertical, but in many instances the inner face was tapered, or progressively thinned by a series of offsets, thus creating a more stable structure (**36**). Examination of the better-preserved forts enables a good understanding of the building methods (see **colour plate 18**). A course of small shaped stone blocks (*petit appareil*) or flint was laid to form the inner and outer face of the wall, creating a trough that was then infilled with a mixture of rubble and mortar, which was subsequently compressed by trampling or ramming. The next course of facing stones was then laid, and the process repeated. Once the wall reached heights of around 1.5m and above, higher than could be comfortably reached by a standing man, scaffold became necessary. At the lowest levels this probably consisted of free-standing trestles, but as the wall rose higher some type of engaged scaffold was used. Evidence for such scaffold is preserved in the forts at Richborough, Lympne and Pevensey, where the sockets for the insertion of the horizontal timbers ('putlog holes') remain as open cavities in the facing. The total height of the defences is not known for certain, because at no location does Roman masonry still stand to its original level. The ancient writer Vitruvius recommended that the wall walk should 'be so made that

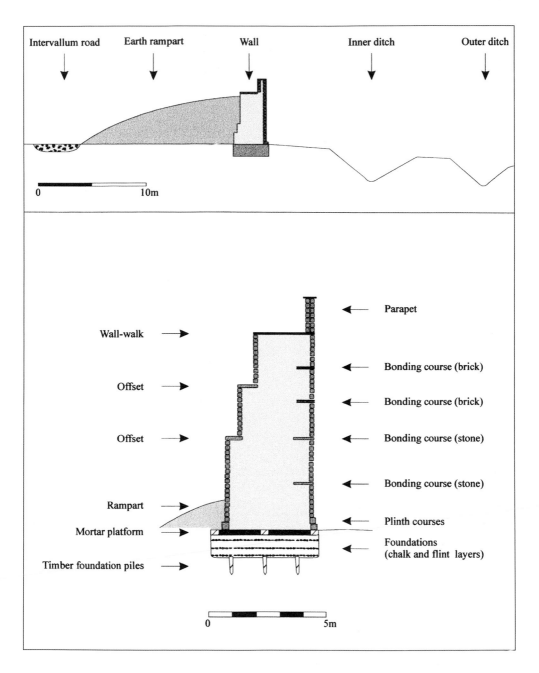

Intervallum road   Earth rampart   Wall   Inner ditch   Outer ditch

0   10m

Parapet

Wall-walk →

Bonding course (brick)

Offset →

Bonding course (brick)

Offset →

Bonding course (stone)

Bonding course (stone)

Rampart →

Plinth courses

Mortar platform →

Foundations
(chalk and flint layers)

Timber foundation piles →

0   5m

36 Sections through the Shore Fort defences. The traditional style of narrow, rampart-backed fortifications at Reculver (top) contrasts with the more massive freestanding wall of the later fort at Pevensey (below)

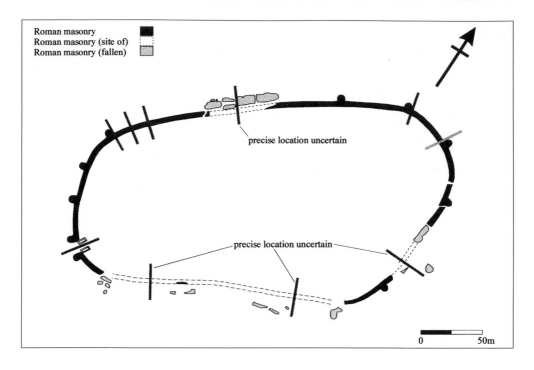

Roman masonry
Roman masonry (site of)
Roman masonry (fallen)

precise location uncertain

precise location uncertain

0   50m

37   Construction sections at Pevensey. The short building sections on the north wall feature in text figure 21

armed men meeting one another ... can pass without hindrance',[2] and thus the thickness of the highest surviving section of wall at Burgh Castle (1.5m) suggests that here the defences stand close to their full height. Adding a parapet of 1.6m, comparable to that excavated at Wörth (Germany) suggests that the complete height of the defences was around 6m. Other forts had wider, taller defences. Roman masonry survives above 8m at Richborough and Pevensey, and it is evident that here, and at Portchester, the full height of the wall was probably in excess of 9m. Although the original parapet does not survive at any Shore Fort, Roman defences elsewhere are known to have been crenellated.

It can be seen that several of the Shore Forts were built in numerous distinct parts, divisions that are often termed 'construction sections', where each stretch of wall is not keyed into the adjacent piece. Of those monuments with well-preserved superstructures, only Burgh Castle seems to have been built as a single unit. These are generally understood to be the work of individual gangs of labourers, and are apparent from the use of different materials, changes in the levels of the masonry courses, and in the varying heights and alignments of putlog holes. At Portchester these divisions appear uniform, with each gang responsible for one section of wall and a bastion. At Pevensey and Richborough, however, the building units are far less systematic; at both forts, the north walls exhibit a series of particularly short sections (**37, colour plate 11**).

Design

Although the methods of construction were broadly similar, the architecture of the forts is actually far from uniform.[3] Particular differences can be observed between the installations built early in the third century (Caister, Reculver, and probably Brancaster) and the group of eight constructed after *c*.260. The early Shore Forts adhere to what might be termed a 'traditional' design, one that continued in the military building traditions of the second century. In plan the defences were rectangular and round-cornered, with walls backed by an earth rampart which extended to the base of the parapet (see Reculver, **36**). Internal towers were present at some or all of the angles, while gates tended to be relatively simple in their design and only lightly defended. Inside the forts was a regular layout of roads and buildings, with the *principia* located within the central range (see **65 & 66**). Such a design directly compares with that of the vast majority of second-century forts in the British province, and indeed elsewhere in the Empire.

During the later third century defensive architecture in the western Roman world as a whole was to change. Drawing directly on influences from the eastern Empire, new defences – both military and urban – in Gaul, Italy and elsewhere were built on an altogether more massive scale. Walls became thicker and higher than had previously been the norm, probably reflecting the insecurity of the times as much as anything else. Increases in scale were accompanied by architectural innovation. Bastions or towers were built at intervals around the new defensive circuits: projecting from the outside of the walls, these provided platforms for archers or artillery, thus giving the perimeters greater protection from attackers (**38**). Entrances also became more heavily defended, often with flanking bastions on either side of the gate, and gatehouse designs also became more complex.

Other more minor, but nonetheless significant, changes can also be seen, foremost of which was the introduction of bonding courses. These normally consisted of one or several horizontal courses of brick (or reused tile) built into the face of the wall at regular vertical intervals (**39**). The principal function of these courses was to key the shallow facing stones into the mass of the rubble-mortar core – a significant structural improvement on the techniques of the past – in addition to serving as a means of levelling the wall during construction. Brick was already widely used in the ancient world by this date: it had started to become common in Rome during the late Republican period, and *opus mixtum* (brick and stone) construction had been introduced into Gaul and Britain by the second century AD. However, its use in military architecture at this time was a new phenomenon in the North-West Empire.[4] In Italy the emergence of the new architecture can be seen in the walls of Rome, begun under the auspices of Aurelian in 271; its adoption in Gaul can be observed in early-dated town walls such as Dijon, whose defences, described by St Geoffrey of Tours, were also attributed to Aurelian.[5]

These defensive improvements are also apparent in Britain within the later series of Shore Forts. Gone were the comparatively simple designs seen in the earlier coastal forts, and in their place were much more substantial, modern defences. In certain cases the regular rectangular plan, which had typified (with a few exceptions) the forts of the early

38 Bastion on the north wall, Portchester. This example is built of flint rubble, and exhibits many bonding courses of thin stone slabs

Empire, was superseded by a variety of polygonal arrangements (e.g. Burgh Castle, Bradwell, Dover) and in the case of Pevensey, an irregular oval. Not all were irregularly planned, however: Portchester and Richborough were designed as rectangles, although the latter fort suffered from minor surveying errors on its north and west walls. Also notably absent from the later Shore Forts are any indications of a planned arrangement of buildings within the perimeter: this subject is one to which Chapter 7 will return.

The architectural innovation seen in the later Shore Forts is in marked contrast to the innate conservatism found in most contemporary building within the British

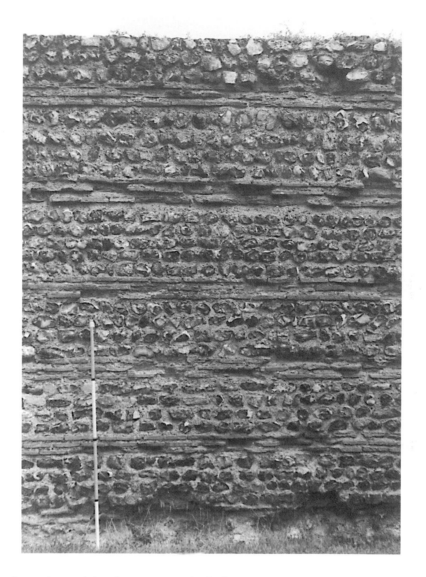

39   Burgh Castle. Brick bonding courses and split flint ashlar on the exterior face of the south wall

province. On the northern frontier, reconstruction of existing forts from AD 270 onwards was undertaken along second-century lines, while the new forts at Piercebridge (Co. Durham) and Newton Kyme (Yorkshire) were also built according to traditional design. Only at a relatively small number of sites – notably in coastal locations – does the architecture demonstrate late-continental influences. A pertinent example is that of Cardiff, which in plan is strongly reminiscent of Portchester, while the late third-century addition of bastions to the estuarine site of Brough-on-Humber also brought this latter site up to the most modern standards. Contemporary town fortifications in Britain were also largely unaffected by continental trends, continuing to employ narrow, rampart-backed walls without external bastions. An interesting example is that of Canterbury, which was fortified in approximately 270. Unlike many other urban centres where the stone defences evolved from earlier earthen ramparts, there was nothing at Canterbury to influence the form of the new perimeter wall, but here, as elsewhere, the defences were built as a narrow-gauge wall with an internal rampart. It would therefore seem that the Shore Forts (and perhaps coastal installations over a wider geographical area), with their characteristic designs, must be viewed as a unique development within the British province, somehow divorced from the other defence-building programmes of the period.

Each of the later group of eight Shore Forts was of somewhat differing design. Even the most basic aspect, the thickness of the wall, varied very considerably between sites, from 2.3m in parts of the circuit at Dover to 4.2m at Pevensey and Lympne. Given these differences, the final height of the defences was probably also very variable. The manner in which the new defensive features were designed and incorporated into each structure was also markedly different, the bastions being a case in point. Normally the bastions were semi-circular or rounded, though at Burgh Castle they are better described as 'pear-shaped'. In most instances they were solid (as for example at Pevensey, Lympne and Burgh Castle) but in rare cases they were hollow (e.g. Portchester). Usually there is consistency within an individual monument, but at Richborough this is not the case, the corner bastions being round and solid, with those on straight sections of wall being rectangular and hollow. Gate designs, too, were quite distinct at each site, both in their arrangement, and in the massiveness of their defences. There is a considerable contrast, for example, between the simple west gate of Richborough and the more elaborate bastion-flanked east gate at Lympne, or the complex inset Landgate at Portchester (**40**). These three forts were broadly contemporary, and yet the detail of the design was markedly different at each.

Crucially too, there appears to have been some confusion as to how many of the new architectural concepts were to be incorporated into the design. The bastions once again provide a case in point. Those at Burgh Castle were only joined to the wall in the upper courses, giving the appearance of having been 'tacked on', perhaps as an afterthought to the original design (**colour plate 19**). Moreover, at this particular site the corner bastions are imperfectly designed, for they do not project far enough to have been able to provide cover for the stretches of wall on either side. At Dover, several of the known bastions were built as an integral, original part of the perimeter wall, but others were added at a later stage, as if it was realised that the spacing between the original bastions was too great. Other inconsistencies can be observed. For example, there sometimes seems to have been a failure to appreciate the fact that the new, thicker defences had rendered the rampart behind the wall unnecessary. This is certainly the case at Dover, although here the wall was relatively narrow (2.3–2.6m), and in fact the rampart may have been used as a means of protecting the chalk facing of the interior from the weather.[6] However, at Bradwell a rampart was present behind a wall 4.2m thick at the base. So too at Pevensey, although here the rampart extends only a very short way up the wall.[7]

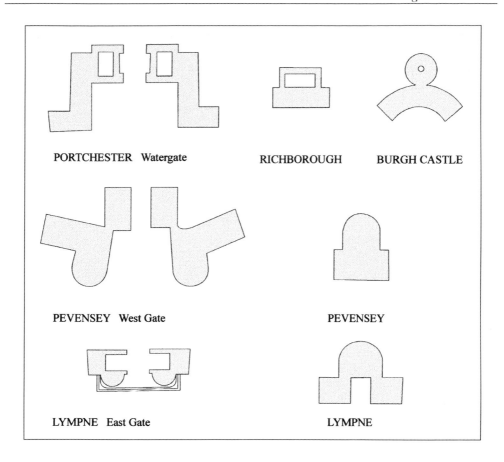

40 Gate and bastion designs

Several explanations exist as to why the architecture of the Shore Forts is so varied. The most widely accepted theory was first proposed by Cunliffe, and has been further elaborated upon by Johnson.[8] The essential plank of their argument is the idea that the design of the Shore Forts evolved during the course of the century, beginning with simple structures that continued the traditions of second-century design, and ending with the most massive and complex defences. According to this model, Reculver, built along traditional lines and dated by archaeology to the first decades of the third century, was seen as the first of the series. Although the archaeological evidence for the date of Brancaster is less conclusive, the 'playing card' plan of its defences, internal rampart and the absence of external bastions also led to the fort being assigned to the early stages of the third century. Caister, still thought to be a civilian port, was not considered as part of the scheme, but would be similarly placed within this initial group of installations. The second phase of Shore Fort construction was seen to begin with Burgh Castle and Dover, built no earlier than the reign of Gallienus (253-68). These forts, which rather imperfectly incorporate external bastions, are said to represent a transitional phase in fort design. It is suggested that the remaining forts were built in close succession, in a phase of construction that began with the erection of stone defences at Richborough from 275. Completion of the series culminated in the building of Pevensey, which until recently was thought to have occurred around the reign of Constans in the mid-fourth century.

Any such scheme awaits proof in the form of conclusive dating evidence for the individual sites, though a temporal separation between the three early-style forts, and the eight more complex monuments built after *c*.260, seems reasonably clear. At present, however, the archaeological data are simply not sufficiently precise to confirm or deny the proposed sequence for the later group's construction. Problems also exist because the idea of a basic, linear typological evolution, from simple to complex, may itself be fundamentally flawed. In his study of Roman fortifications, von Petrikovits concluded that:

> ... different methods of fortification were employed side by side, simultane-
> ously and in the same areas, so that we should guard against any tendency
> to date late Roman fortifications on typological grounds. This method, if
> cautiously employed, is useful for dating the forts of the Principate, but (with
> few exceptions) is worse than useless in the late Roman period.[9]

The conclusion that ancient architecture did not evolve in linear fashion is borne out by examination of other, wider, aspects of Roman building. One example that can be cited is the Pompeian house. Here, studies have shown that 'traditional' design aspects persisted up until the destruction of the town in AD 79, alongside the suppos-edly 'later' features that were once thought to have superseded them in the mid- and late first century AD.[10] It is quite possible, therefore, that improved dating evidence for the forts will dispel, rather than confirm, any typological scheme.

An alternative solution to the architectural question may lie in the transmission of the design. It has been commented that the architecture of the later forts was so different that they 'did not emerge from a single stereotyped blueprint from central authority'.[11] However, the very lack of standardisation might in fact argue for many, if not all, having been virtual contemporaries. Stephen Johnson, architect of the typological scheme, has commented elsewhere that, 'if not actually planned together, they show all the hallmarks of different sets of military architects and surveyors shown an original blueprint and told to go off and apply the new methods to what was built'.[12] It is quite plausible for designs in the Roman world to have been transmitted verbally: elevation drawings in particular might well only have been used for complex constructions.[13] What we may see, therefore, in the architecture of the later group of eight Shore Forts, are the attempts of several contemporary (or near contemporary) groups to grapple with some new and unfamiliar concepts. Why certain groups were more successful than others is not clear. Perhaps some of the architects had recently worked on the continent, and thus had first-hand knowledge of the new architec-ture, while others did not. Alternatively, the most advanced installations may indeed have been the last to be commissioned, and thus their builders could draw directly on the experience of earlier, and slightly less successful, efforts at the other forts. To a very large extent, however, only improved dating evidence for the Shore Forts' construction will shed light on whether this second theory is any more or less valid than the typological scheme.

Raw materials

The scale of demand

Each Shore Fort required a large volume of raw materials for the construction of the perimeter defences.[14] Calculations suggest that the total volume of stone needed for the construction of the perimeter defences of the 11 installations was to the order of 200,000 cubic metres. This equates to roughly 500,000 tonnes of stone, to which must be added a lesser (though still significant) tonnage of other items such as brick and timber. In themselves such figures are, admittedly, somewhat meaningless. However, when compared to other large-scale construction projects of the time we can begin to gain an impression of the relative scale of the Shore Fort project. Calculations made for Hadrian's Wall, for example, suggest that the construction of the curtain wall, milecastles and turrets required some 1,178,000m^3 of material.[15] Large though the demands imposed by the Shore Forts were, it becomes apparent that they required considerably fewer building materials, in fact under one-fifth of that which was necessary for Hadrian's Wall.

When we examine the individual forts, it is possible to see that the estimated volume of raw materials needed for each differed very markedly (**41**). Installations with lower, narrower walls generally required between 12,000m^3 and 14,000m^3, while those with more substantial defences consumed far greater volumes. Contrast, for example, Burgh Castle (14,300m^3) with Pevensey, which has the longest and widest

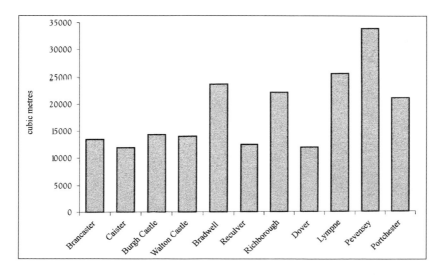

41   Raw material demand for the Shore Fort defences

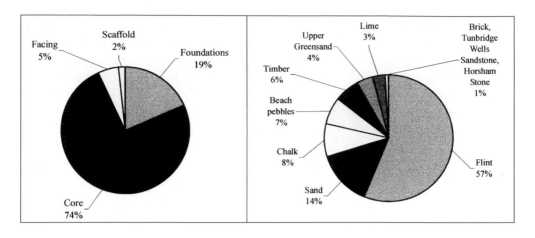

42   *Raw material use in the defences at Pevensey*

superstructure of any Shore Fort (33,710m³). It has been argued that the new, larger style of the later Shore Fort defences, as at Pevensey and Portchester, was a case of Britain imitating the latest continental 'fashion'.[16] The massive increase in the raw materials consumed by such forts indicates that this is rather unlikely; while fashion can be expected to come at a price, a nearly threefold increase in materials (and, consequently, in manpower) seems too extravagant a cost to have been justified.

On the level of the individual fort, the estimates are informative about the significance of the various types of material used in the structure, as can be illustrated by the example of Pevensey (**42**). Here, the rubble core comprised the overwhelming proportion of raw materials, accounting for 74% of the total volume. Within the core itself, rubble stone was the dominant material, followed by the components of the mortar (sand, beach pebbles and lime). By contrast, the facing stones account for only 5% of the overall demand. So too timber, which constituted only 6% at Pevensey, and still less at sites such as Caister (2%) where it was not used in the foundations, but only for scaffold. This situation contrasts greatly with the wooden forts of the early Empire, which used vast quantities of timber in all aspects of the structure.[17] The innovation of bastions was moderately significant, increasing the overall material requirement by 7%. However, the introduction of bonding courses, although a striking aspect of the design, did not create a great demand for brick: within the defences at Pevensey, only 80m³ of brick had been used (0.0023% of the total volume of building material). Of course, any timber-built, tile-roofed structures in the interior would have added significantly to the demand for both timber and tile, and to a lesser extent, mortar, iron and other sundries.

Sources of supply

The materials for building the Shore Forts were drawn from far and near.[18] In most cases, however, local supply was the dominant factor. Lympne was the most compact project in this respect, for here the Roman builders had virtually all their materials immediately to hand. Limestone from an outcrop within a few hundred metres of the building site was used for the core rubble and the facing stones, and was also burnt to produce the lime for the mortar. Sand and pebbles were procured from the beach at the base of the slope below the fort, while the small quantities of timber needed could also have been felled locally. Much of the brick and tile in the bonding courses had been recycled from an earlier structure – probably the suspected fort on or near the new site. In most cases, however, the materials were not quite so conveniently located. Reculver is perhaps rather more typical of the Shore Fort projects as a whole: here nearly 90% of the perimeter was built using materials probably procured within 20km (12 miles) of the fort. In this instance the only stone to travel any distance was Kentish ragstone from the Maidstone district, which was transported some 70km (43 miles) for use in the facing of the defences.

Reused building materials were an important resource, and their incorporation in the Shore Fort defences made a virtue of necessity, effectively combining site clearance with quarrying. The recycling of materials can be best seen at Lympne and Richborough, where old roof tiles (*tegulae*) were incorporated into the bonding courses (**43**). Reused stone is far less easy to identify than tile, and the amounts that are positively detectable in the Shore Fort defences are minimal. However, some can be seen at both Lympne and Richborough, where second-hand monumental blocks formed part of the foundations of the east and west gates respectively (**colour plate 22**). The reuse of old stone may in fact have provided a very large proportion of building materials at certain sites such as Dover, and above all at Richborough. Here, calculations suggest that the great first-

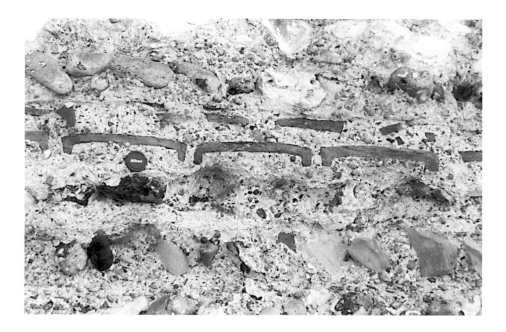

43 Reused tegulae *in the west wall at Richborough*

century monumental arch incorporated some 16,000m³ of material.[19] Given that this structure may have remained substantially intact at the time of the Shore Fort's construction (a general, albeit unproven assumption) it could have provided up to 70% of the raw materials for the new defences. Some of the rare stone types originally used in the arch can certainly be observed in the north wall of the fort, such as tufa and marble. However, most stone in the arch was flint, and this cannot now be distinguished from any flint freshly quarried at the time of the Shore Fort's construction.

In most instances it was the coast that provided the vast majority of stone for the defences. Opportunist exploitation of unconsolidated deposits was of prime importance: beach stone (particularly flint) was extremely widely used, as were septarian cementstones, the latter being abundant on the coasts of Essex and north Kent. Beach platforms were also extensively exploited, with slabs of stone simply being levered up from foreshore deposits: the Upper Greensand used in the facing and bonding courses at Pevensey is one example of stone procured by this practice, as is the Bembridge Limestone quarried on the Isle of Wight for use at Portchester (**44**). These and many other rock types in the Shore Fort defences exhibit the borings of modern marine creatures, such as the worm *Polydora ciliata* and the bivalve *Pholas* (piddock). The occasional example still has barnacles attached, further evidence of their coastal origin. Sand and pebbles for the mortar could also be procured from beaches, and when one looks at coastal exploitation as a whole, it can be seen that the practice provided virtually three-quarters of all raw materials for the Shore Fort programme.

The traditional view of Roman quarrying is of the cutting of stone from inland pits, but the example of the Shore Forts shows that the importance of coastal materials as a resource should not be underrated (**colour plates 20 & 21**). Coastal quarrying has been a widespread activity in more recent periods, and examples can be cited from all around Britain, for example in Devon, South Wales and Scotland to name only a few instances.[20] Roman practices were undoubtedly similar to those of the nineteenth century: much loose stone was probably picked up directly from the beaches, but some may have been dredged from shallow waters. By way of illustration, we can turn to a recent account of the history of Lyme Regis:

> ... a new local industry did arise in the 1820s. This was sea-quarrying ... The toughness of the workmen, known locally as stoneboatmen, has become legendary. They developed a special double-hulled boat, rowed by two long sweeps, called the stoneboat, and akin to the Portland lerret. Having broken the ledge-stone at low water, they then rowed it back ... Notoriously independent, these titans worked in all conditions, often up to the waist in water, and of course needed great physical strength. One did not lightly start a quarrel with a stoneboatman.[21]

Some materials were, however, still procured from inland. Bricks are one example, and many of those supplied to the Kent and Sussex forts could well have been produced in the Weald, depending on how long the *classis Britannica* tile industry persisted into the later Roman period. This would seem to be the case at Reculver,

44 *Doggers of Thanet sandstone at Reculver Bay, Kent, exposed by the erosion of softer material in the cliffs above. Beach platforms such as these were widely used as a source of building stone for the Shore Forts. Thanet sandstone itself was extensively used at Reculver and Richborough. The twin towers of the medieval church of St Mary, built inside the Roman defences at Reculver, are visible immediately to the left of the cliff line*

where tiles made from Wealden clays are present in the east gate of the fort and in reused form within St Mary's church.[22] Most chalk was probably dug from small inland pits, a practice that persisted well into the nineteenth century in areas such as the Sussex Downs. A Roman or Iron Age chalk quarry is known at Birchington on the Isle of Thanet, only a short distance away from Reculver, on the opposite side of the Wantsum Channel.[23] Of course, whether it was used for the Shore Fort project is entirely beyond proof. Although most flint was collected on the coast, some was gathered from inland sources. Nowhere is this more apparent than at Portchester, where most was freshly quarried from the nearby chalk cliffs of Portsdown Hill, with a smaller proportion of orange-stained flints gathered from fields where they had been ploughed up during farming (see **23**).

The pattern of supply

Local materials were, in nearly every case, completely adequate for the purpose of building. As discussed above, the rubble core consumed the vast majority of the raw materials, and for this purpose one stone type is quite as serviceable as the next. At Dover, even old sculpture and the occasional lump of iron slag was used as core fill. Only where the quality of the stone was more crucial was it necessary to bring it from further afield. This was the case for more specialist aspects of the design, for example the facing, the bonding courses, or where monumental masonry was required for impressive gateways. Quarries owned or operated by the State may have supplied some of this higher quality material. Kentish ragstone from the Maidstone district, present at the Shore Forts of Reculver, Richborough and Bradwell, is one example where this may have been the case. This stone had been quarried since the first century AD, and from the second century onwards it had been widely exported across south-east Britain.[24] Early in the third century it was used to build the town walls of both London and Rochester, and some decades later it was quarried for the new London riverside wall (*c*.255-70).[25] The association between Kentish ragstone and these large-scale defences may be coincidental; it is, notably, one of the few lithologies in the region of any reasonable quality. However, it may be that some or all of the Medway quarries were imperial property, devoted to the production of stone for public and military projects. The Blackfriars I vessel, sunk in London with its cargo of stone still on board, may have been in imperial service, although it might equally have been a private vessel under contract.[26]

Only at Bradwell is there definite evidence for the transport of stone over distances on an extra-regional scale (**45**). The bulk of materials used in the Shore Fort defences was still local – mostly foreshore-gathered septarian cementstones weathered from the London Clay cliffs. However, the walls of St Peter's chapel, built on the site with Roman stone, exhibit a wide array of materials from far-flung sources; Lincolnshire Limestone (an estimated journey of 300km/190 miles), Kentish ragstone from the north and south coasts of Kent, and tufa, also probably from the same region. We must expect these imports to have been used for specialist aspects of the design, and indeed the Lincolnshire Limestone is found in the chapel in very large blocks, which were probably once part of a monumental gateway. Similarly the Kentish ragstone and tufa may have been employed in the facing of the wall, perhaps at a prominent point such as the gates.

Nevertheless, why Bradwell was exclusive in incorporating such a proportion of extra-regional material is extremely curious. It is perhaps an indication that stone was travelling alongside other construction goods, such as brick and timber, or food and other consumable supplies for the workforce. Iron was another vital commodity and one that would have been used in significant quantities in any timber buildings within the fort. Interestingly, the area to the west and north of the Roman town of *Durobrivae* (Water Newton), from which the Lincolnshire Limestone was quarried, is one also associated with iron production. By the time that Bradwell came to be built, the iron industry in the Weald of Kent had all but perished, and perhaps in the presence of Lincolnshire Limestone at Bradwell we are seeing evidence that the demand for iron was now being met from elsewhere. All this is unlikely to be established with certainty, but it is clear that Bradwell provides evidence for a complex pattern of supply, and one that indicates something far more than a locally administered, locally supplied project. Why the stone in the walls of the other Shore Forts does not attest to a similar over-arching administration awaits explanation.

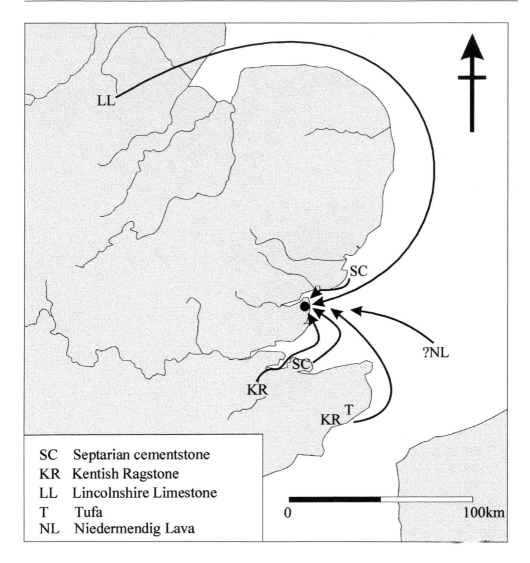

45   *Stone supply for the building of the fort at Bradwell*

SC   Septarian cementstone
KR   Kentish Ragstone
LL   Lincolnshire Limestone
T   Tufa
NL   Niedermendig Lava

Transport

Modes of transport

The large quantities of raw materials posed a significant logistical challenge, and there would have been a number of options open to the Roman commander as to how this task was to be achieved. The primary decision would have centred on whether raw materials were to be transported by land or by water, but the balance between these modes of transport cannot now be established with certainty. In some instances, however, the provenance of the building materials does offer a clear answer to this question. At Portchester, for example, the flint and chalk were quarried from inland sources and had to be transported by land to the building site. Conversely, the Bembridge Limestone quarried on the Isle of Wight for use in the bonding courses could only have been carried to the fort by boat.

The coastal location of the forts and their supplying quarries strongly suggest that water transport was the likelier of the two options to have been chosen. This is supported by the fact that transport by boat has been shown to be by far the most efficient way of moving goods in the ancient world – approximately 28 times more cost-efficient than movement by land.[27] Studies of Romano-British pottery production, such as the Alice Holt/Farnham and Oxfordshire ware industries, have also demonstrated both the importance, and the commercial advantages of river transport.[28] Only for projects where inland sources were being exploited, or where the quarries were very close to the building site, as at Portchester, Dover and Lympne, were carts or mules likely to have been the dominant mode of transport. To some extent, however, any idea of a rigid division between land and water transport is overly simplistic, as all materials which were not quarried directly on the coast would have required a short journey over land to the nearest navigable water source. This distance was unlikely to be great: many of the Kentish ragstone quarries, for example, must have lain within a few hundred metres of the River Medway, while chalk pits on the Isle of Thanet or the South Downs could easily have been dug close to the beaches. Stone such as Lincolnshire Limestone probably had a journey of some complexity: a load from the Clipsham quarries, for example, would have needed to be carried some 5km (3 miles) to the River Glen and thence via the River Welland to the Wash, a further 25km (16 miles). At this stage it was probably transferred to a larger vessel for the southward coastal journey.

Although there is no direct evidence for the types of vessel used for the Shore Forts' construction, the discovery of Roman ships from British waters does provide some impression of the types that might have been employed. The subject of Roman shipping in the province is discussed further in the next chapter, and one of the vessels described is the Blackfriars I vessel, a ship known to have been used for the transportation of stone. Another example, the smaller boat from Barlands Farm (Magor, Gwent), was also discovered with a few stones in the hull, and these have also been suggested to be the remnants of the cargo.[29] Such vessels, capable of operating in inshore waters, and whose shallow draft enabled them to sail in shallow waters and to be drawn up on a beach, would have been ideal for a coastal construction project of this type.

Meeting the transport demand

The estimated transport demand required for the Shore Forts' construction is shown in **Table A**. Calculations of boat loads are based on the Blackfriar's I vessel, which it is suggested was able to carry around 30 cubic metres of cargo, to a maximum weight of 50 tonnes.[30] For the overland movement of goods, the calculations arbitrarily assume that 'post-wagons' – large four wheeled vehicles, drawn by a team of six or eight oxen – were employed. (Such vehicles were one of several types described in the *codex Theodosianus*, where weight limits for cargoes on imperial highways were specified.) The calculations assume that a post-wagon could carry a load of 0.850 tonnes. The speed of such a vehicle has been estimated at 3.2km/h (2mph), and that loading and unloading could be carried out in $1\frac{1}{4}$ hours.[31]

Table A   Estimated requirement for transport of raw materials between the quarries and the Shore Forts

	Boat loads	Cart loads
Brancaster	560	0
Caister-on-Sea	520	0
Burgh Castle	620	0
Walton Castle	470	0
Bradwell	870	0
Reculver	530	0
Richborough	960	0
Dover	0	13540
Lympne	220	21980
Pevensey	1580	660
Portchester	240	15530
Total	6570	51710

Any suggestion of an annual size of a fleet is rather conjectural, particularly as we must not dismiss the scale of the support activities required to maintain a labour force, often working in localities that were rather remote from the main areas of Roman occupation. For example, it has been calculated that a Roman soldier would eat half a tonne of wheat during the course of a year. To sustain a labour force of 100 men, therefore, required the transport of 50 tonnes of grain – equivalent to one entire boat load of the Blackfriars I vessel – and this was but one component of the diet. When we consider all the other logistical demands it becomes clear that the scale of the transport demand must have been somewhat larger than our basic calculations might suggest.

Under favourable circumstances it has been estimated that the Blackfriars I vessel could have achieved speeds of 7 knots (8mph). Such a figure suggests that in the course of a day's sailing a vessel of this type could travel between 85km (53 miles) and 140km (87 miles), depending on the amount of available daylight. Such figures ignore many of the practicalities of seafaring in the ancient world,[32] but it is reasonable to suggest that, under normal conditions, all the major quarries provisioning the Shore Forts lay within a day's reach, and indeed many were far closer. Wind direction and tides probably meant that only a single journey to or from the quarry was possible in any one day.

For the sake of argument, let us assume that a vessel operating on a coastal route can complete a return journey in three days; one day to reach the quarry, a second day to be loaded and a third to make the return trip. Using this model, the 1580 boat loads postulated for Pevensey equates to the continuous operation of 17 vessels over a season of 280 days. Using the same model, we can demonstrate that for the eight later forts, a fleet of 70 ships was required if all the raw materials were to be moved during a single season. These are necessarily broad estimates, but they at least suggest the order of magnitude of any fleet. If construction spanned several years then the required number of vessels would have fallen correspondingly.

The size of the transport fleet needed for the Shore Forts' construction can never have been very great, and certainly in the case of the early third-century installations we can expect the *classis Britannica* to have played a major role. This organisation had, after all, a history of involvement in logistical tasks (including support of the contemporary or very recent Severan campaigns), and would have been well suited to the task of provisioning a military building project. Despite the disappearance of the British fleet from the archaeological record during the latter parts of the third century, we must assume there was a considerable volume of maritime traffic on Britain's east coast at this time. However, whether supply to the northern frontier was conducted by a military agency (i.e. a successor organisation to the *classis Britannica*) or by chartered civilian ships is unclear. Whatever the mechanisms, we might expect that vessels existed which could have been diverted to the task of supplying the Shore Forts.

As we have already seen, the number of ships required was not particularly large. However, a major construction programme might have raised demands for shipping above normal levels, and perhaps above that which the existing resources of the State could meet. In this situation the Roman commander had two options – to construct new vessels, or to contract or commandeer ships from civilian operators. Episodes from Julius Caesar's invasions of Britain provide examples of both activities on a massive scale.[33] In 55 BC, for example, some 80 vessels were mustered from the territory of the Morisi, most probably from the River Somme. In the following year, some 600 were built during the winter period, despite shortages of raw materials. In total, Caesar writes that 800 seagoing vessels were constructed or commandeered for the expedition to Britain in 54 BC, enough to transport five legions across the Channel. Four centuries later, similar figures are quoted for Julian's Germanic wars, some 600 vessels being assembled of which 400 were specifically built.

Although such claims may be apocryphal, they nevertheless demonstrate the abundance of shipping on the Atlantic coast during the Roman period. They also show that seagoing vessels could be built in a relatively short space of time, and even more significantly, by non-specialists, in this case by legionaries. However, while the task of building boats was in no way insurmountable, one cannot simply create experienced sailors to handle such craft. For this reason, in a situation where the army could not sustain the transport burden using its own resources, it is perhaps more likely that existing vessels and their civilian crews were chartered or commandeered for the task.

The demand for manpower

Although the Shore Fort defences were comparatively simple structures, they were nevertheless the product of many individual actions and processes (**46**). These cannot be understood or modelled in their entirety at this distance in time, but it

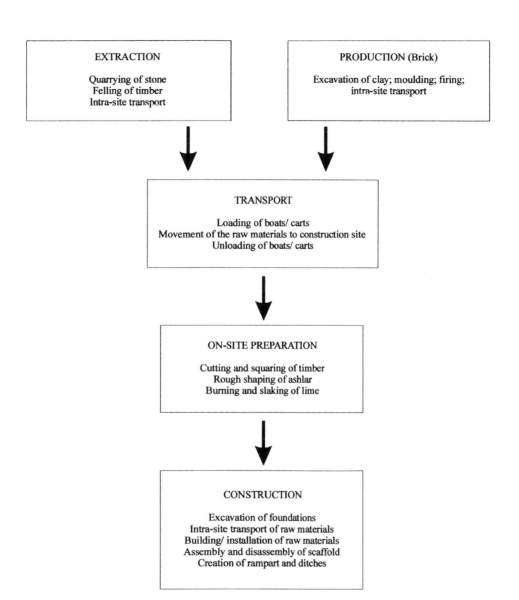

46   A simplified flowchart of the construction process, as analysed in the manpower study

still remains possible to establish a broad estimate for the labour requirement.[34] These estimates concern only the perimeter defences, and do not take into account other known or possible components of the installations, principally internal buildings, the presence and form of which is largely unclear for most of the forts. The analysis envisages an unrealistically streamlined construction process, excluding many activities that were essential to, but not directly part of, the actual processes of production, quarrying and construction. These include planning and administration, logistical operations such as the supply of food and clothing for the workforce, the supply of animal fodder and the manufacture and maintenance of tools and plant. Neither have inefficiencies within the project been considered: the movement of the workforce to and between building sites and quarries, inclement weather, sickness and incapacity, unforeseen difficulties, and mistakes or failure of teamwork. All these can have a major impact on the speed and efficiency of a construction project. The proposed figures (shown in **Table B**) do not therefore claim complete accuracy. Nevertheless the exercise does establish an order of magnitude by which we can appreciate (if only in broad terms) the scale of the labour requirement. Given the omissions outlined above, however, the figures must be considered to represent a *minimum* estimate.

Table B   Estimated labour requirement for the construction of the Shore Fort defences

Shore Fort	Man days
Brancaster	44000
Caister-on-Sea	40000
Burgh Castle	47000
Walton Castle	47000
Bradwell	78000
Reculver	41000
Richborough	72000
Dover	39000
Lympne	85000
Pevensey	103000
Portchester	69000
Total	665000

To equate these manpower figures to the actual size of the workforce required every year, we must first establish the length of the building season. Evidence from pre-industrial Britain demonstrates that climate played a major role in dictating the amount and nature of work that took place at different stages of the year. Most building work seems to have been carried out in the reasonably clement period between April and November. The winter might have been used as a time for procuring raw materials, and indeed, this is the ideal season for the felling of timber. However, transport during the winter months was a very difficult prospect, either by land or sea, and thus it seems likely that little work of any kind was undertaken during this period.[35] We can therefore suggest a season length of approximately 280 days, which for our smallest and largest building projects equates to the *average* labour forces shown in **Table C**.

Table C   Average labour forces required for the building of the Shore Forts at Dover and Pevensey

Project duration	Average labour force	
	Dover	Pevensey
1 year	140	360
2 years	70	180
3 years	46	120
5 years	28	70
10 years	17	35
20 years	7	18

As we have already seen, however, such figures undoubtedly represent an unrealistic minimum. The greatest unknown question relates to the presence and form of any internal buildings. Calculations for Pevensey demonstrate that if a regular arrangement of timber buildings had existed within the defences (perhaps a dubious assumption), then the labour demand for the fort would be increased to 160,000 man days.[36] Thus, the labour force is increased by over one-half, that is to say 570 men in a single season, 285 in two seasons, and so on.

It is particularly interesting to note that most of the tasks did not required skilled workers. The majority of labour was absorbed by the quarrying process, and by tasks such as the intra-site movement of the raw materials (both at the quarry and the building site). Only approximately 6% of the workforce needed to be skilled craftsmen, for example masons and sawyers; the remainder of the men on site were simply needed to carry out basic physical tasks. This fact takes on some considerable importance in the following section, when we examine the possible sources of manpower for the building of the Shore Forts.

Human resources

When considering how the labour demand might have been met, it is evident that manpower could have been drawn from both the Roman army and from the civilian population. That the army played a central role in the construction of the Shore Forts cannot be doubted: these were, after all, military projects and we must envisage that at the very least the army was involved in a supervisory capacity.

Construction and the Roman army

Throughout the history of the Empire, the army's resources were widely utilised for civil, as well as military building. Although construction work was traditionally a role fulfilled by the legions, it was not uncommon for auxiliary regiments (including cavalry units) to carry out building work.[37] In addition to providing a valuable pool of labour, the army also possessed within its ranks a significant number of skilled craftsmen. The second-century jurist Tarruntenus Paturnus, a writer on military law and later praetorian prefect under Marcus Aurelius, makes this clear. His list of *immunes* (those soldiers excluded from normal duties because they carried out a specialist role) included 'architects ... shipwrights ... cartwrights ... stone-cutters, men who burn lime, men who cut wood, and men who chop and burn charcoal'.[38] Here, evidently, is the complete range of skills necessary to build the Shore Forts, from the construction of a transport fleet, through quarrying, to the actual processes of building.

Unit identities

The identity of the army units involved in the construction of the Shore Forts is often uncertain, and only the early-dated forts of Reculver and Brancaster have yielded any physical evidence that sheds light on the issue. At these sites stamped tiles of *cohors I Baetasiorum* (at Reculver) and *cohors I Aquitanorum* (at Brancaster) have been found, providing direct evidence of the involvement of these units in construction work at the forts.[39] Both units had previously been stationed on the northern frontier: before its move south, *cohors II Baetasiorum* is last recorded at Maryport (during the last years of the second century), while *cohors I Aquitanorum* had been at Brough-on-Noe, where it had also recently been engaged in building work.[40] The presence of Wealden tiles at Reculver has already been noted, and the involvement of the *classis Britannica* in raw material production, the transport process, and perhaps even in building work, is also to be suspected for the group of three forts built early in the third century. Some caution is required, however, for we cannot necessarily assume that any of these units were responsible for the original construction of the installations. Brancaster, Caister and Reculver all lack bonding courses in the defences, and therefore the tiles that have been found were almost certainly used in the roofs of internal buildings. Some of these structures may post-date the construction of the fort defences by a number of years, and so the tiles may attest to subsequent building work of a somewhat later date.

Where material evidence is lacking, the identity of any units involved in construction is a matter of conjecture. The late date of the *Notitia Dignitatum* listing limits its usefulness, and, as described in Chapter 7, it is clear that many of the units that it records at the Shore Forts are not the original garrisons. Unless new archaeological evidence emerges, we are unlikely to know for certain who was responsible for the work.

The size of the Roman army in Britain

Although the army's involvement is clearly established, could it have provided the entire labour force for the Shore Fort programme? The army represented only a small proportion of the total Roman-British population (perhaps around 3.5%), but at the start of the third century the military presence was probably at least as large as it had been under Hadrian, and perhaps larger still. This was mainly a consequence of the introduction of new units during the Severan campaigns, which had more than made good the reductions caused by Clodius Albinus' removal of troops for his continental war in 196/7. It has been estimated that in AD 210 some 55,000 troops were present in Britain, the vast majority stationed in the Highland Zone.[41] Given this situation, it would not be unreasonable to expect the army to have supplied most (if not all) of the manpower for the building of the early Shore Forts, and indeed the other coastal installations of the time. The direct involvement of *cohors I Baetasiorum* and *cohors I Aquitanorum* at Reculver and Brancaster respectively provides strong support for this idea. Other regiments (or detachments) might also have been removed from the northern frontier specifically for the task of building the new coastal forts: we can certainly postulate that such units also constructed Caister. These troops would probably have been expendable in the north, as the Severan campaigns not only restored the army in Britain to its full strength, but also seem to have pacified the northern frontier for the remainder of the century.

For the later group of eight Shore Forts, built in the period after *c*.260, the situation becomes somewhat less clear. As the third century progressed the army presence in Britain was greatly reduced, such that by the end of the century the number of troops is likely to have been more than halved. The greatest single reduction probably resulted from the departure of vexillations from *Legio II Augusta* and *Legio XX Valeria Victrix* in AD 255, which were probably accompanied by auxiliary units.[42] Further withdrawals to the continent are likely to have occurred during the reigns of Postumus and Victorinus. It has been estimated that by AD 300 there were 25,000 troops stationed in Britain, but if arguments regarding reduced unit sizes in Diocletian's army are correct, then such a figure could be halved again to 12,500.[43] Crucially, the composition of the army had also changed during the course of the century, with some traditional auxiliary regiments being replaced by units of *numeri*. Raised from barbarian tribes both within and outside the Empire's borders, *numeri* are first known in Britain during the third century. Such units seem to have performed specialist tasks, but are unlikely to have possessed the building skills of the legions and older style auxiliary units. In absolute numbers, therefore, and in terms of the available skilled craftsmen, the army can be seen to be a much-reduced resource after the middle of the third century. Despite these reductions, the army in Britain may not have been overly stretched. The province was largely unscathed by the upheavals on the continent, and it is likely that the running down of the garrison in Wales and its transfer to other locations in Britain at least partially offset the departure of troops from the province during the 250s and 260s.

The later group of Shore Forts, not only greater in number but also with more massive defences, accounted for some 80% of the manpower demand for the series as a whole (as shown in **Table D**). In a longer-term scenario for the construction of the later Shore Forts – perhaps five years or more – it is quite plausible that the army provided the whole workforce. The necessary labour could be met by the redeployment of one or two auxiliary cohorts or a legionary vexillation. Any troops introduced from the continent during the episode of Carausius and Allectus would also have boosted the potential labour force. However, whether the army could have met the demand in the shortest of timescales is dubious. We can probably envisage the need for a very urgent programme of one or two years to have arisen only within the Carausian-Allectan period. If, as has been proposed, some seven forts were built during the brief reign of Allectus, then the task was almost certainly beyond the army's resources. After the recapture of the Gallic littoral by Constantius, the threat of invasion must have been clear to the usurpers, and the dispersal of troops around the coast on construction duties is unlikely to have been perceived as a wise option. The use of barbarian mercenaries by Allectus probably highlights the fact that military manpower was at a premium during this period.

Table D   The average labour requirement for the building of the later Shore Forts (Burgh Castle, Walton Castle, Bradwell, Richborough, Dover, Lympne, Pevensey, Portchester)

Project duration	Average labour force
1 year	2000
2 years	1000
3 years	660
5 years	400
10 years	200
20 years	100

The civilian population

In a situation where the army was unable, or unwilling, to provide the entire labour force for the Shore Forts, the civilian sphere offered an alternative (and by no means inferior) source of manpower. Any such workforce would certainly have operated under military supervision. Estimates of the province's population have varied from 0.5–6 million,[44] and when looked at in these terms the prospect of being able to draft a few thousand labourers does not seem unrealistic. Although there are no indications of civilian involvement in the Shore Forts, there is evidence for the use of non-military labour on Hadrian's Wall. Here, inscriptions that probably date to the Severan reconstruction record the work of men from, amongst others, the civites *Dumnoniorum* (Exeter) and *Catuvellaunorum* (St Albans). There is little doubt that skilled workers existed in significant numbers within the civilian population. This fact is illustrated by one of the panegyrics written for Constantius, describing events of 296/7:

> The city of Autun … received … immediately after the victory of Britain, a multitude of its craftsmen who abounded in these [British] provinces, and, at that hour, the restoration of its old dwellings, the rebuilding of public buildings and the restoration of its temples began in the ruins.[45]

The terms under which any such workforce could have been drafted is not entirely clear: workers, particularly the skilled artisans, could have been paid by the State but it is equally possible that some or all could have been forcibly recruited. Parallels can be found in the medieval and Early Modern periods, where the right of governments to require military service was one way by which labour could be recruited for public works. Although no record of the appropriate legislation survives from Roman Britain, the evidence of civilian workers on Hadrian's Wall demonstrates that similar measures were available to the British authorities. Legal codes from the continent illustrate how such laws might have worked, the prime example being the *Lex Irnitana*, a municipal law code of Flavian date from Spain. Here provision is made for up to five day's labour per year from every man in the *municipia* aged between 15 and 60 years and every yoke of animals.[46] Given the distances involved between the towns and the Shore Forts, and the general scale of the project, a figure of five day's labour is rather too low to have been practicable. We should perhaps envisage compulsory service that was rather more draconian, as was the case for Edward I's Welsh castles, where 40 day's work was demanded of every labourer impressed for the project.[47]

The degree of disruption to urban life would have varied according to the number and economic role of those recruited. In overall terms, however, the effects of a draft were unlikely to be keenly felt, particularly if the burden was evenly spread between the towns of Britain. The population of London, estimated at 30,000, would be best placed to absorb such losses, while the *civitas* capitals, which are suggested to have accommodated between two and five thousand, could also have supplied a significant number of workers. Towns such as Canterbury could perhaps have supported the labour demand for the completion of one Shore Fort during a single season, but not more. The labour required to build the forts of Richborough, Lympne and Dover in the course of a year would almost certainly have exceeded the adult male population of a major town such as Canterbury.

The context of construction

When the history of third-century Britain and Gaul is examined, it becomes immediately evident that the Shore Forts were not the only major construction projects of the time; indeed, this is far from being the case. Some of these – the coastal defences in both provinces – have already been described in Chapter 3 (**47**). In terms of other military building within Britain, it is possible to identify two episodes of repair on the northern frontier. The first was the restoration begun under Septimius Severus, which continued for the next quarter of a century or more. During this time Hadrian's Wall underwent significant modification, while new forts were built in forward positions in the eastern sector at Risingham and High Rochester. Existing bases, including Netherby and Bewcastle, were also renovated. Other contemporary repair work can be found elsewhere in the province, for example at the fort at Caernarvon, where an inscription records the restoration of an aqueduct broken down by age. Early in the fourth century renewed building activity on the northern

47 *The east wall of Cardiff Castle, an installation that was built at around the same time as the later group of Shore Forts. The defensive perimeter, originally constructed during the late third century, was rebuilt at the start of the twentieth century, and provides a good impression of how many of the later Shore Forts would have appeared*

frontier has also been detected: Constantius probably initiated such work, as is indicated by inscriptions from Housesteads and Birdoswald that date to before 305.

Probably the largest building projects in the south of Britain took the form of town walls. By the end of the second century many towns and some smaller settlements had been provided with linear defences, normally earthworks with masonry employed only for the gateways. The conversion of these defences to stone appears to have begun early in the third century, although, as with the Shore Forts, the dating of such features can normally be established only in broad terms.[48] It is evident that certain towns had been provided with walls early in the third century, but it seems probable that much construction work at other sites took place rather later. Many town defences, including Canterbury and Silchester, whose defences have been dated respectively to 270-300 and 260-80, may be contemporary with the later group of eight Shore Forts (**48**).[49]

One other large-scale civil project deserves particular mention, and that is the structure at St Peter's Hill, London. When the site was excavated only the foundations remained; their size indicated that a massive superstructure was intended, although it was not possible to determine whether the building was actually completed. Dendrochronology shows the foundation piles to have been felled early in 294. The complex has been interpreted as a 'palace', built for Allectus after his seizure of power

48   A stretch of the defences built around the Roman town of Silchester (Hampshire) in approximately AD 260-280. The walls employ bonding courses of stone slabs, but are otherwise of traditional design

from Carausius, which could have incorporated such features as a mint, treasury and supply depot. Here is specific evidence that the Shore Forts were not the only building project to concern the rulers of Britain during the late third century. The methods of construction are described as being closely comparable with Pevensey, indeed so similar are they that it has been suggested that 'resources were diverted from the Saxon Shore … to assist in the construction of the complex in London'.[50]

Large-scale building in Gaul can be discussed in two principal parts: town walls and coastal defences. As outlined above, a number of the defences on the Gallic coast can be shown to date to the latter parts of the third century. This is true in part also for town walls in Gaul, although once again the dating evidence is often poor. Over 80 Gallic towns were provided with walls from 260 onwards.[51] Archaeology is able to confirm that a number of town defences were built in the later third century, and it does indeed seem likely that a great deal of construction work took place under the auspices of the Gallic Empire and the Tetrarchy. We must note, however, that the process of fortification was much lengthier than was once assumed. Certain sites can now be shown to have been provided with walls at a much later date; the defences of Tours now have a *terminus post quem* of 364-75, while Auxerre has one of 350-3. Evidence from Beauvais suggests that the defences were built around 320, and it has been proposed that the other stylistically similar town walls in *Belgica* such as Soissons and Senlis may be of a comparable date.[52]

An overview of the building project

The Shore Forts, if considered as a series, represented the largest military building project within Britain since the construction of the Antonine Wall during the mid-second century. However, even when the basic transport and manpower figures are adjusted upwards towards a more realistic estimate, the Shore Forts still emerge as a modest enterprise. In terms of human and material resources, as well as in the physical sense, the Shore Forts were dwarfed by the great buildings of the central Empire. Individual projects such as the Baths of Caracalla in Rome can be cited: built between AD 211 and 216, this structure required an average labour force over four years of 7200 men, with approximately 13,000 workers employed during the early stages of the project.[53] The British province was, admittedly, far removed from Rome, with its exceptional levels of financial and human resources. To relate the Shore Forts to structures such as the Colosseum, the Baths of Caracalla, or even with the Aurelian walls of Rome, is simply not to equate like with like.

Within Roman Britain, the building of the first-century legionary fortress at Inchtuthil (Scotland) bears greater comparison to the entire Shore Fort series, at least in terms of the necessary manpower. In this case, however, the fortress was built (and demolished) in a maximum period of four years, and probably rather less. As many as 5000 men might have been working on the fort, if (as is possible) it was completed in a period of $2\frac{1}{4}$ months.[54] When we look for comparisons with an individual Shore Fort, examples can easily be found for building projects of the late third century that were a significantly larger undertaking. Many of the Gallic town walls could be mentioned at this point: Châlons, for instance, was provided with a circuit of walls 2.5-3.5m thick and 950m in length. Only Pevensey is likely to have come close in terms of economic magnitude. Turning to the medieval period in Britain, concentrations of labour can also be cited that were far greater than those required by the Shore Forts, albeit normally under rather extraordinary political or military circumstances. Historical records relating to Edward I's castle-building programme in Wales, for instance, show over 2700 workers engaged in the construction of Beaumaris during the year 1295, and this was only one of seven major fortresses being undertaken at the time.[55]

The difficulties of finding the resources to build the Shore Forts, even within a comparatively short period, therefore seem far from insurmountable. Labour resources were the key factor, and we have seen that a pool of workers existed in both the military and civilian populations. Significantly, we find that skilled workers (a small but absolutely essential component of the workforce) were present both in the army and the civil sector. The fact that the raw materials were likely to have been moved by water is also significant, as the efficiency of water transport greatly reduced the logistical problems that dogged inland projects such as Hadrian's Wall.

In Chapter 6 theories regarding the reasons for the Shore Forts' construction will be examined. Some envisage a lengthy period of building, while others entertain the idea that the later forts were built within a very short length of time, perhaps within one or two seasons. The findings of this study suggest that either

1   Robbed facing stones from the Brancaster Shore Fort, reused (together with other, later material) in the south chancel of St Mary the Virgin, Brancaster

2   The site of the Brancaster Shore Fort, looking north towards the coastal marshes. The fort's east ditch can be seen as a marked depression on the right hand side of the photograph

3   The south wall and south-east angle bastion, Burgh Castle

4   Burgh Castle. Fallen bastion on the south wall

5   *The seventh-century chapel of St Peter, Bradwell*

6 St Peter's chapel, Bradwell. This view of the north wall shows very clearly the Saxon reuse of Roman brick and stone – particularly notable are the large blocks of Lincolnshire Limestone employed as quoins. A rectangular lewis hole, cut by the Romans for the insertion of lifting equipment, is evident on the second block above ground level

7   *The east wall, Reculver. Stone robbing in later periods has greatly reduced the Roman perimeter, and in this portion the facing blocks have been entirely removed, leaving only the core rubble in place*

8   *The south wall of the Shore Fort at Reculver. At the base are two courses of Kentish ragstone facing blocks – rare examples that survived the attention of stone robbers. Above these only the core remains, built of local beach flint. The light patches of mortar relate to a recent restoration of the defences*

9 *The south gate, Reculver. These three blocks, which once formed the base of a monumental arch, are all that now remains of the gateway above ground level*

10 *The west wall, Richborough. In the foreground the line of Watling Street crosses the
double ditches of the Shore Fort*

11 *The north wall, Richborough; view east from the postern gate. This beautifully preserved stretch of masonry was built in two parts, the break between the 'construction sections' being clearly evident. Much reused stone from earlier Roman buildings was employed in this portion of the defences*

12 *View south-west across Romney Marsh from the medieval castle at Lympne. In the foreground, between the trees, are the ruins of the Roman fort. The installation, positioned on the slopes of an ancient, degraded sea cliff, originally overlooked a wide expanse of tidal water and marsh*

13 *The remnants of a bastion on the north wall of the Roman fort at Lympne. This is a rare instance where the facing of Kentish ragstone blocks and brick still remains* in situ

14 *The west wall of the Shore Fort at Pevensey*

15 *Bastion on the north wall, Pevensey. The lower portion is clearly of Roman date, exhibiting construction methods identical to those used elsewhere in the defences. However, the part of this 'tower' that projects above the level of the adjacent section of perimeter wall is almost certainly a post-Roman addition*

16 *The north wall, Portchester Castle. In recent decades, the medieval and later overburden was cleared away from the perimeter wall, and the original Roman facing was found to have been preserved. The Roman plinth is visible at ground level, above which are seven courses of flint and two bonding courses of thin stone slabs*

17 *The Dover lighthouse, which now stands within the defences of the medieval castle. The uppermost masonry is a later repair, but the lower levels (the bottom three-quarters of the structure) are of Roman date*

18 The west wall, Richborough. Here can be seen many of the characteristic features of late Roman defensive architecture. At the base of the wall are two courses of large stone blocks forming the plinth. Immediately above, stone robbing has left the core rubble exposed; a layer of chalk rubble set amidst the flint and septaria illustrates how the core material was laid down in successive courses. At higher levels the small facing stones remain in situ, bonded to the core of the wall by periodic brick bonding courses. Two horizontal lines of square putlog holes, left open when the scaffold was removed, can be seen between the third and fifth bonding courses. At this location the Roman wall presently stands 7m high, but it would originally have been somewhat taller

19   *Interval bastion on the east wall, Burgh Castle. The vertical break between the bastion and the adjacent section of wall shows that they were built as virtually separate components; the bastion is only bonded to the wall in the very uppermost courses*

20 Building stone for the Shore Forts. In rare cases, stone was quarried from inland pits. These blocks of limestone ('Clipsham Pink Stone') used at Bradwell and recycled in St Peter's chapel were imported over 300 km (190 miles) from quarries to the north-west of the Roman town of Durobrivae (Water Newton, Cambridgeshire)

21 [Building stone for the Shore Forts]. However, local coastal sources provided the vast majority of materials for the building programme, including this beach cobble of Kentish ragstone used in the defences at Lympne

22 The west gate, Richborough.
These monumental blocks
forming the foundations of the
gateway were recycled from an
earlier structure on the site —
probably the first-century monumental arch

23 Coastal erosion on the north Kent
coast; the medieval church of St
Mary, Reculver. During Roman
times the fort lay approximately
1km south of the coast. Erosion,
only halted by defences built from
the nineteenth century onwards,
has since brought the sea to
within just a few metres of the
church, which stands in the centre
of the Roman fort

24 *The church of Saint John the Baptist, Reedham (Norfolk). Very large quantities of Roman building material, principally brick and tile, can be seen in the church's fabric. This evidence, and other finds in the locality, indicates that a substantial Roman site existed here. It would have lain on the shores of the Great Estuary, and has been suggested to be a lighthouse or watchtower*

25 *The walls of the inner bailey of Pevensey Castle, built in the south-east corner of the Roman perimeter during the mid thirteenth century. A medieval castle had been present on the site since Norman times – just one instance of the extensive reuse of the Shore Forts during the post-Roman era*

scenario is quite plausible, and certainly there is nothing that rules out the idea of a rapidly realised construction programme.

The building of the forts did not take place in isolation. As described above, they were part of a much larger phenomenon of building in Britain and the near continent during this period. Many contemporary projects were larger, and in cases such as the Allectan palace in London, also intended to be far grander. Let us conclude, therefore, by considering the possible place of the Shore Forts within this context. One scholar to recently address the question is Richard Reece, who has proposed a framework for the use of military manpower in third-century Britain.[56] Reece suggests that in the early 200s the army was engaged in the repair of the Northern and Welsh frontiers, before moving to the building of urban defences by around the middle of the century. Finally, after these had been completed, he sees the military builders being transferred to the Shore Forts and other coastal defences.

In his argument Reece rightly stresses the need for what might be termed 'displacement activities'. The army in Britain had a history of major disciplinary problems, and from the time of Clodius Albinus through to the early fifth century it involved itself in the political intrigues of the Empire.[57] The danger it posed must have been especially acute during the third century, for although Britain was relatively peaceful, it was certainly not a time of political stability. Elsewhere in the Empire the army was making and deposing emperors on a regular basis, and thus the issue of how to keep the army occupied (and consequently out of trouble) must have been a serious concern for the British authorities. In more general terms too, a restless soldiery could be problematic. The difficulties caused by the peacetime army, particularly with regard to the civilian population, are well documented.[58] One example is given by Tacitus, who recorded that after the suppression of the Boudiccan Revolt of AD 60/1, 'the troops, accustomed to campaigns, got out of hand when they had nothing to do'.[59] A military presence had to be maintained on the northern frontier, but other tasks had doubtless to be found. The diversion of troops to construction projects was a well-tried solution to the problem of keeping the army occupied, and perhaps this, as much as any military threat, is what prompted the building of the British town walls, and later the Shore Forts.

Reece's chronology is perhaps a little simplistic. It certainly glosses over the vagaries of the dating evidence for many sites, both urban and military, and omits to mention the early third-century forts on Britain's east coast. Nevertheless, this model offers one very plausible explanation as to why the architecture of the late third-century coastal forts in Britain is distinct from virtually all other defensive building in the province, as was discussed at the beginning of this chapter. Perhaps the Shore Forts were indeed built very late in the century, and were also the first structures in the province to adopt the new architectural innovations from the continent. If this was the case, and the walls around the British towns had already been completed, then those innovations would not have found their way into the urban defences. The traditional style of the late third- or early fourth-century repairs on Hadrian's Wall (which almost certainly post-date the Shore Forts) admittedly causes some problems for this argument. However, this might be explained by the northern legions not yet having come into contact with the new architectural styles from the continent. Alternatively, it may reflect a general conservatism amongst military architects on the northern frontier. Nevertheless, the argument certainly still holds for the south of the province, and though not yet fully supported by solid archaeological dating, it is still tempting to view the Shore Forts as the last of the many construction projects of third-century Britain.

5 The landscape setting

The physical settings of the Shore Forts, that is to say their landscape and topography, have been much changed since Roman times. The visitor to the sites at Pevensey, Lympne and Richborough is often bemused by the fact that these 'Shore Forts' are in fact now firmly land-locked. By contrast, Walton Castle has fallen victim to the encroachment of the sea, while Bradwell and Reculver have been partially destroyed by the same process of coastal erosion. Only Portchester retains an environment similar to that in the third century (**49**).

The setting of the Shore Forts is an issue of major significance. At the outset of the construction process, the choice of the site on which to build was a crucial decision. This choice would influence, more than any nuance of the architectural design, how well the installation could fulfil the role for which it was intended. Over the longer term the Shore Forts may or may not have served as ports in a commercial sense, but it remains important to understand how each was situated, and why this may have been so. Considerations of defence, the spatial relationship with other Roman sites, accessibility and communications may all have played a part. As Milne has commented:

> Each port requires its own study since the local topography, ancient river and sea-levels, tidal effects and the rate of siltation and erosion all need to be determined before a meaningful evaluation of the potential of the port can begin.[1]

We might also consider whether there was a common strategy behind the siting of these installations, with similar types of locations being sought for each fort. Certainly this could be borne out by the findings of this chapter, which suggest that the installations display a remarkable uniformity of setting.

The changes to the Shore Fort landscapes have long been recognised. The Tudor scholar and topographer John Leland, who visited Richborough during the 1530s, commented that '… the main sea [once] came to the very foot of the castle. The main sea is now off of it a mile by reason of wose, that hath there swollen up.'[2] Similar comments about Richborough can also be found in William Camden's *Britannia*, first published in 1586:

> This city seemed to have been seated on the descent of an hill, the Castle there stood overlooking from an higher place the Ocean which is now so farre excluded by reason of sandy residence inbealched with the tides, that it hardly comes within a mile of it.[3]

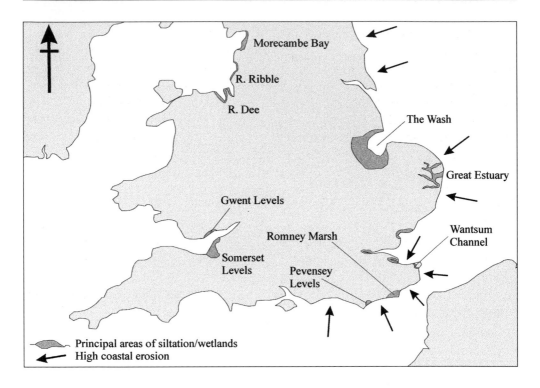

49   Coastal change during the post-Roman period in southern Britain

In the modern day, sea defences have tended to reduce the rate of coastal change in the vicinity of these ancient monuments. However, the processes that have transformed the landscape of the forts have sometimes been dramatic, and were readily apparent to the earliest commentators on the forts. One such example can be found in the first and second editions of Kirby's *Suffolk Traveller*, published in 1735 and 1754 respectively. The original edition merely noted the remains of a Roman monument on the cliff top north of Felixstowe. The second edition, however, recorded the final destruction of the site by the sea:

> How much larger it [the fort] was we cannot judge. Part of the south end being washed away: and the sea, which is daily gaining upon this coast having swallowed up the ruins. Such was the condition of it about the year 1740: but since then the sea hath washed away the remainder of the Foundation.

The first serious attempts to understand the original landscape of the forts were made during the nineteenth century. A particularly credible attempt was Elliott's reconstruction of the environment of Romney Marsh, made in conjunction with Roach Smith's investigations of the Shore Fort at Lympne during the 1850s.[4] These early studies were hampered by the limited amount of evidence available, but an increasing corpus of geological and archaeological data in the modern era now enables at least a partial understanding of the ancient setting of the Shore Forts. There remain, however, widespread misunderstandings about the landscape setting of the installations, both in academic texts and also in less formal literature. This chapter attempts to put the worst of these misconceptions to rest, by summarising the data that relate to the landscape of the Shore Forts during their operational lifetime. The only prior overview of the subject is that of Burnham in 1989,[5] but this discussion was very brief, with the individual forts dealt with in only a cursory fashion. Little was said about Pevensey, and nothing regarding Caister or Portchester. Moreover, since the time of Burnham's writing, significant new research has also been undertaken, particularly on the East Anglian coast, which directly relates to the setting of Bradwell, Caister and Brancaster.

The following sections, therefore, offer the first detailed synthesis of the landscape of our forts. In some instances there is little to add to what is already present in the literature: Hawkes' 1968 discussion of the physical geography of Richborough, for example, remains a perfectly adequate summary.[6] The forts of Portchester, Lympne and Dover have also been outlined in considerable detail, and these sites are included here for the sake of completeness, and not because it is possible to say anything particularly novel about their setting.

Factors influencing coastal change

Before we can reconstruct the original settings of the Shore Forts, it is first necessary to understand the physical processes that have shaped the south and eastern coasts of England during the past few millennia. Changes in the relationship between the land and the sea are the result of numerous factors, which operate on a global, regional and local level, and over both the long and the short term.[7]

Sea-level change

The underlying factor influencing coastal advance and retreat during the Flandrian period (the most recent interglacial stage in Britain, which covers the past 10,000 years and continues to the present day) has been changing sea-levels. When the Devensian glaciation reached its peak around 15,000 BP (Before Present) sea-levels in Britain and north-west Europe were approximately 100-130m below those of the present day.[8] Since that time there has been a large overall rise, due (in simplistic terms) to the melting of the ice sheet, which has occurred on a global scale. These sea-level rises have been neither constant, nor achieved at a uniform rate. Rather, coastal history has been shaped by phases of transgression (the incursion of the sea) and regression (the re-emergence of the land surface). During the Boreal period (*c*.9000-7000 BP) rapid changes brought sea-levels to around -23m OD (Ordnance Datum; modern sea-levels are at +4m OD). These rises overwhelmed the Straits of Dover and so severed the land-bridge to the continent, as well as flooding inlets such as the Wantsum Channel on which the Shore Forts would later be situated. Very rapid changes ceased around 5000 BP, by which time the sea reached its approximate modern level. Since then the total rise in relative sea-level in south-east England has been of the order of 8m, and estimates for an overall rate of change in this region during the last two millennia vary between 0.1m/century and 0.2m/century.[9]

Sea-levels in south-east England during the first century AD were approximately 3-4m below those at present.[10] Studies of the inner Thames estuary, for example, have shown that mean sea-level in Roman London around this date was approximately +1.5m OD.[11] Sea-levels appear to have been relatively stable during the early Roman period, but from the late second or early third century they may once again have risen by a significant amount, and quite rapidly. Scientific data suggest the possibility of a marine transgression, the onset of which in the inner Thames has been dated to *c.*1750 BP (AD 200), with relative sea-levels rising by over 1m during the late Roman period.[12] There is similar evidence for this event from elsewhere in southern Britain, from the Dengie and Foulness region of Essex,[13] and from Romney Marsh.[14] Archaeology might also provide evidence for such an event, for example in the abandonment of settlements in the Fenlands, Romney Marsh and the Somerset Levels at about this time. However, the existence of such a widespread marine transgression during the late Roman period still awaits conclusive proof. The scientific data are beset by various difficulties, not least the fact that the dating of these sea-level changes has not been precisely established. The archaeological evidence is also open to question. The abandonment of a few sites does not constitute substantive proof for a widespread inundation of land by the sea, and in any case settlements may be given up for reasons other than flooding. Nevertheless, if such an event did indeed take place, it could have had profound effects on the Shore Forts. The relationship of the forts – and in particular their harbours or beaching points – to the sea could have been significantly altered, perhaps to such an extent that the installation at Lympne had to be abandoned before the close of the fourth century. Even if the forts themselves remained operational, it is possible that much of the coastal settlement and industry in their locality could have been seriously affected by episodes of flooding.

Erosion, siltation and drainage

From the preceding discussion it can be seen that sea-levels have changed comparatively little between the Roman period and the present day. In such a situation, the impact of local coastal processes can often have a more immediate and pronounced effect on the landscape than changes in relative sea-level. These processes can be broadly divided into the destruction of the coast – erosion – and mechanisms of accretion – the siltation or drainage of land – which result in the retreat of the sea.

Erosion

The Saxon Shore is almost entirely composed of soft Cretaceous and Eocene geological formations, and as a result this portion of the British coast is particularly prone to erosion. The process of erosion is well in evidence in the modern day, as witnessed by the major cliff falls at Beachy Head and Thanet during storm surges in the winters of 1999 and 2000 (**colour plate 23**).

Erosion in southern Britain is greatest where cliffs are subjected to almost continuous wave attack. The worst affected part of the south coast, the Brickearth cliffs around Middleton (Sussex), are eroding at an average rate of 1.08m/year. Erosion of the chalk coastline is less, at a maximum of 0.58m/year on the south-west Isle of Wight. Such losses are matched on the north Kent coast, where the London Clay formations are eroding at average rates of between 0.64m/year (Reculver) and 0.91m/year (north-east Sheppey). The chalk cliffs of Thanet demonstrate rather slower rates of erosion.[15] The London Clay and glacial till formations of the East Anglian coast are also extremely vulnerable. Studies of the cliffs of north-east Norfolk have shown that, prior to the erection of sea defences, they were retreating at an average rate of 1m/year. In the worst affected sections of the coast, for example around Overstrand, the average rate of loss was 1.8m/year.[16]

These modern rates of erosion cannot, however, be uncritically used to infer the losses in the past. Erosion is accelerated by a number of factors, principally high sea-levels, wide extremes of high and low water, excessive rainfall, shrinkage cracks and nocturnal cooling.[17] The relation of sea to land is particularly important: during a tidal regression when sea-levels are low, the cliff is protected by the beach platform and by weathering talus (eroded rock debris at the base of the cliff). Relative sea-levels are likely to have been low during the so called 'Saxo-Norman regression', which has been proposed for eastern Britain between the eighth and fourteenth centuries.[18] Erosion is likely to have been minimal, and we can envisage that the coastline was comparatively stable throughout this period. This fact can be illustrated by a study of the lost villages of Norfolk, which found that of those settlements in the region destroyed by erosion, the vast majority were lost *after* the medieval period. It is probably the case, therefore, that modern rates of loss can only be inferred for the last 700-900 years. Furthermore, erosion of the Kent, Essex and Suffolk coasts in recent centuries may have been exceptionally rapid, because quarrying of septarian cementstones from the foreshore during the eighteenth and nineteenth centuries has denuded the London Clay cliffs of their natural breakwaters.[19]

Siltation

Equally significant alterations in coastal morphology have resulted from depositional processes – the siltation of rivers and estuaries and the drainage of lands previously open to the sea. The deposition of alluvium has been occurring since the tidal inlets were created, and continues to the present day in some places such as Romney Marsh. The process of siltation was accelerated by forest clearance from the Neolithic period onwards, which led to greater soil erosion in agricultural regions. Deforestation in the uplands surrounding Romney Marsh, for example, led to an increase in the sediment load and aided valley fill accumulation.[20] Furthermore, it has been suggested that large-scale felling of timber, to provide fuel for the kiln-drying of grain during the deteriorating climate in the third and fourth centuries AD, led to further erosion and siltation in Roman times.[21] Siltation is quite likely to have been well advanced by Roman times – certainly the area occupied by alluvium in the modern day would not all have been open, navigable water in the third century AD.

In this respect, any illustration that simply substitutes alluvium for a completely open channel would be rather misleading. As we shall see in the following discussion, many of the Shore Forts were situated on the margins of the alluvium, which by the Roman period would have been a combination of tidal marsh, shallow water and deeper channels. Only the latter would have been navigable, thus providing the means of communication between the forts and the open sea.

Coastal barriers

Tidal scour can maintain channels and inlets, especially those that are open at both ends, such as the Wantsum or the modern-day Solent. However, when blocked by coastal barriers, normally a result of the longshore drift of eroded cliff-material, siltation of shallow marine environments can be rapid. A number of these barriers or spits are known to have been present during the Roman period, partially blocking the estuaries on which the Shore Forts were situated. As will be seen, the sheltered anchorage they offered seems to have been a major factor in the choice of the site on which to build a coastal installation. These spits have continued to migrate since the Roman period, particularly in recent centuries when increased rates of erosion have removed a greater volume of stone from local cliffs. Such barriers have been responsible for the blocking of the former inlets of the Dour, Rother, the Waveney-Yare estuary and the Wantsum Channel. Similarly, the growth of a new spit since medieval times has led to the closure of the Pevensey Levels from the open sea.

Drainage

The building of coastal defences and the embankment of rivers, often in conjunction with the natural siltation process, have reclaimed large regions for agriculture. In regions such as the Fenlands and Romney Marsh very large areas of land have been recovered, and the area of tidal influence has diminished greatly since prehistoric times. Reclamation on a smaller scale has taken place on the Pevensey Levels, the Broads, and the former Wantsum Channel.[22] Some drainage work is believed to be of Roman date, for example in the Lincolnshire Fenlands,[23] but most was begun during the medieval period. The process of enclosure and defence was largely completed by the seventeenth century.

The geomorphology of the Saxon Shore

Illustration of the ancient coastline

Any process of reconstruction must be approximate. A precise figure for sea-level cannot be ascertained for any site, with the possible exception of Dover, and in all cases the rates of erosion and the deposition of alluvium are uncertain. These issues present particular difficulties in terms of illustrating the Roman landscape, because such pictorial representations require decisions to be made about the precise relationships between land and sea, when the data do not exist to support such accuracy.

Furthermore, water levels may well have been changing significantly during the late Roman period and, in addition, alter rapidly with tide and season. As Hawkes noted in her discussion of the landscape of Richborough:

> … even if the Roman shoreline could be plotted on the map, it would not give a true picture of the Wantsum Channel at the period. Marsh formation was probably far advanced in Roman times, and we have no way of knowing the amount of open water in the channel.[24]

Illustrations remain valuable, but should be accepted as approximate, and only as the basis for a more subtle discussion of the evidence. On the figures accompanying this chapter, the convention in most cases has simply been to depict the landscape in terms of the pre-Flandrian land surface and alluvium, the latter labelled 'tidal water and marsh'.

Brancaster and north-west Norfolk

The north-west coast of Norfolk between Old Hunstanton and Blakeney is comprised of a complex of coastal sand-gravel barriers and marshland (see **colour plate 2**). A major feature of the coast is Scolt Head Island, a formation of dunes, shingle ridges and marshland that extends for some 6km (4 miles) between Burnham Overy Staithe and Brancaster Staithe.[25] The sand dunes that constitute the most westerly extension of the island provide protection for the coastline from the North Sea, including the modern harbour at Brancaster Staithe. Scolt Head Island has a strong tendency for westward extension and migration, and in general the sedimentary structures at its eastern end are older than those on the west. There is reasonable evidence to suggest that the island has largely developed within the last two millennia: during the Roman period it seems unlikely to have been a significant feature, and was probably located several kilometres to the east of Brancaster Staithe.

The fort at Brancaster is now located on a raised platform, roughly half a kilometre from the North Sea (**50, 70**). In between fort and sea is a broad swathe of tidal marsh, which stretches some 5km (3 miles) to the west, and over 20km (12 miles) eastwards. The accretion of the alluvial sediments on which the marsh rests has kept pace with sea-levels that have risen approximately 3m since 3000 BP. The southern extremity of the marsh extends to the Roman extra-mural settlement, and has enveloped the northern parts of a double-ditched rectilinear enclosure, seen by some scholars as a precursor to the Shore Fort. The marshes immediately north of the fort and those further seaward, on which the golf course is situated, are bisected by Mow Creek, a tidal channel that exits eastwards into the inlet known as Brancaster Harbour.

Borehole evidence from near to the Roman fort combines to suggest that it originally lay on the shores of an eastward-opening tidal inlet. Boreholes on a line north from the fort found a shallow depression between the mainland and a sand/gravel barrier that lay just to the south of Mow Creek.[26] Other boreholes on the site of the nearby golf course also revealed evidence for an east-west channel, some 6m deep and up to 400m wide. This channel cut through peat deposits that have been dated

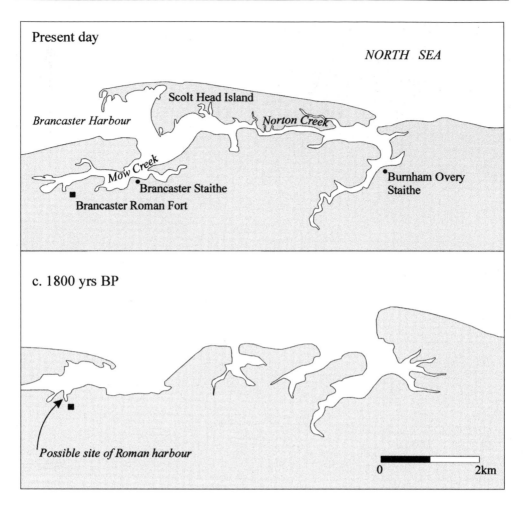

50 The ancient and modern coast at Brancaster. After unpublished work by C. Bristow

to *c.*3470 BP – 2790 BP, and is thus very likely to have been present during Roman times. The tidal inlet, which adjacent to the fort was around 250m in width, may well have been defined to the north by a substantial sand and gravel spit. This feature is known to have been present by AD 1000, and it is quite plausible for it to have formed by the Roman period.[27] The depth of water close to the fort could never have been very great, due to the fact that the depth of the depression between the fort and Mow Creek is no more than 3m at any point. The siting of the settlement and fort at Brancaster may have owed much to the shallow profile of the beach, which would have allowed flat-bottomed or shallow-keeled vessels to be drawn up close to the shore, or perhaps hauled up onto the beach. In this respect, there may well have been no need for wharves or a deep-water harbour. The inlet would have allowed convenient access to the Wash, while providing a sheltered anchorage that was not directly on the North Sea.

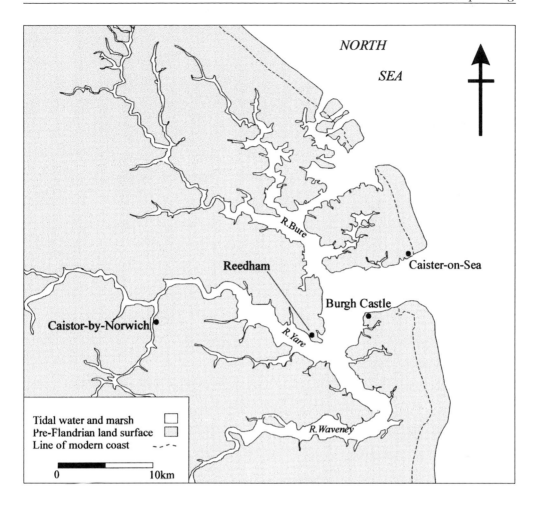

NORTH

SEA

R.Bure

Reedham

Caister-on-Sea

Burgh Castle

Caistor-by-Norwich

R.Yare

R.Waveney

Tidal water and marsh
Pre-Flandrian land surface
Line of modern coast

0   10km

51   The Great Estuary, showing the Roman sites at Caister, Burgh Castle and Reedham

The Great Estuary: Caister-on-Sea and Burgh Castle

The Roman installations at Caister-on-Sea and Burgh Castle faced one another across the 'Great Estuary', a major tidal inlet that opened to the sea in the area now occupied by Great Yarmouth (**51**). The mouth of the Great Estuary had once been some 7km (4 miles) wide, but by Roman times the centre had become partially blocked by a sandbank known as the 'Cerdic Sand', which would have acted as a substantial breakwater. Channels to the north and south, however, enabled continued access to the estuary.[28] The lower reaches of the Rivers Yare, Bure and Waveney were much wider than in modern times, and estuary conditions extended in the Yare to within 7km of Norwich. Siltation of the estuary was probably well advanced by the late Roman period, but navigation of the rivers and probably some of the tidal channels in the mudflats would have remained practicable. The presence of salt works in the late Saxon period around Runham demonstrates that sea water regularly penetrated at least 7km inland, although the industry seems not to have survived long after the Domesday Survey.[29] During the early parts of the Flandrian period the coast lay several miles to the east of its present position, but by the Roman period erosion had brought the coastline to within approximately 1km (0.6 miles) of that of the modern day.[30]

In Roman times the North Sea, Great Estuary and the enlarged River Bure had created an island roughly 10km (6 miles) square. The fort at Caister lay close to the south-east tip of this island, located at the end of a ridge of Boulder Clay on a gently sloping rectangular spur on the 15m contour. The open sea would have been approximately 2km (1.2 miles) distant to the east, but the shoreline of the estuary probably lay 335m to the south of the fort's south gate.[31] Here, an embayment 300m across seems to represent a plausible location for the beaching of shallow-drafted vessels. Protected on all sides apart from the south-east (a direction from which gales are rare), yet still close to the open water of the Great Estuary, this haven was well situated. Another small bay further to the east has also been proven, but it seems unlikely to have provided a suitable landing-place due to its extremely shallow-shelving beach.

On the opposite shore was Burgh Castle, standing on the north-west side of Lothingland, a tract of higher land bounded on the east by the North Sea and by the alluvial flatlands to the north and west. The fort was built on a tongue of land 30m above the fenland, and its site retains something of its original setting. The opening in the perimeter created by the fall of the west wall overlooks the River Waveney, and beyond that the River Yare. In the Roman period the extent of water was much greater, with an expanse of navigable water and tidal marsh extending several kilometres to the west of Burgh Castle. Breydon Water, immediately to the north of the fort, is the last vestige of the open estuary.

No harbour-works or staithes have been discovered at either site. The masonry at Burgh Castle identified by Morris at the base of the slope at the edge of the marsh clearly relates to the fallen west wall of the fort, and not to a harbour. The find of anchors in the locality suggests that some larger vessels used the Great Estuary and anchored in deeper water,[32] and in a situation in which many vessels were merely being beached, while larger-draft ships were anchored off the shore, elaborate facilities were unnecessary.

At least one other Roman site was located on the shores of the Great Estuary close to Burgh Castle and Caister. This is at Reedham, where on a slight rise close to the River Yare a small enclosure and the foundations of a tower were reported during the nineteenth century. Although nothing now remains that can be identified as a Roman structure, a large number of Roman finds have been made in the locality. Some buildings certainly did exist, for the parish church contains a large quantity of reused Roman brick in its fabric, a fact that only recently became apparent when a serious fire destroyed the overlying render (**colour plate 24**). In the past Reedham has been proposed as the site of a lighthouse, or of a signal station or fortlet intended to protect the River Yare – possibly a minor installation intended to work in concert with Burgh Castle and Caister.[33]

Walton Castle

Precise reconstruction of the coastline around Walton Castle is made difficult due to the severe extent of coastal erosion. Much of what can be deduced is readily apparent on the modern geological map of the region.[34] The site of the fort now lies some 250m out to sea, and as the last masonry was washed away in approximately 1750, we can infer that the cliffs have been retreating at an average rate of approximately 1m/year. Given this likely rate of loss, it is possible to see that the Saxon Shore Fort at Walton Castle was actually built quite some distance inland. If we adopt an average figure for loss of 1m/year over the last 17 centuries, this would place the site of the installation approximately 1.5km (1 mile) inland at the time of its construction. If such rates of loss have only been sustained since later medieval times, however, then the distance between the fort and the Roman coast would be significantly less. In either case, the notion that the fort was omitted from the *Notitia Dignitatum* because it had already started to collapse into the sea is implausible.[35]

Walton Castle was built on a broad, flat tract of land, a promontory now partially occupied by the modern town of Felixstowe. It is defined to the north by the Deben estuary, and to the south by the outflow of the Stour and the Orwell Rivers, which combine in the Orwell Haven (modern day Harwich harbour). The present cliffs stand to a height of about 30m, which must mark the approximate height of the land on which the fort once stood. The ground to the north descends gently to an alluvial basin, through which the Deben flows to the North Sea. A promontory that extends southwards from Bawdsey, comprising a line of cliffs, provides the basin with considerable shelter from the open sea. This natural breakwater, now only 300m wide, has been very significantly reduced by erosion.

There is a strong tendency for shingle spits to form along this section of coastline, created by the south-westerly longshore drift of material eroded from the cliffs. Orford Ness, a shingle spit some 15km (9 miles) in length, is a particularly prominent example. Growth of another spit has led to the formation of Landguard Point, which extends south from Felixstowe, protecting, and partially closing, the Orwell Haven. A similar, though much less developed barrier is present on the north-east side of the mouth of the Deben, visible only at low tide. Burnham thought it to have been present during the Roman period,[36] but this conclusion seems unlikely given that most spit-formation in the region has occurred from the High Middle Ages to the present day. Its presence or absence at Walton would probably not have been critical to the function of the site as an anchorage, however, since the southward extension of the cliff-line offered a great deal of protection.

The Shore Fort can be envisaged as having occupied a position on higher ground that overlooked a sheltered, tidal basin (**52**). The Deben itself would have been navigable for some distance inland, and other deeper channels probably laced the alluvial marshland. One of these, the King's Fleet (formerly the Walton Haven), branches south-west from the Deben about 2km (1.2 miles) distant from the site of the fort. It seems likely that any anchorage associated with the fort would have been somewhat closer, but although there have been a substantial number of Roman finds in the vicinity of the fort, none has indicated a harbour or beaching site.

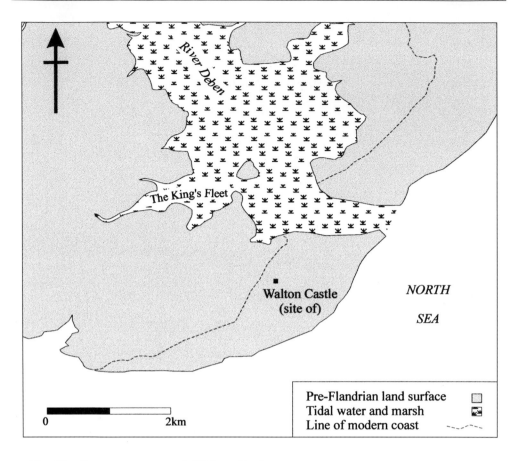

52   The Roman coast around Walton Castle

Bradwell

After major changes during the Flandrian period that continued until Neolithic times, the Dengie peninsula, on which Bradwell is situated, and the estuaries of the Blackwater and Crouch attained roughly their present form during the Bronze and Iron Ages.[37] The fort of Bradwell was constructed near the end of a promontory, the eastern extremity of which in post-Roman times was first eroded by the sea, and later enveloped by a salt marsh (**53**). The eastern defences of the Shore Fort have been destroyed by this process. St Peter's chapel presently overlooks a swathe of tidal mudflats, which stretch eastwards for approximately half a kilometre from its walls (**colour plate 5**).

In Roman times substantial tidal inlets to the north and south defined the promontory on which the fort stood. Both are now obscured by fine alluvial sediments, deposition of which had probably already commenced by the Roman period. The mouth of the northern inlet was a significant distance from the fort, and has been proven during borehole investigations close to the site of the Bradwell power station. A number of 'red hills', small mounds associated with Roman salt production, were situated on the margins of the alluvial fill of the inlet.[38] The inlet to the south, which shows clearly as

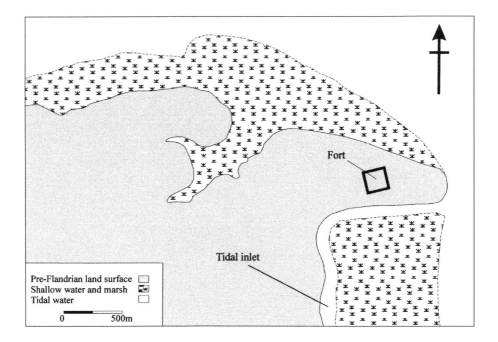

53   The Roman coast around Bradwell

a sinuous vegetation mark on aerial photographs, lay much closer to the fort, approximately 100m from its south wall. Its mouth may have been partially blocked by a shell ridge or chenier, a southern extension of which has been dated to the sixth or seventh centuries AD.[39] Had this particular ridge been present during Roman times it would have afforded significant protection for shipping in the southern inlet.

The Wantsum Channel: Reculver and Richborough

The rising sea-levels that overwhelmed the Dogger Bank around 7600 BP also flooded a shallow syncline ('u'-shaped depression) in the Chalk of east Kent, creating the Wantsum Channel and separating Thanet from the mainland. The Wantsum was a large tidal channel, into which the Stour and other rivers drained, and in its early stages it was probably open at both its north and east ends, in much the same way as the Solent is today. However, the formation of shingle barriers across both ends has since partially closed off the channel. The barriers at the eastern mouth, the inner bank (the Stonar Bank) and the outer spit (the Brake Bank), now extend between Ebbsfleet, to the north-east of Richborough, and Deal. The precise date and cause of their formation is the subject of debate, but it is evident that the barriers were present by the Roman period. Roman coins and pottery were found on the bar, and the shingle was itself used for the mortar in the Richborough Shore Fort.[40] The eastward longshore drift of eroded London Clay from the Reculver cliffs led to the formation of another barrier across the northern mouth of the Wantsum Channel, which finally closed this entrance at the end of the eighteenth century. This barrier was also likely to have partially formed by Roman times.[41]

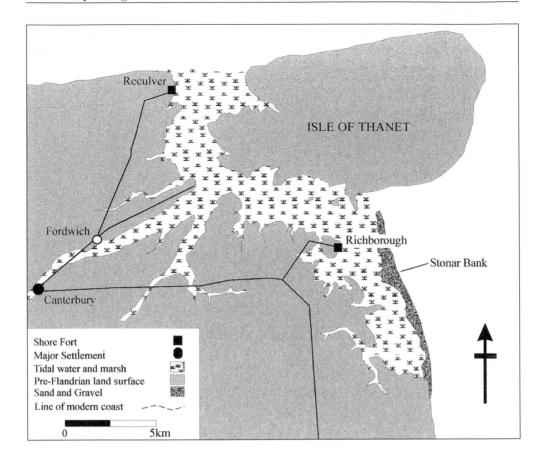

54 The Wantsum Channel

While the Wantsum was open at both ends it is likely that the tidal scour, suffi-cient to remove the Thanet Sands from the lap of the syncline, also prevented the build up of alluvium in the channel. The formation of the shingle barriers, however, would have led to siltation that was probably quite well advanced by the early Roman period, and still further by the third century.[42] Nevertheless, the River Stour remained navigable as far inland as Fordwich, 5km (3 miles) from Canterbury, where Roman wharves have been discovered.[43] The barriers them-selves provided a breakwater from the North Sea, and a sheltered anchorage for vessels within the channel.

The forts at Richborough and Reculver both lie on raised ground bordering the western margins of the alluvial fill of the Wantsum syncline (**54**). Reculver was located on a low, well-drained hill that overlooked a small embayment to the south, which may have provided a sheltered anchorage for shipping (see **74**). Although now situated precariously on the cliff edge, the fort was significantly further inland at the time of its construction. One recent reconstruction of the Wantsum Channel assumed that modern rates of erosion had been in operation since the Roman period, leading to a southward coastal recession of some 3km (2 miles).[44] Such a calculation may be an overestimate, but if rates of erosion have been consistent from later medieval times to the present day, then losses of the order of 1km (0.6 miles) are quite plausible.

Richborough was built at the end of a peninsula, joined to the mainland to the west by a strip of clay marsh. The 'Fleet Causeway' – a raised road linking the fort to the mainland proper – was built on this strip, probably during the third century.[45] At some point after its construction the causeway was buried by alluvial sediment, but although it is tempting to ascribe its submergence to a late Roman marine transgression, there is no evidence that clearly points to such a conclusion. In recent times the course of the Stour has shifted westwards, gradually eroding the end of the Richborough peninsula and ultimately causing the fall of the fort's eastern wall. It has been suggested that the original area of the Claudian beachhead was of the order of 40ha (100 acres).[46]

No traces of harbours have been identified at either site. In 1792 Boys claimed to have located a 'landing place' at Richborough close to the foot of the slope '40 rods [200m] to northward of the castle'. Roach Smith's subsequent investigation of the same area found no evidence to support Boys' claim, and the position of any harbour remains unknown.[47]

Dover

The modern town of Dover is situated at the mouth of the Dour valley, flanked by the chalk cliffs of Castle Hill to the east, and the Western Heights. The River Dour flows to the sea through a shallow alluvial basin, its course diverted to the south-west by a sand and gravel barrier that has accumulated since the medieval period. Traditions regarding the ancient landscape of Dover have proved to be relatively accurate. Leland claimed that there had once been a haven at Dover, while the antiquary William Stukeley depicted an inlet, where the River Dour meandered through a wide, flat valley: the Roman town (fancifully depicted with defensive wall and forum-basilica) was situated close to the sea on the western bank. Two light-houses were illustrated, on the eastern and western cliff tops overlooking the valley. The coastal form of Roman Dover was debated on several occasions during the twentieth century, and all authors reached similar conclusions.[48] The most complete discussion is that of Rigold, and although it pre-dates the major discoveries of the *classis Britannica* and Shore Forts it remains valid.[49]

The Roman coast was defined by a small spit (which Rigold referred to as the 'old spit'), extending south-westwards from what was probably the line of the ancient coast (**55**). The presence of samian ware and other pottery on the shingle land surface, buried by alluvium, demonstrates the spit's existence in the Roman period. The mouth of the inlet was closed on the western side by a small promontory, thus creating an entrance to the basin approximately 50m in width. Behind the inlet lay a wide, shallow basin, now occupied by alluvium up to the 7m contour. The Dour itself does not appear to have been tidal to any great distance, as it is freshwater alluvium that occupies the floodplain inland from Dover.[50]

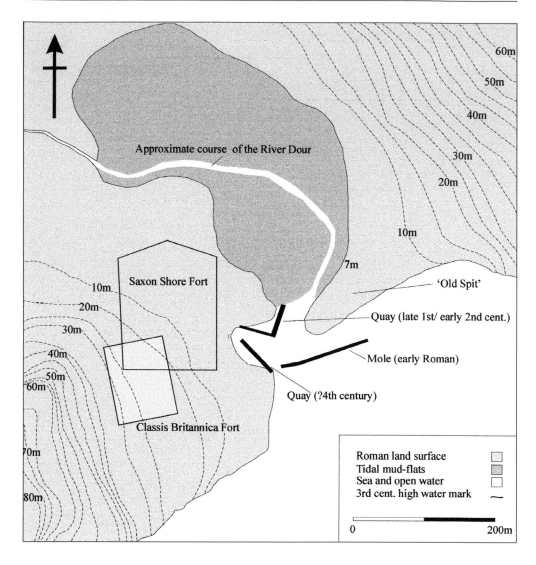

55   Roman Dover. Based on Rigold (1969)

In 1855 a timber-faced and timber-laced mole or breakwater was discovered, filled with shingle, positioned slightly to seaward of the old spit. A probable second section was located during the 1920s, and Rigold has suggested that the mole extended across most of the estuary mouth, creating two artificial inlets around the breakwater's east and west sides. The mole itself is undated, but most commentators seem to favour an early Roman interpretation. Immediately behind this breakwater on the western shore a quay has been found, and a jetty projecting from it, both dated to the late first or early second century AD. A later quay, possibly of the fourth century, but on balance more likely late second, has been discovered a little further to the south, still under the lee of the breakwater.

All substantial Roman structures thus far encountered in the town have been on the western shore, although the find of samian pottery on the old spit does suggest at least a small amount of early to mid-Roman activity on the far bank. Settlement appears to have occupied the reasonably gently sloping ground between the 7m and 14m contour, above which the terrain rises sharply. The Shore Fort itself was built roughly adjacent to the mole, commanding the mouth of the inlet, its eastern wall being situated adjacent to the margins of the alluvium. Taking coastal erosion into consideration, its south wall was probably slightly inland from the sea. Rigold also suggested the presence of an inner basin extending around 500m behind the inlet, which he proposed as an anchorage, perhaps one which was dredged. However, the present evidence tends to dispel such a notion. Although some scatters of second-century pottery have been found on the western margins of the alluvial fill, there is no indication of substantial activity, and no material from the late Roman period.

The differing height of the two Roman quays has attracted comment, the top of the late second- to fourth-century structure being approximately 0.5m above the top of the earlier quay. This was suggested to be a reflection of rising sea-levels in the interval between their construction.[51] There are also a significant number of second-century land surfaces in the town that have been buried under alluvium, including those around the 'inner basin'. Relative water levels have clearly risen since the early Roman period, but the abandonment of certain areas of the basin after the second century may relate to the contraction of the Roman settlement, rather than to any late Roman marine transgression. Support for this latter view might come from houses south of the fort sites, which were apparently deliberately destroyed around AD 200.[52]

Romney Marsh: Lympne

The Shore Fort at Lympne is situated on the upland margins of Romney Marsh, the latter being a region of gravels, sands, silts, clays and peats that has formed in its entirety during the Flandrian period.[53] Early postglacial sea-level rises created a wide embayment on the south Kent coast some 30km (20 miles) wide, bordered on the west, north and east by the higher land of the Wealden scarp. During the later parts of the Flandrian period, sediment accumulation led to the formation of a shallow lagoon, protected from the sea by a sand bar. By the Roman period a substantial shingle bank was present, anchored on Fairlight Head (near modern Hastings) and extending eastwards to a cuspate head immediately to the south of West Hythe. Early Bronze Age axes found on the Lydd Shingle attest to human activity on the bank from an early date, which, as we shall shortly see, was also occupied during the Roman period.[54] The evolution of the Dungeness spit, now a major feature of the region, began much later, probably in late Roman or early Saxon times.

The Roman landscape of Romney Marsh is only partially understood. Reconstructions rely heavily on an extensive soil survey of the region that differentiated between areas of decalcified (older) and calcified (younger) marsh.[55] The evidence suggests that the younger marsh was not drained *earlier* than the Saxon period; by contrast, it seems that natural or artificial processes had reclaimed the older marsh well before the Saxon occupation of the region. A series of archaeo-

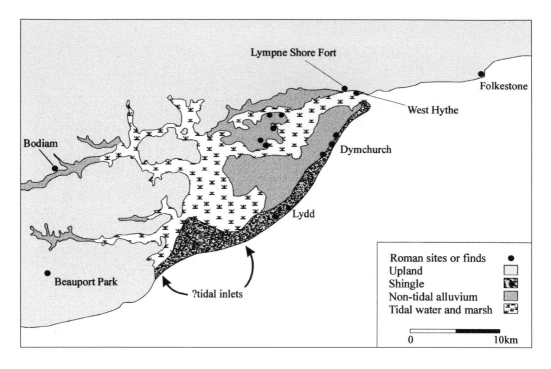

56 Romney Marsh in the Roman period. After Cunliffe (1980b)

logical finds have been made on the decalcified marsh that date to the first century BC or first century AD, on or adjacent to the shingle barrier at Dymchurch, St Mary-in-the-Marsh and Lydd, and inland at Snargate and Ruckinge. The Roman debris within the storm beach at West Hythe has already been discussed in Chapter 1.[56] These sites, probably associated with salt and perhaps in some cases pottery production, indicate that dry land already existed in some places by the early Roman period. Water continued to penetrate quite far inland, however, and the River Rother was navigable at least as far as Bodiam, where as we have already seen, a first- or second-century Roman port existed. The major tidal inlet was located at the eastern end of the Marsh at West Hythe. There exists the possibility that there were two other outflows to the sea (through breaks in the shingle barrier) around New Romney and Rye, though their presence in Roman times has yet to be conclusively proven.

In his study of the Romney Marsh landscape, Cunliffe tentatively adopted the decalcified marsh as the Roman land surface, the 'new' calcified marshland indicating the extent of marine influence in the region at that time.[57] In so doing he was able to depict an expanse of marshland sheltered behind the shingle barrier, which was dissected by the drainage channels of the Rother, Tillingham and Brede Rivers (**56**). A recent field walking survey has shown Cunliffe's work to be slightly inaccurate, since it detected some settlement or activity on the areas of 'new marshland', which the model proposed to have been entirely inundated by water.[58] Nevertheless, Cunliffe's

*57   View north from Romney Marsh towards the Shore Fort at Lympne. In the left of the
picture the tumbled ruins of the Roman defences lie scattered on the hillside; the medieval
castle and church are visible to the right, at the top of the slope. During the Roman period,
a tidal inlet would have occupied the position from which the photograph was taken*

general conclusions still appear valid, although our understanding of the Roman
landscape is likely to be further altered or refined as new discoveries are made.

Importantly, there is evidence that the landscape of Romney Marsh may have
altered significantly during the late Roman period. All the known occupation sites
are of first- and second-century date, and there is little to indicate any activity on the
Marsh during the third, fourth or fifth centuries. One explanation might lie in rising
sea levels, which could have led to the inundation of settlements by tidal water. These
too could have brought about the abandonment of any second-century fort in the
area of Lympne or West Hythe, if it had been situated at a lower altitude than the
later Shore Fort. Future research may perhaps show this apparent lack of late Roman
activity to be illusory, or that the abandonment of settlements was for reasons other
than flooding. If rising water was to blame, it remains to be seen precisely how well
Cunliffe's reconstruction holds up for the later Roman period.

The Shore Fort at Lympne was built on a degraded sea cliff, which slopes
downhill from north to south at around 9°. The site once overlooked the major tidal
inlet that opened to the sea near West Hythe, but now offers an impressive view
across Romney Marsh (**57, colour plate 12**). The cliffs to the east and west of
Lympne are between 90-100m in height, and the Shore Fort appears to have been
situated at a similar altitude. Geotechnical investigation of the cliff has revealed much

about the siting of the fort; it is clear that by Roman times major land-slipping had already occurred, and the terrain differed little from its present form.[59] The fort was built on the lower part of the slope (the 'accumulation zone') rather than the unstable, slipping surface (the 'degradation zone'). As such it was reasonably well situated, although (with the benefit of hindsight) it should ideally have been positioned 50m further to the west. Investigations of the site have identified two potential beaching sites at the base of the slope, one to the north, and one to the south of the present slide toe. Landslipped material and marsh sediments overlie the beaches, which tend to suggest their presence during the Roman period. The height of the beach 35m north of the present slide toe is approximately -3m OD. Estimating water levels to be roughly equivalent to those of the modern day, it was concluded that the depth of water over the beach would have been 5.0m–6.4m at high tide, and 0m–1.3m at low tide. The more southerly beach was at a higher altitude (-1.5m OD), and the depth of water was correspondingly lower. Either location could thus have served as a beaching site in Roman times, although the southerly site would not have been accessible at low tide.

The Pevensey Levels

The Roman fort at Pevensey presently stands land-locked on a slightly elevated tongue of land, overlooking the Pevensey Levels, approximately 1km (0.6 miles) from the East Sussex coast. At the time of its construction, however, its situation was greatly different (**58**). The Pevensey Levels have a complex history of coastal advance and retreat during the later stages of the Flandrian period, the environment varying from a shallow marine environment to one of freshwater.[60] During post-Roman times the eastward longshore drift of debris from the chalk cliffs to the west has created a shingle barrier. This barrier, which in modern times stretches from Eastbourne to Bexhill, cannot be dated precisely by any current technique. However, historical records show that its formation was well advanced by the thirteenth century, being part of the wider phenomenon of the siltation of many East Sussex harbours behind drifting gravel. It is thus possible to envisage the original setting of Pevensey Castle, positioned at the end of a raised peninsula and surrounded by a shallow coastal marsh. Although not yet protected by any coastal barrier, the region was nevertheless a sheltered, low energy marine environment, as indeed it had been throughout the Flandrian period as a whole. In contrast to Romney Marsh, there is no evidence of Roman settlement in the land behind the modern coastal barrier, strongly suggesting that the whole region was marsh during the Roman period.

Navigation of this marshy embayment was possible only along the courses of a number of deep-water channels. Some of these would have been blind-ended tidal creeks, while others would have been the tidal lower reaches of rivers, carrying freshwater run-off from the gentle slopes to the west, north and east that defined the marsh. The choice of the Pevensey peninsula for the site of a Shore Fort must have owed much to its proximity to one such channel, a tidal creek that opened onto the sea close to modern-day Eastbourne. Although this waterway, the 'Pevensey Haven',

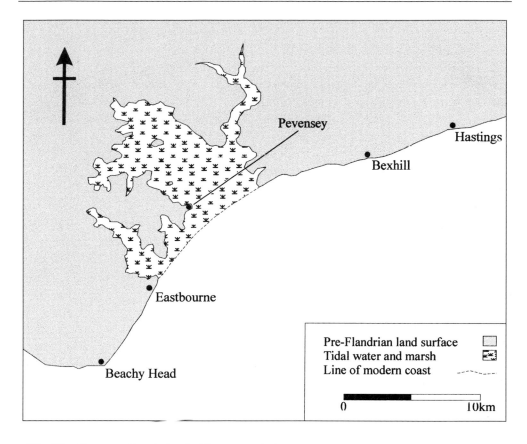

58 The Pevensey Levels in the Roman period

now flows a considerable distance to the east of the castle, tenth-century records suggest that its course was originally much closer to the fort, quite possibly running along the edge of the peninsula on its south-eastern tip.[61] This channel is likely to have been of primary importance to the fort, connections with the sea being funda-mental to its existence. Indeed, there could have been no other reason for the siting of such a major installation on the isolated and probably rather inhospitable Pevensey peninsula. Although access to the fort by sea may have been restricted to times of high or rising tides, vessels of considerable size have in the past been able to operate within the channels of the Levels. The Domesday Survey records a large number of salt works on the Pevensey Levels, indicating that seawater regularly reached consid-erable distances into the marsh even during medieval times. The industry had declined by the early thirteenth century, however, probably as a consequence of the formation of the coastal barrier. A programme of drainage during the medieval and Early Modern periods has since reclaimed almost the entire marsh for farmland, a process that led directly to the decline of Pevensey as a port by the fourteenth century.[62] Only in the modern place name of Pevensey [*Pevens + island*] is the marine context of the site now preserved.

Portchester

Portchester Castle, situated in Portsmouth Harbour, occupies a position that is probably the least-changed of any of the Shore Forts (**59**). Siltation is likely to have kept pace with rising sea-levels, and thus the only major alteration is that brought about by the erosion of the promontory on which Portchester Castle was constructed. On this subject there is relatively little to add to comments made in the first report on the excavation of the fort:

> The sea lapped the east wall at high tide until the modern retaining wall was built to prevent damage by undercutting, but extensive erosion can still be observed along the south side of the promontory. Several feet of land have been lost in some places since the excavations [1961-1972] began, and it can only be assumed that encroachment by the sea has gone on over a long period of time. Documentary accounts record serious flooding and erosion during turbulent weather in the early decades of the fourteenth century.[63]

The east wall, in particular, demonstrates the level of damage to that quarter of the fort: both the south-east angle bastion and the next one to the north have been destroyed, presumably by the action of the sea, and much of the adjacent wall has also needed extensive repair. The total extent of the erosion is unclear, but if the modern rates of loss are representative of those in the past, then the shoreline may well have extended several hundred metres to the south-west.

Access to the fort in the modern day is possible even at low tide. A deeper water channel is present about 150m from the fort's east wall and it is unlikely to have changed its course greatly since Roman times. At low tide the fort is largely surrounded by mud flats, with small sailing vessels anchored a few tens of metres from the perimeter walls.

Beaches, harbours and Roman shipping

The preceding discussion demonstrates that, in general terms, all the Shore Forts occupied locations of a similar nature. They were positioned in sheltered, tidal environments that lay close to, but not directly on, the open sea. In many cases they were protected by natural barriers, as at Brancaster, Reculver Richborough, Lympne and possibly at Walton Castle and Bradwell. Only at Dover do we know of an instance where an artificial breakwater was provided, and given the natural protection afforded to most of the forts, such measures were probably deemed unnecessary. The physical situations of the Shore Forts are comparable with many other Roman coastal sites in Britain. The fort at Cardiff, positioned on the River Taff, a little removed from the Severn Estuary, is but one pertinent example. This finding in itself is not surprising, because exposed harbours on the open sea have never been thought favourable, and the Roman period is no exception in this respect.[64] Nevertheless, it emphasises the

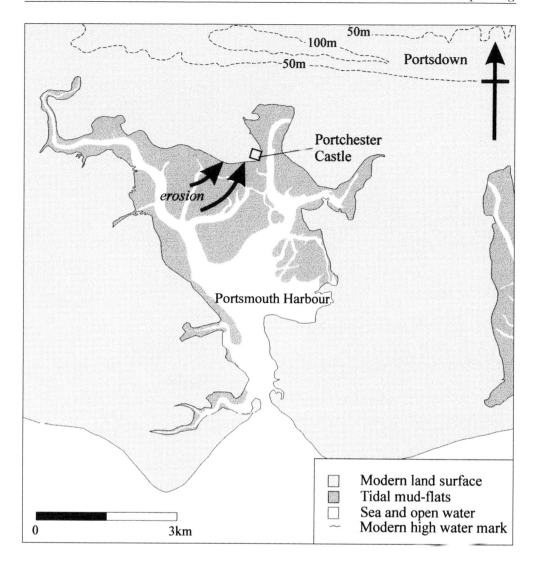

59   The coast in the area of Portchester Castle

point that the sites were carefully and correctly selected, even though later coastal changes mean that only a few have continued as successful ports.

The conclusions also prompt a reassessment of the manner in which these installations might have operated as ports and harbours. Previously the most specific attempt to deal with this question was made by Mann. He proposed an arrangement whereby the Shore Forts were grouped into pairs, with one site possessing a deep-water harbour, while the other was a place where vessels would have to be hauled ashore onto a shallow-shelving beach. In order to work at all, Mann's system relied on a specific order for the forts (based on the earlier work of Stevens) in which the Roman site of *Portus Adurni* had to be Portchester not Walton Castle (see Chapter 6).[65] Caister was not considered by either scholar to be a part of the Saxon Shore and was not included in the discussion. Mann's scheme, based on Stevens' order for the forts, is as follows:

Dover	harbour
Lympne	beach
Brancaster	beach
Burgh Castle	harbour
Reculver	beach
Richborough	harbour
Pevensey	beach
Portchester	harbour
Walton Castle	beach
Bradwell	harbour

The present findings suggest that there is nothing whatsoever to recommend this scheme, as there appear to be no fundamental differences between the coastal settings of any of the Shore Forts. Furthermore, although in several instances evidence has come to light that was interpreted at the time as relating to a harbour or landing place (for example at Richborough and Burgh Castle), most of these identifications have proved false. Only at Dover do we have genuine evidence for deep-water harbour facilities. In fact, it may well be that such features will not be detected at the Shore Forts simply because they did not exist. This becomes more apparent when we examine the types of vessels that could have been operating from or visiting the Shore Forts.

There is evidence for a wide variety of vessels having operated in British waters during the Roman period. In his discussion of the traffic in the Port of London, for example, Marsden is able to list evidence for local riverboats and barges, fishing boats, seagoing merchantmen and for warships.[66] Merchant ships of a considerable size probably carried much of the commerce between Britain and the Empire. Examination of Classical wrecks from the Mediterranean suggest that such vessels were capable of carrying a cargo of between 170 tonnes and 600 tonnes, most lying in the 200–350 tonne range. The more prominent keel of such vessels, while enabling them to operate at sea, prevented them from navigating in shallower waters. Unless deep-water quays were available (as in Italy at Ostia and Portus) the cargo would have to be transferred to smaller river vessels for unloading.

Smaller vessels with limited seagoing capabilities are also known from Britain, such as that from St Peter Port, Guernsey, the Blackfriars I ship from London and most recently the boat found at Barlands Farm (Gwent). These belong to the Romano-Celtic (or Gallo-Roman) tradition of boat-building. The Blackfriars I ship was a small single-masted sailing vessel, which was capable of carrying a maximum cargo of about 50 tonnes (**60**). It is thought to be comparable to the coastal vessels of the Veneti tribe that operated on the Gallic coast, which were described by Caesar. The Barlands Farm boat, though of a similar basic design, was about half the size of the Blackfriars I vessel.

Most of the Romano-Celtic vessels discovered in Britain have been small river-boats and barges, whose shallow draught and keel-less profile rendered them unsuitable for service at sea. One such is the vessel from New Guys House, Bermondsea, which is thought to have been a lighter involved in the trans-shipment of goods from larger ships visiting the Port of London.[67] Although no examples have yet been found in Britain, it seems likely that log-built barges, constructed using the same techniques as the Roman wrecks from Zwammerdam (Netherlands) and Pommeroeul (Belgium), were also present on estuaries such as the Thames.[68] The cargo capacity of the New Guy's House lighter is estimated at 7 tonnes, while the largest of the Zwammerdam barges could have carried approximately 50 tonnes.

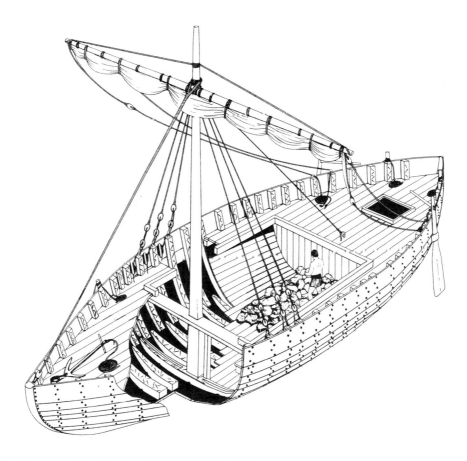

60 *Reconstruction drawing of the Blackfriars I ship.* Copyright English Heritage, Museum of London, C. Caldwell

It has already been suggested in the previous chapter that ships of a type similar to Blackfriars I would have been well suited for the transportation of building materials during the construction of the Shore Forts. Relatively flexible in their operational abilities, they would have been able to sail close to shore, while also being able to undertake limited coastal journeys. The shallow draught and strengthened keel planks of the Blackfriars I vessel would have allowed it to be drawn up onto a beach for loading and unloading, thus avoiding the trans-shipment process required by larger seagoing vessels. If similar vessels used the Shore Forts over the longer term, then there would simply have been no need for more elaborate harbour facilities to be provided. The beaching of ships was a widespread practice up until recent times, a relevant example to this study being the barges that carried stone from the Kentish ragstone quarries on the River Medway during the nineteenth century. These were loaded while drawn up on the foreshore and then re-floated on the rising tide. Ships of considerable size, well in excess of the Blackfriars I vessel, have been regularly beached in the past. However, it is not known whether warships, or the small scouting craft (*pictae*) described by the late Roman writer Vegetius, were capable of being beached in a similar fashion. Galleys, in particular, are likely to have had a much more pronounced keel than many coastal merchant craft, and may of necessity had to be anchored offshore. This is obviously an important point in the discussion of the operation of the Shore Forts as military harbours, but as the wreck of a Roman fighting ship has yet to be found the question must remain open.

The largest merchant vessels likely to have operated in Romano-British waters could certainly not be beached, but there was still no necessity for deep-water harbours to have been provided, as the cargoes could have been trans-shipped to smaller vessels, perhaps to lighters of the New Guys House type. We might even consider the possibility that the great ships of the ancient world visited Dover exclusively, and that their cargoes were moved onwards along the south and east coasts of Britain by smaller vessels. It certainly seems likely that very large ships would not have visited certain of the Shore Forts: Pevensey, for example, was situated some distance from the open sea and the waterways leading to the site were probably not navigable by vessels of major size.

In a sense much of the preceding discussion about the use of the Shore Forts must be speculative, as the findings of this chapter can tell us little about the precise function of these sites. However, what is abundantly clear is that maritime communications were of paramount importance to the Shore Forts, and that their physical setting would have served them equally well as commercial harbours or as bases for small war fleets. There is, of course, no reason why the installations could not have simultaneously fulfilled both of these functions.

6 Strategy

In the previous chapters many aspects of the Shore Forts have been considered, but the core question of their function has yet to be addressed. In the absence of any specific historical references, or of overwhelming archaeological evidence, the role of the Shore Forts – and indeed late Romano-British coastal installations as a whole – is to a large extent a matter of conjecture. The previous chapter demonstrated that our sites occupied sheltered locations that lay in the coastal zone, though not on the open sea; their general role as ports or harbours is clear, but no more detailed conclusions can be drawn from their physical setting.

As has been observed elsewhere, 'no better example can be found of the difficulties in determining the tactical and strategic use of Roman forts than the problem of the Saxon Shore',[1] but over the years several theories have been advanced. It is not the purpose here to argue specifically for any one of these in particular; there is as yet too little evidence – particularly from the fort interiors – to enable confident conclusions. Arguments for a single function may in any case be too simplistic, for it is quite possible that the installations fulfilled several (and perhaps many) different functions simultaneously. Neither is it necessarily the case that the Shore Forts functioned in the same way throughout their operational lifetime; their role in the late fourth century may have been markedly different from that originally intended at the time of their construction. A glance at the post-Roman histories of the forts, where we see them fulfilling a variety of tasks, illustrates this point.

Britain in the fourth century

The fourth century in Britain started in much the same way as the third century had done, with campaigning on the northern frontier. Constantius had been absent from the province since 297 but returned in 306, now as Augustus following the retirement of Diocletian and Maximian in the previous year. The precise reasons for the warfare are obscure, as is the course of the campaign. Literary sources allude to penetration by Roman forces far into the north, and pottery of the period at both Cramond and Carpow once again suggest the use of a fleet in support of operations. A victory over the Picts ('the painted men') was claimed, the first instance where a Highland tribal confederation appears under this name in the historical record (**61**).

Constantius died unexpectedly at York in 306. In violation of the Tetrarchy's rules of succession, his son Constantine (who had accompanied Constantius to Britain) was proclaimed Augustus by the army, and shortly afterwards departed the province

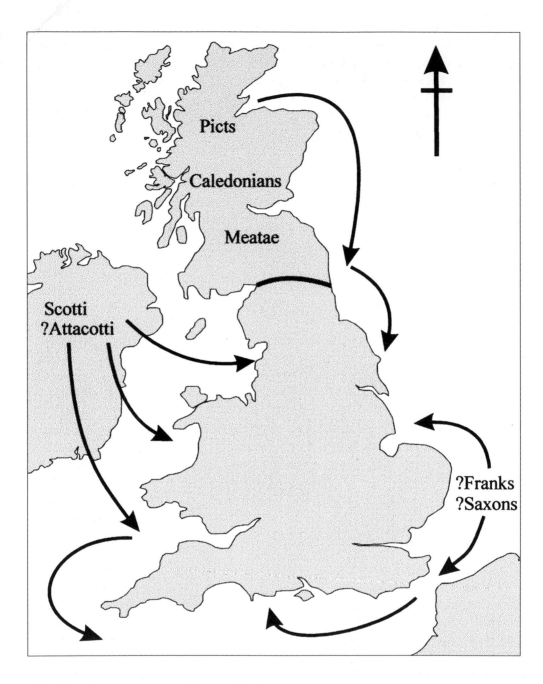

61 Changing threats to late Roman Britain

to pursue his imperial claim. 17 years of intermittent civil war ensued before Constantine emerged as sole ruler of the Roman world, but during this period, and indeed for most of the first half of the fourth century, Britain appears in the literary record as something of a backwater. Problems begin to surface in 342/3, when Constans (joint emperor 337–50) visited Britain in winter. For the emperor to have personally risked a crossing during this season hints at serious trouble. The exact nature of any crisis is not clear, but was probably of a military nature, and likely to have been concerned with the Picts. Constans' coinage of that year shows him on a warship steered by Victory, from which we might reasonably suppose that the difficulties in Britain had been dealt with successfully.

The overthrow of Constans by the army in 350 brought about the proclamation as emperor of Magnentius, an army officer from Britain. Although defeated at Mursa (Osijek), Illyricum, his regime was not finally suppressed in Britain and Gaul by the legitimate emperor Constantius II until 353. Reprisals followed in Britain, not least against pagans, who had enjoyed a respite under Magnentius. Largely as a result of the distraction of the civil war, the Rhine frontier had been overrun briefly in 353. Other dangerous incursions by the Franks and Alemanni followed. The barbarians initially proved difficult to dislodge from Gaul and Germany, but successes by the young Caesar Julian between 355 and 359 ousted them from the Empire and restored the integrity of the frontier. During 359, in advance of campaigns on the lower Rhine, Julian assembled a large fleet for the transport of grain from Britain. Accounts vary, but something of the order of 600 ships were built or commandeered for the task.[2] This was seemingly an attempt to reopen an imperial supply route that had ceased to function. For the next half-century there is no record of any serious breach of the Rhine *limes*.

The historian Ammianus Marcellinus describes how, early in 360, the Picts and the Scots (the latter still based in Ireland at that time) broke the terms imposed on them – presumably by Constans – and began to plunder lands close to the northern frontier in Britain. Julian did not follow Constans' precedent of a winter sea crossing, but instead dispatched his *magister militum* Flavius Lupicinus at the head of four units of the field army. Once again the details are not made clear, but any immediate difficulties within the province appear to have been swiftly remedied. However, throughout the early and mid-360s Ammianus continues to hint at troubles in Britain, and matters came to a head in 367, when an allegedly co-ordinated attack (the so-called *barbarica conspiratio*, or 'barbarian conspiracy') was mounted on Roman Britain and the near continent. Some recent scholars have cast doubt on the extent of the troubles, and whether the attacks were in fact in any way co-ordinated.[3] However, if we follow the traditional view, the Picts, Scots and Attacotti (the latter probably from Ireland or the Western Isles) assaulted north and west Britain, while the Franks and Saxons are recorded as having attacked the coasts and frontiers of Gaul. In Britain a senior officer named Nectaridus, *comes maritimi tractus* ('count of the maritime region') was killed, and duke Fallofaudes (probably the Roman commander in the north) was also killed, captured or otherwise incapacitated. The army disintegrated under the pressure, and as the barbarians split into small bands to pillage the province, order rapidly broke down.

The emperor Valentinian (364-75) dispatched another senior officer, count Theodosius, once again at the head of four units of the field army, to restore order in the province. Despite the apparent seriousness of the situation, this appears to have been achieved fairly quickly, for by 368 or 369 Theodosius was able to embark on a broad programme of restoration in the province, reorganising the army and setting in hand repairs to the northern frontier. A small number of new military installations, notably the Yorkshire signal stations, might be attributed to Theodosius, although these could well have been built a decade or so after this point in time. The external towers that were added to the existing defences of many of the British towns are also frequently associated with the Theodosian restoration.[4]

After the 360s the historians of the Empire seem little concerned with the British province, although it is known that it was twice out of the control of the Central Empire: for five years under the usurper Magnus Maximus (383-8), and for two more under Eugenius (392-4). It is likely that barbarians continued to threaten, however. A passage in the sixth-century work of the British writer Gildas specifically talks of wars against the Picts, both during and after the revolt of Magnus Maximus.[5] The sources on which Gildas based this assertion are not known, but even if not factually accurate, his writings probably serve as a useful reminder that not all was peaceful during the last decades of the century. Other slightly enigmatic references to troubles can be found in the works of the eulogising poet Claudian, where Britain is portrayed as having been under attack from Picts, Scots, and also by Saxon pirates. Although no campaigns are mentioned, Stilicho, the Vandal-born general who was effective ruler of the Roman west during the early reign of Honorius, is given credit for rescuing the province in or around AD 400.

Despite the various military difficulties of the period, the image of fourth-century Britain is one of reasonable prosperity. Some scholars go further, citing it as a 'golden age' on the basis of the large number of sites of all types that were occupied, and the quantity of finds recovered from them. Somewhat against this view, a body of evidence is now accumulating that suggests a decline in activity in Roman Britain during the last quarter of the fourth century. There is, however, little doubt that the fabric of the province – military, administrative and material – remained substantially intact at this time. The catastrophic collapse of Roman civilisation that befell Britain during the early fifth century was certainly very unlikely to have been anticipated.

The military role of the Saxon Shore

The Notitia Dignitatum

A convenient starting point for the discussion of the role of the Shore Forts is the late Roman text known as the *Notitia Dignitatum*. Here, and only here, do we find a historical reference to the 'Saxon Shore'. For this reason, the document has rightly or wrongly assumed a central place in debates about the function of the coastal forts of both Britain and Gaul, and therefore examination of its character and content is necessary.

The *Notitia Dignitatum* (translated as 'List of Offices') essentially comprises a list of civilian and military commands in both the eastern and western parts of the Empire; this much is understood, but little else is known for certain. Its date is much disputed, but a reasonably widely held view is that it was compiled from other documents (some of a substantially earlier date) in approximately 395. It was subsequently corrected and updated for the next 25-30 years, and the copy that has come down to us perhaps dated to around the year 425. The view that it is a single, coherent document now seems unfounded.

The *Notitia* was probably an official document that originated in the *primicerius notariorum*, the official registry of the Empire, or another central record-keeping office. Its intended use has been hotly debated, but it can never have been an effective working document. Many of the commands listed had ceased to exist even before 395, while others were rendered obsolete by uncorrected promotions and re-postings. One theory is that the surviving version is in fact an unofficial copy, updated with inadequate information by a private individual, perhaps for research into military history.

Three chapters of the *Notitia* are of direct relevance to the coastal defences of the North Sea and English Channel. Chapter 28 refers to south-east Britain:

> *Sub dispositione viri spectabilis Comitis Litoris Saxonici per Britanniam*
> *Praepositus numeri Fortensium, Othonae*
> *Praepositus militum Tungrecanorum, Dubris*
> *Praepositus numeri Turnacensium, Lemanis*
> *Praepositus equitum Dalmatarum Branodunensium, Branoduno*
> *Praepositus equitum Stablesianorum Gariannonensium, Gariannor*
> *Tribunis cohortis primae Baetasiorum, Regulbio*
> *Praepositus legionis secundae Augustae, Rutupis*
> *Praepositus numeri Abulcorum, Anderidos*
> *Praepositus numeri exploratum, Portum Adurni*

Under the command of his excellency, the Count of the Saxon Shore
The commander of the unit of Fortenses, at *Othona* (?Bradwell)
The commander of the Tungrecanian troops, at *Dubrae* (Dover)
The commander of the unit of Turnacenses, at *Lemanis* (Lympne)
The commander of the Branodunensian Dalmatian cavalry, at *Branodunum* (Brancaster)
The commander of the Garriannonensian Stablesian cavalry, at *Garriannonum* (?Burgh Castle/Caister)
The tribune of the first Baetasian cohort, at *Regulbium* (Reculver)
The prefect of the second legion, the Augusta, at *Rutupiae* (Richborough)
The commander of the unit of Abulci, at *Anderida* (Pevensey)
The commander of the unit of scouts at *Portus Adurni* (Walton Castle/Portchester)

129

Two further chapters refer to defences on the coast of Gaul, which are also described as being 'on the Saxon Shore'. Chapter 37 details the command of the Duke of the Armorican region and the Nervian Frontier, which encompassed coastal forts and towns in the provinces of Aquitania Prima and Secunda, Lugdunensis Senonia, Secunda and Tertia. Chapter 38 lists a further three sites under the command of the Duke of Belgica Secunda. Interestingly, there are no naval forces listed in any of the chapters referring to Britain: the former Pevensey fleet (the *classis Anderetianorum)* is recorded, but by the time of the *Notitia's* compilation this unit had been transferred to Paris.[6] The Welsh sections of the list are missing, or perhaps were never compiled.

The British chapter presents several difficulties. First there is the basic matter of linking each fort to its Latin title (**62**). In most cases this proves straightforward: Brancaster retains enough of its original name for identification to be reasonably simple, while other sites feature in a variety of Roman documents, such as the *Antonine Itinerary*, the *Ravenna Cosmography* and Ptolemy's *Geography*, or in later texts. However, the identification of Bradwell as *Othona* has yet to be fully accepted by all philologists, and there is no conclusive evidence as to whether *Portus Adurni* is Walton Castle or Portchester. The *Garrianus* river was mentioned by Ptolemy, and is almost certainly the Great Estuary; there is, however, no evidence to determine whether *Garriannonum* is Burgh Castle or Caister.[7] A further problem lies in the fact that the chapter lists only nine sites, when there were at least eleven forts in existence on the 'Saxon Shore' between the Wash and Solent. Which element of both the Burgh Castle/Caister and Walton Castle/Portchester pairs is not included, and why? The most obvious solution is that those sites omitted from the list had been abandoned by the end of the fourth century. Certainly this is a distinct possibility, but any such interpretation requires great caution. The *Notitia* is a notoriously unreliable guide to the occupation of a site, because the picture it paints is often at variance with the real situation on the ground, as demonstrated by the archaeology of a site. This is nowhere more clearly demonstrated than by its inclusion of Lympne, which, as will be seen in Chapter 8, had been abandoned for several decades by the time that the *Notitia* was compiled. Conversely, other sites are omitted that are known to have been occupied; one example is the Yorkshire signal stations, which although probably still operational at the time do not appear in the chapter for the *dux Britanniarum*.[8]

What was the Saxon Shore?

The actual meaning of the term 'Saxon Shore' is a matter of debate. There are two principal interpretations, either that the name refers to a shore that was 'settled by', or 'under attack from', the Saxons. The notion of Saxons or other barbarians being settled in south-east Britain during the fourth and early fifth centuries is in itself perfectly plausible. The official settlement of barbarians within imperial boundaries was not uncommon during the late Roman period, and federate troops came to form an increasingly important aspect of the imperial army during this time. There is, however, little to support the idea of the settlement of Saxons in fourth-century Britain, or indeed in Gaul. Of the *foederati* settled within the Western Empire that

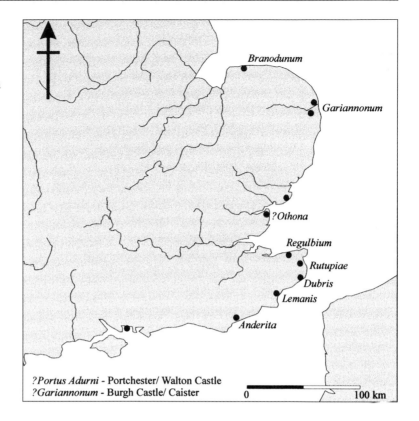

62 *The Shore Forts in the* Notitia Dignitatum

Branodunum

Gariannonum

?Othona

Regulbium

Rutupiae

Dubris

Lemanis

Anderita

?Portus Adurni - Portchester/ Walton Castle
?Gariannonum - Burgh Castle/ Caister

0   100 km

are named by late Roman writers, none is Saxon. The notion that the British garrison was reinforced by federate barbarian troops during the fourth century – evidence for which was once seen in the presence of 'Romano-Saxon' pottery and barbarian metalwork (such as belt fittings and shoulder clasps) on military sites – also seems more doubtful. Such artefactual evidence has now been discredited as a definite indicator of the presence of Germanic soldiers, and therefore it has not yet been determined whether barbarians of any ethnicity (much less Saxon) were employed as troops within Britain.

A variation of the same idea has been proposed by Hind, who suggests that by the late third century a part, or perhaps the entire, Germanic Ocean (North Sea) had become known as the Saxon Sea.[9] In this context *litus Saxonicum* becomes the 'shore on the Saxon Sea', and thus the requirement for us to find extensive barbarian coastal settlement within the Empire becomes unnecessary. Again there are problems, for if the North Sea was so named we should expect to find other references to the Saxon Sea occurring within contemporary historical records, but none is known to exist.

Most scholars, both past and present, tend to accept the alternative view of a coastline attacked by the Saxons. Despite its widespread following, this theory is also far from secure. The argument rests on the notion that Saxon raiding was prevalent during the later fourth century, and was of such intensity that the frontier came to bear their name. As we will see below, while seaborne assaults on Gaul can be proven

131

at this time, the evidence for barbarian raids on Britain is far from compelling. Furthermore, the naming of a Roman frontier after its attackers is a phenomenon that is otherwise unknown, and the whole idea must be treated with caution. As has been commented elsewhere, 'the meaning of the "Saxon Shore" must remain what, in reality, it always has been: an open question'.[10]

Defences against seaborne raiders

The idea of a coast under barbarian attack is the most enduring, and certainly the most popular explanation of the Shore Forts. It is one that first found expression during the sixteenth century in Camden's *Britannia*:

> The honorable, Earle or Lieftenant of the Saxon Shore along Britaine, whose office was garisons set upon the shore in places convenient, to represse the depredations and robberies of Barbarians, but of Saxons especially, who grievously infested Britaine.[11]

This image persists, little changed, within many modern histories of Roman Britain:

> [Britain] was under threat of raiding and piracy from peoples along the North Sea littoral outside the Roman frontier on the lower Rhine, the forebears of the Anglo-Saxons. This resulted in the building of the Saxon Shore from the early third century on, and at the time of his rebellion in 286 Carausius was commander of the fleet charged with keeping the British seaways clear.[12]

In this latter statement can be found all the elements of the argument for the Shore Forts as an anti-pirate scheme. It envisages a threat from seaborne barbarians – principally Franks and Saxons – and normally assumes that such a danger existed from an early date. Connections with the military crisis of the Empire in the mid-third century are often made, and the forts themselves are generally viewed as part of an evolving system designed to counter an increasing threat from beyond the Rhine frontier. The Roman response is often suggested to have been accelerated by the barbarian invasions of Gaul in 260 and 276.[13]

In the *Roman Forts of the Saxon Shore*, Stephen Johnson addressed the question of how such a system would actually have worked in practice.[14] In his view, the coastal forts on both sides of the English Channel represented a co-ordinated scheme for the defence of both Britain and Gaul – one which ultimately evolved into the command of the Count of the Saxon Shore that we find listed in the *Notitia Dignitatum* (**63**). In Johnson's model the forts on both sides of the Channel functioned as fleet bases and also housed garrisons of land troops with a high degree of mobility. Because of the primitive nature of the raiders' boats and their navigational technology, they would have been compelled to follow a predictable route along the Gallic coast as far as the Straits of Dover. From this point they could either continue east and south to raid *Gallia Belgica* and the *Tractus Armorica*, or cross the Channel to southern Britain. The Roman naval patrols acted as a screen, intercepting the pirates before they could

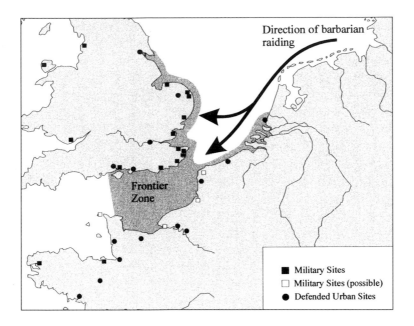

63 The Shore Forts as an anti-pirate defence? In this model the installations form a military frontier intended to combat the depredations of seaborne barbarians. After Johnson (1976, Fig. 70)

attack, while those that slipped through the net were dealt with by the land-based forces. As a last resort, the fleet would catch any that escaped these two tiers of defence before they could reach the North Sea. The forts themselves were positioned at the head of important waterways, and combined with the defended urban centres on the coast, denied access to the interior of the province.

A barbarian threat to Britain?

The writers of the late Roman period make clear the danger posed by barbarians to the north-west provinces of the empire. Britain is described as an island beset by enemies, which increasingly come to be represented by the Picts and Scots during the fourth century. In Gaul, the dangers from beyond the Rhine frontier are clearly set out on numerous occasions. The majority of references are concerned with land-based threats posed to Gaul by the Franks, and to Britain by Scottish and Irish tribes. Many scholars, however, and Johnson in particular, have no doubts as to the existence of a maritime danger to Britain:

> ... another tribe of seafarers had established what was a virtual control of the sea-lanes between Britain and the Continent ... Contemporary sources graphically describe the Franks and the Saxons, both sea-faring tribes, infesting the seas and posing a dangerous double threat to the shores of Britain and of Gaul.[15]

133

Johnson viewed the 'Saxon Shore' as being a defensive system of long standing. The episode of Carausius was used to argue that piracy was manifest in the English Channel by the 280s, and the large number of coin hoards recovered in southern Britain and Gaul dating to the period *c.*270-85 were thought to be archaeological evidence of these troubles. Here, it seemed, were good indications that piracy had existed for some years prior to Carausius' appointment to reclaim Roman control of the seas. Johnson argued that the command of the 'Saxon Shore' was conceived many years prior to the compilation of the *Notitia Dignitatum*, perhaps as early as the reign of Constantine (307-37). He was inclined to see the office of the *comes maritimi tractus*, mentioned in connection with the events of the barbarian conspiracy of 367, as a direct precursor of the *comes litoris Saxonici* of the *Notitia Dignitatum*, if indeed they were not one and the same. Whether the British and Gallic coasts ever came under a unified command is not known, but Johnson contended that this was the case, and that the command was only confined to the island of Britain later in the fourth century.

Documentary references to a seaborne threat to Gaul are, if not abundant, still sufficient to demonstrate that such a danger did exist. The fourth-century historian Eutropius, writing about the usurpation of Carausius, specifically identified the areas under attack as being *Belgica* and *Armorica*.[16] Prior to his recapture of Britain, Constantius is found dealing with Germanic seafaring tribes in the Rhineland area of Batavia, campaigns which were repeated in the mid-fourth century by both Julian and count Theodosius. The panegyrist Nazarius, speaking in 321, stated that the Franks had raided the continental Atlantic coast as far as Spain.[17] Ammianus Marcellinus writes of the attacks on Gaul by Franks and Saxons during the barbarian conspiracy, and for the year 370 relates the tale of a party of seaborne raiders, captured in Gaul and given safe passage out of the empire, only to be later ambushed and slaughtered.[18] Ambrosius hints at further piracy during the 380s,[19] and campaigns on the Rhine by Stilicho during the 390s may well have been directed against maritime barbarian tribes.

For Britain there is no such explicit historical evidence, and in fact it is impossible to find where a barbarian threat is 'graphically described' as Johnson thought it to be. Close examination of the (admittedly slender) sources relating to the Carausian usurpation tends to suggest that in the late third century the threat of piracy extended only to Gaul. In addition to Eutropius' description of the danger to north-west Gaul, one of the panegyrics specifically states that Carausius '... carried off the fleet that defends the Gauls'.[20] In none of the sources relating to this episode is Britain directly mentioned in the context of piracy. The references to barbarian troubles in fourth-century Britain are concerned with threats from Scotland and Ireland, providing a *raison d'être* for the coastal defences on Britain's west coast, but piracy on the south and eastern shores of the province is never specified. The poems of Claudian come closest to doing so, and it is notable that in one passage he described Britain as being harassed by Saxons, while Gaul was oppressed by the Franks. This would seem to indicate that Claudian was not (as in so many fourth-century sources) talking generally about the north-west Empire and including Britain for the sake of completeness, or using the province simply as a literary device for the far reaches of the world. It is also notable that contemporary sources describing the later third and the fourth centuries perceived the Germans in the Channel to be Frankish, and not Saxon.[21] Only from the last decade of the fourth century do the Saxons appear to have been viewed as the principal enemy. For this reason it seems rather unlikely that the command of the 'Saxon Shore' could have existed under that particular name until the very last years of Roman Britain when the *Notitia* was compiled.

Significant doubt can therefore be cast on the historical evidence for maritime attacks on the south and east coasts of Britain. However, just because the literary sources are silent or ambiguous we cannot simply assume that piracy was not taking place. Writings that discuss the province are scant, and a nagging problem of raiding could easily have been passed over by contemporary authors writing from Rome or elsewhere in the Empire. Nevertheless, it is also the case that the archaeological record does not support the idea of barbarian attacks from the sea. The coin hoards of the 270s and 280s, for example, may in fact have had nothing to do with warfare. The hoards comprised mostly base *antoniniani* of the Gallic Empire, and their monetary value was low. The fact that they were concealed by their owners was quite likely a result of the enforcement of Aurelian's currency reforms, and not because they were hidden during an attack. They may never have been recovered simply because it was not worth the effort.[22] As a whole, Roman sites in the south of the province do not provide positive evidence for there having been widespread destruction at any given time that could be attributed to pirate raids. This said, at least one of the Yorkshire signal stations (Goldsborough) does appear to have come to a violent end, though the most likely culprits would be enemies from Scotland, rather than barbarians from the continent (**64**).

Other factors also argue against there having been widespread maritime attacks on south and east Britain during the late Roman period. Not least are the practical obstacles to raiding the province from a starting point beyond the Rhine. Calculations show that a return voyage from Jutland to Britain would probably have

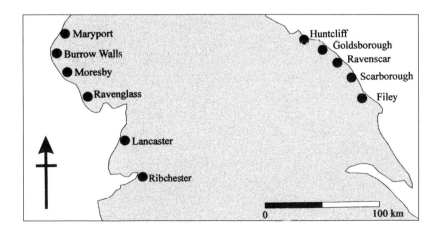

64 Late fourth-century coastal defences. The Yorkshire and Cumbrian signal stations were built to warn of attacks from the sea

taken at least two months, and perhaps longer.[23] On this basis it has been argued that, prior to the collapse of the north-west frontier in the early fifth century and the advent of widespread Saxon settlement south of the Rhine, the distances were simply too great for pirate raids against Britain to have been practicable. Cotterill makes this case very strongly, stating that 'it would have been physically impossible for the Germanic seafarers to have raided the coasts of Britain in the late Roman period'.[24]

Defences against Rome

Scepticism regarding the reality of this barbarian threat – particularly during the late third and early fourth centuries – led some scholars to search for a different reason for the Shore Forts' presence. As already noted, the initial role for which the forts were intended may not have been the same as the one that they fulfilled in the later years of their operation. One author to have disengaged the Shore Forts' earliest years from their later function was D.A. White.[25] In the first modern book to address the installations, White questioned the extent of barbarian raiding in Britain during the late third and early fourth centuries, and reasoned that while the Rhine frontier faced a very real threat at that time, no such danger was posed to Britain. Furthermore, he argued that the scale of the Shore Fort defences was indicative of an enemy with a capacity for siege warfare, and as such they over-engineered to meet a threat from pirate raiders or *bagaudae*. As he stated, 'a band of pirates would not stop to reduce them even if they were capable of it'.

White therefore sought other reasons for the building of the installations, and presented them as a scheme built entirely during the reign of Carausius, intended to protect south-east Britain from invasion by Imperial armies. In this they were clearly a failure, and the defeat of the Allectan regime brought the immediate usefulness of the new forts to an end. White contended that they lay dormant until after the middle of the fourth century, from which date they were reactivated to meet a threat of piracy that, in his view, had only then grown to serious proportions.

White's scheme has found little support amongst scholars. One glaring problem is the fact that any notion of a purely Carausian scheme is ruled out by the archaeological evidence. Caister (a site admittedly not considered by White), Reculver and Brancaster all pre-date the 280s, while Pevensey is now known to belong to the Allectan regime. Secondly, White based his arguments for an early fourth-century abandonment purely on his interpretation of the slender documentary evidence for the period. This notion is largely unsupported by the archaeology of the sites, but it is worthy of note that activity at Portchester does appear to diminish temporarily during the last years of the third century. It is also true that the history of occupation at most of the forts is poorly understood, though the coin series from the sites do not indicate abandonment at this time (see Chapter 7).

Despite these criticisms, the idea that the Shore Forts originated for reasons other than pirate raiding still has merit. Indeed, in recent years Fulford and Tyers have revived White's theories, at least in part. In their reassessment of the origin of the Shore Forts, they have suggested that only with the loss of Boulogne, late in Carausius' reign or early in that of Allectus, did a seaborne invasion become a viable threat.

Fulford and Tyers argue that the usurpers inherited a coastal defence which already comprised Brancaster, Caister and Reculver, and that it may have been they who augmented the system by the addition of the other forts during the period *c*.293-6. The historical argument is sound, and such a scheme is not contradicted by the archaeological evidence from the sites themselves, although the balance of evidence perhaps suggests that Lympne, Dover and Richborough pre-date the usurpation. However, there is nothing that definitely precludes the idea that these three sites, and others of the later Shore Forts, contributed to a Carausian-Allectan defensive scheme that was converted for a different use after the recapture of the province.

Fortified ports

Some scholars see no link at all between the Shore Forts and piracy. In a wide-ranging critique of the notion of Saxon raiding in late Roman Britain, Cotterill argues that not only is the historical and archaeological evidence unsatisfactory, but that Johnson's scheme for the operation of the Shore Forts is also flawed.[26] In particular he argues that the units stationed at the forts, as listed in the *Notitia Dignitatum*, were ill-suited for any anti-piracy role. The majority were infantry, rather than cavalry: hardly a rapid reaction force capable of intercepting a fast-moving and unpredictable enemy. The lack of a fleet, apart from the *classis Anderetianorum*, was also seen by Cotterill as a crucial aspect absent from any such defensive scheme.

As an alternative, Cotterill developed the ideas of Wood, Milne and others,[27] proposing an entirely different role for the forts, which placed considerable emphasis on their economic function. This alternative view sees the Shore Forts, combined with the other elements on the north-east, south, and west coasts of Britain, as part of a chain of fortified ports. The location of each Shore Fort, near to the mouth of a navigable waterway, did not arise from a need to protect the interior, but instead to facilitate access for both military and commercial shipping. The installations (which as we have seen were well placed to handle merchant ships of considerable size) were intended as bases where goods en route for inland garrisons could be offloaded. They could also have served as centres where agricultural and mineral products from the region could be collected and shipped onwards for use elsewhere by the army. Many of these goods must have been destined for the northern frontier, but the forts could also have played a major role in conveying supplies to Gaul and Germany. The supply route for British grain reopened by Julian in 359/60 to support his campaigns on the Rhine is perhaps one exceptional example of this logistical network in practice. The forts may also have served as holding camps for troops in transit. Their importance in this respect would have been greatest at times of military crisis when a secure link between Britain and Gaul was required. The use of Richborough by count Theodosius as a place to land his armies in response to the barbarian invasion of 367 illustrates how valuable such defended ports could be.

If the Shore Forts were indeed links in a logistical system it would do much to explain the construction of the forts of Caister and Reculver, many decades before the first historical references to piracy in the Channel. The connection of these sites with supply for the Severan campaigns in Scotland is already well rehearsed, and it is quite possible that the forts continued to fulfil a role in the supply process long after warfare in Scotland was abandoned. Even if they played no role in the defence of the province, the key to understanding the building of a second group of eight forts might still lie in the third-century crisis of the empire. However, it would not be found in the military anarchy, but in the collapse in the value of the Roman currency. Hopkins has argued that, in an era where the coinage was increasingly unstable and valueless, the institutionalisation of taxation in kind came to be the major mechanism for the State to collect revenue. In this scenario the Shore Forts could have been intended to serve as collection points for this tax, from which goods were shipped onwards to the northern frontier, or to Gaul and the Rhine.

The role of the Shore Forts?

Each of the perspectives on the Shore Forts has its flaws and its critics. Despite the silence of the literary sources on the subject of attacks from the continent and the lack of specific archaeological evidence, we cannot necessarily assume that Britain was safe from the Saxons or Franks. As Bidwell observes, despite the practical difficulties, 'journeys by raiders would have been feasible if they had rested in deserted coves and inlets along the Gallic coast, unless we assume that there was immediate Roman supervision and control of every mile of the coastline'.[28] Raids might also have been anticipated from beyond Hadrian's Wall, particularly in the later fourth-century when the danger from Scotland and Ireland seems to have become more serious. The building of the Yorkshire signal stations and the revival of some of the Cumbrian watchtowers would appear to suggest that this was the case; these installations were too small to act as large stores bases or holding points for troops. Nevertheless, the arguments for the Shore Forts having had some economic role are quite compelling, particularly during the third and earlier fourth century, when it surely seems that any piracy could not have amounted to anything more than an intermittent, nagging problem.

Even those scholars sceptical of a maritime threat to Roman Britain are, for the most part, more willing to accept its existence as the fourth century drew to a close. To some extent this may be conditioned by hindsight, dependent on the knowledge that southern England was to become increasingly Saxon during the following centuries, a process largely complete by the start of the eighth century. Large-scale Saxon migration to Britain probably did not begin until at least the early fifth century, and perhaps considerably later. Even if we do see the Shore Forts as a coastal defence during the very last years of Roman Britain, their role (or roles) in the two previous centuries remains very much an open question. That they were utilised as a Carausian defence against Rome (albeit unsuccessfully) seems likely. A longer-term, primary, logistical function is also very plausible, as will become apparent in the discussion of the economic aspect of the forts in the following chapter. We must, nevertheless, accept that the 'Saxon Shore', as recorded in the *Notitia Dignitatum*, did exist within Roman Britain at some point around the late fourth or early fifth century. Given the doubts over the interpretation of the title, however, it still remains to be established whether the Saxons came to the province as official settlers, or as unwelcome pirates.

7 Occupation and economy

In the cases of some of the first installations to be built, for example Caister and Brancaster, the Roman occupation of the Shore Forts spanned nearly 200 years. For others, as will be seen in the final chapter, the end came sooner, and the operational lifetime was much more brief. In the preceding chapter the possible military or official functions of the forts were considered. Below, however, we will examine a different but complementary aspect of the installations, assessing the character of the occupation both within and outside the defences.

Internal buildings

The internal organisation of late Roman forts

There is a great difference between the internal layout of forts of the Principate and those of the late Empire. During the Principate, the area within the defences was almost entirely built over. There would normally have been four gateways, and the two main streets (*via praetoria* and *via principalis*) met at right angles roughly in the centre of the fort. Immediately inside the defences a third major road, the *via sagularis*, ran all around the perimeter. Minor streets linked the buildings to the main roads. In the centre of the fort were the administrative buildings, including the head-quarters building (*principia*), while the remainder of the internal area was given over to a variety of other structures, principally barracks, storehouses and workshops.

Though not without exception, this traditional layout survived more or less into the middle of the third century. What happened during the military troubles of the period *c.*235-70 is not fully understood, but Roman forts designed from the late third century onwards were often significantly different from those that had gone before (**65**). As has already been seen, the defences of new-built forts of the later period differed from those of the Principate, but the internal arrangements of both new and existing installations were also markedly different.

Very few late Roman forts have been sufficiently excavated to produce even a reasonable appreciation of the ground plan; two of the best understood examples in the western empire are Alzey and Altrip (Gemany), but even here the picture is somewhat incomplete.[1] No ground plan of a late Roman fort in Britain has yet been established. This situation is due in large part to the destruction of the uppermost Roman occupation layers at many sites, either by later habitation, or by ploughing. The problem is also exacerbated by the fact that the buildings them-selves, although far from ephemeral, were often of timber construction, and have

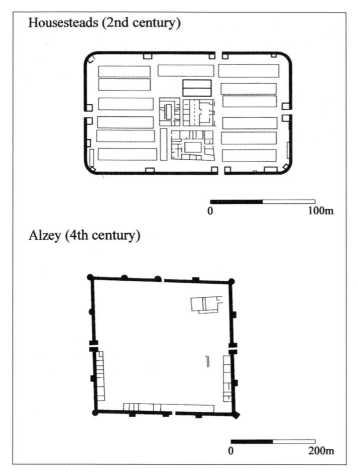

Housesteads (2nd century)

Alzey (4th century)

0   100m

0   200m

65 *Changing defensive styles. The forts at Housesteads (Hadrian's Wall) and Alzey (Germany)*

therefore survived less well in the archaeological record than stone structures, or those with stone foundations.

A general picture can be offered, however. The most striking aspect was the less intensive use of space within the defences. Many buildings tended to be set against the perimeter wall, where previously this had rarely been the case, and then only for store buildings and stables. From the fourth century (increasingly so from the middle decades) barracks were constructed against the defences, probably to protect them from bombardment during a siege. Bath buildings, always exterior to earlier forts, were also moved within the perimeter, despite the potential fire hazard that they posed. The buildings around the perimeter often appear to have enclosed a large open courtyard in the centre of the fort. In some instances there are traces of buildings within these courtyards, but their function is not obvious. The *principia* was often absent (at least in a recognisable plan-form), and certainly no longer provided the focus of the installation.

There is a lack of knowledge about what the internal buildings of late Roman forts were used for, and why the layout was so different from that of the Principate.

The solution most likely lies in the many changes to the army itself. During the Principate each fort was semi-independent, with responsibility for its own administration, storage of supplies, and maintenance of equipment and weaponry. As such, it was necessary for every installation to have substantial facilities for storing food and other goods, as well as workshops for repair and manufacture. During the late Empire much of this changed, with administration and supply becoming more centralised. Equipment was often centrally produced and repaired, and food supply was much more tightly controlled. Granaries and other stores buildings were no longer needed in such large numbers, nor were workshops. Administration was also very much reduced, rendering the *principia* largely unnecessary.[2]

Buildings within the Shore Forts

The contrast between the internal layout of early and late Roman forts is apparent to some extent in the Shore Forts. Reculver offers an almost archetypal plan of an installation of the early third century (**66**). In the surviving portion the metalled surfaces of the *via principalis*, *via praetoria* and *via sagularis* have been uncovered on a number of occasions during excavation. The stone headquarters occupied a central position: although of a standard five-room design, its dimensions (33m x 42m) make it one of the largest buildings of this type known from a British auxiliary fort.[3] An underground strongroom was present beneath the *sacellum*, the central room of the *principia*. A bathhouse was situated on the opposite side of the main east-west road,

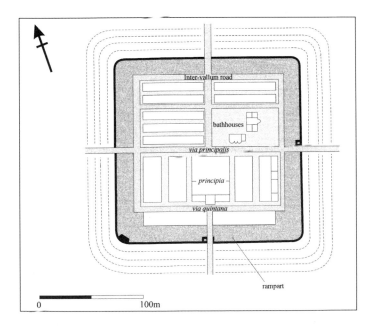

66 *Reconstructed internal plan of Reculver, showing third-century structures. The unlabelled buildings away from the central range served as barracks, stores and in other ancillary functions. Not all were necessarily in use at the same time.* After Philp (1996, Fig. 5)

while a little further to the north was another substantial hypocausted building, which was probably residential in character. Barracks, or living quarters, have been located east of the *principia*. These consisted of clay walls on stone foundations, with a clay floor. At least one was decorated with painted wall plaster.[4] West of the *principia* were two masonry buildings, the larger of which contained several small domestic ovens and many quern fragments, indicating use as a bakehouse.[5] Fragmentary remains of other buildings of uncertain purpose have also been found elsewhere within the perimeter.

The detail of the internal buildings has yet to be published in detail, but the structures described above appear to relate to activity during the third century. The *principia* was probably erected at approximately the same time as the defences, but at least one of the barrack buildings has been dated to a different phase, in the later third century.[6] The reconstructed plan of the fort may not, therefore, entirely reflect the original layout. There is also strong evidence for a decline in occupation from the later third century at Reculver. The *principia* was in a state of ruin by the early fourth century, its strongroom deliberately filled with rubble and tile.[7] The two barracks were derelict by 300, the smaller of them having burnt down after 270. None of these structures was rebuilt, although the excavator did suggest that there might have been more ephemeral timber structures within parts of the fort interior during the fourth century. The east gate was also blocked up at some stage in the late third or early fourth century. As a whole this evidence does much to suggest a reduction in the garrison of the fort at about this time.

Somewhat less is understood of the internal plan of the other early forts at Caister and Brancaster, although stone buildings are known within both installations (**67**). At Brancaster, aerial photographs show the *principia* to have been a large, courtyard building, which was placed in a standard central location, just to the south of the *via praetoria*. Other smaller buildings show as cropmarks in the north-east quarter of the fort.[8] A substantial structure in the same area is on a slightly different alignment, orientated not with the Shore Fort defences, but with the extra-mural settlement. This has led to the very plausible suggestion that it relates to an earlier installation on the same site, although there is no reason why it could not have continued in use during the lifetime of the later fort. None of these structures has been excavated, and thus their date and character remain largely unknown. In the south-west corner of the fort, two successive floors were encountered during St Joseph's excavations, the uppermost floor being associated with the remains of sandstone walls. Finds from both occupation layers dated to the fourth century, and attest to there having been at least two phases of building in this quarter of the fort.[9]

Of Caister rather less is known, though traces of cobbled street surfaces have been found, representing a north-south road (?*via principalis*) and *via sagularis* (**68**).[10] The lower courses of two structures have been discovered in the south-west quarter of the fort (the only area to be intensively excavated).[11] One was quite substantial, consisting of at least ten rooms. Window glass, painted wall plaster, an inserted hypocaust and a possible portico on the southern front of the building indicate that occupation was

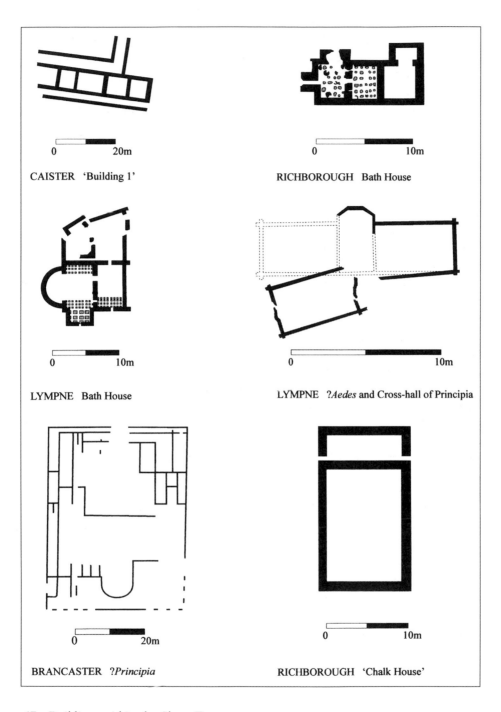

CAISTER 'Building 1'

RICHBOROUGH Bath House

LYMPNE Bath House

LYMPNE ?*Aedes* and Cross-hall of Principia

BRANCASTER ?*Principia*

RICHBOROUGH 'Chalk House'

67 Buildings within the Shore Forts

143

68   The internal buildings at Caister, looking west

initially of luxurious, domestic character. A possible addition of rooms to form a west range would have created a courtyard building that opened onto the main road through the fort. The finds of large quantities of animal bone, combined with the presence of hearths in certain rooms, suggest a later change in use to an industrial function – perhaps butchery and tanning. Neither the construction date, nor a chronology for the building, has been established, but it is thought to have existed by the late third century. It was at least partially in ruin by the later fourth century. In the same area was a second structure, a flint building onto which a series of small timber rooms had been attached. It has been severely damaged by ploughing and its function is enigmatic, but once again it is known to have been at least partially demolished during the fourth century. The only other structural evidence from within the fort was in the south-east corner, where a heating flue was discovered, presumably belonging to a building close to the east wall.[12] The central parts of the fort, where the *principia* and other administrative buildings might be expected, lie under modern housing.

Some structures have been excavated within the enceintes of the later group of Shore Forts. These, however, appear to be isolated structures set amidst vacant areas of ground, though once again it must be stressed that later use of the sites may have destroyed any traces of less durable structures, in particular those built of timber. We must also immediately dispel the notion that any wooden buildings present would necessarily have been less substantial, or somehow inferior to stone structures. In reality, however, the argument for all such 'lost' buildings is made from archaeological

69   *The Roman bathhouse at Lympne during excavations in 1850*

silence, and it remains the case that there is at the present time no evidence for the intense use of space that is seen in the early phases of Reculver.

At Richborough, the *principia* is suggested to have been situated on the levelled foundations of the monumental arch, though this appears simply to be an assumption based on its central position within the fort, rather than on any physical evidence for such a structure. A small three-roomed bathhouse was built on the site of the former *mansio*, and two other small stone structures of uncertain purpose were also present, each with a small porch, one opposite the *principia* and the other just inside the west gate.[13] Despite the intensive use of the fort during the late third and fourth centuries, attested by a series of large rubbish pits and deep wells, and by the vast quantities of coins and other material culture of the period, no other structures were identified. The excavators of the 1920s were of the opinion that timber structures had existed, but failed to identify any such buildings: all evidence will now have been removed by those same excavations.

Two stone buildings were encountered at Lympne during excavations in 1850.[14] Close to the east gate was a small hypocausted structure, interpreted at the time as a domestic dwelling, but which was almost certainly a bath block (**69**). In the northern part of the fort was a three-roomed building. Although somewhat deformed by landslipping, the plan suggests it to be an apsidal shrine flanked on either side by a small rectangular room, such as would be found behind the cross hall and tribunal of a headquarters building. Although not centrally positioned, this structure appears to be a rare example of a *principia* within a late Roman fort. The broken fragments of a building that may have 'formed originally a series of long, low edifices' were found in the north-east corner of the fort, but the excavator could make little sense of the remains.[15]

Despite the total excavation of fully one-eighth of the fort interior at Portchester, little convincing evidence for structures *in situ* has been discovered.[16] During the initial phase of the site (*c*.285-90) occupation was of very superficial character: the 'streets' within the fort were only lightly gravelled, and the sole evidence for structures was in the form of rectangularly-arranged gullies, suggested to be for drainage around tents. During the period *c*.325-45 the roads were more heavily metalled, and occupation was attested by a large number of rubbish- and cess-pits. Light timber structures were suggested to have been laid out in the undisturbed areas between the roads and pits, but there was no conclusive evidence for such buildings. From *c*.345 the interior was reorganised, and at least one (and probably a second) square building was erected in this part of the fort. These have been identified from slight traces of the sill-beams on which they are thought to have stood: the nature of the superstructure is unclear, but was probably of wattle and daub. Neither resembled barracks.

The excavations did, however, produce some convincing evidence for the existence of substantial Roman structures, though these probably stood elsewhere in the fort. Bricks and tiles were commonly recovered from occupation layers and pits, and from post-Roman buildings on the site. As well as *tegulae* and *imbrices*, hypocaust- and box flue tiles were present in significant quantities, suggesting not only structures with tiled roofs, but at least one which had a heating system. The most likely parallel would be a small bathhouse similar to those known at Richborough and Lympne. A small quantity of window glass was also found, indicating that glazed windows were present.

Limited excavations of Pevensey in 1907 encountered a series of hearths spaced approximately 6m apart in the area adjacent to the postern gate of the north wall. No other structural features were found, but the excavator suggested that the hearths related to regularly spaced barracks.[17] A timber-lined well was also discovered in the north-west quarter of the fort during excavations in the following year, but no traces of structures were identified on that occasion.[18] Later investigations have produced other evidence for possible timber-framed, mortar-floored structures at several locations. Several appear to have been present immediately inside the east gate, while traces of others were found close to the fallen south wall, approximately 20m west of the gatehouse of the medieval castle. None of these buildings seem to have been of substantial character.[19]

The interior of the Dover Shore Fort has been incompletely excavated, and the details only scantily published. However, at least 11 timber-built structures of late Roman date have been found within the perimeter, of circular, square, oval and sub-rectangular plan. As many as seven separate phases of such structures were discovered at one location, presumably indicating a lengthy period of occupation.[20] In the south-west corner of the fort is one of the most remarkable buildings known from any of the installations: a 'squalid' circular wattle and daub hut that 'would have fitted well into an Iron Age village'.[21] Other scattered elements known within the Dover Shore Fort are metalled roads, a postern gate with a footbridge, ovens and pits. The second-century bathhouse, built outside the *classis Britannica* fort, was reused within the Shore Fort, albeit in a modified form.[22]

Neither Burgh Castle nor Bradwell has produced much evidence for internal structures, an unsurprising fact given the limited excavation within each, and the extent of
post-Roman damage to both sites. In the north-east corner of Burgh Castle, mortar
floors and daub fragments were discovered, perhaps belonging to timber-framed
buildings. These burnt down during the middle years of the fourth century, and it has
been suggested that clay and other debris found overlying the destruction layers could
have been a platform for replacement timber structures, of which no other trace now
remains. In the south-west corner of the fort a Roman masonry building was found
immediately adjacent to the defences, and above the rubble of this demolished structure
were fragmentary traces of other, possibly Roman, floors. Mortar and plaster fragments
found during excavations in the north-east, north-west and south-west corners of the
fort also imply the presence of structures in these areas.

A 'single fragment of a foundation-wall' in the south-east part of Bradwell is all
that attests to buildings within the fort. However, as the excavator observed, the
extensive destruction of the site, which had rendered even the perimeter defences
untraceable at points, made it unlikely that internal structures would have survived.
Geophysical survey possibly located the line of a barracks building up against the
north-western corner of the fort.[23]

Garrisons

Although there are few elements of the internal buildings surviving within the Shore
Forts, some must originally have existed if the forts were to have been garrisoned.
There is a certain amount of archaeological and historical evidence for this aspect of
the installations. As discussed in Chapter 4, stamped tiles of *cohors I Aquitanorum* and
cohors I Baetasiorum have been found at Brancaster and Reculver respectively. These
have tentatively been suggested to be the units responsible for the original construction work, and if this were the case we can also expect them to have formed the
initial garrison. Apart from these finds, no other archaeological clues on this matter
have yet emerged: only two inscriptions have been recovered from the Shore Forts,
and neither sheds any light on the issue.

The only other source of information is the *Notitia Dignitatum*, although its late
date and the difficulties of using this document limit its usefulness. As discussed
above, the absence of a cavalry component at every Shore Fort has been cited by
Cotterill as evidence that the troops lacked the mobility to fulfil the anti-pirate role
envisaged by Johnson.[24] The reality, however, may well have been rather more
complex than the *Notitia* listing would suggest. Mann argued that the military units
recorded in the document were most probably present at more than one place: only
a single fort was actually listed for each because that was where the main headquarters (and records) would be kept.[25]

The *Notitia* records that *cohors I Baetasiorum* was still in place at Reculver at the
end of the fourth century, but that *cohors I Aquitanorum* had been replaced by a cavalry
unit, the *equites Dalmatae Branodunenses*.[26] Another mounted force, the *equites*

Stablesiani Gariannonenses, was present at either Burgh Castle or Caister. Both of these cavalry units are thought to have been raised by Gallienus and transferred to Britain after the collapse of the Gallic Empire in 274. If these were not in fact the original units to garrison the forts after their construction, then certainly their association was enduring enough for the installation's name to form a part of each unit's title. The *numerus Fortensium* began life as a vexillation (detachment) from *Legio II Traiana*: this legion was honoured on coins of the Gallic emperor Victorinus alongside others of the continental legions. It is quite possible, therefore, that the *numerus Fortensium* was also deployed to Bradwell from the continent shortly after 274.

Except for these instances, the picture of the initial garrisoning of the Shore Forts is not specifically understood. In general terms, however, a southward redeployment of troops in Britain during the third century can be observed, although the details are obscure. Frere, for example, equates the smaller number of occupied forts on the northern frontier from the mid-third century onwards with the advent of the Shore Forts, as well as the departure of units to the continent:

> Under Probus part of *Legio II Augusta* can be assumed to have occupied Richborough if not other new Shore Forts as well; *Legio XX* may also have been involved in similar duties, since about this time there is evidence for a reduction in the size of the Chester garrison.[27]

It is possible that detachments of *Legio II Augusta* were actually responsible for the construction of Richborough. The legion is last recorded at Caerleon in the period 253-9, and by the end of the century it no longer garrisoned this fortress.[28] However, although vexillations may have been deployed for the building of Richborough, the actual headquarters of the legion is argued to have been transferred initially to Cardiff – where, by implication, it must have been directly involved in the construction of the new coastal fort there.[29] The legion has been associated with maritime trade on the west coast of Britain, and it is suggested that the headquarters was relocated to Richborough only after these activities had been scaled down, or had entirely ceased, during the later fourth century.

Several of the units recorded by the *Notitia* at the Shore Forts in the late fourth century were certainly not the original garrisons. This is particularly clear at Pevensey, where units bearing the fort's name are found on the continent. The *classis Anderetianorum* (the only recorded naval unit from Roman Britain after the demise of the *classis Britannica*) was listed as being at Paris, while the *milites Anderetiani* was at Mainz.[30] The *Notitia* notes the *numerus Abulcorum* as being present at Pevensey and it is likely that this unit, along with many others in Britain, was put in place during the period immediately after 367. As such they were but one part of a wide reorganisation of the army following count Theodosius' restoration of order in the province in the wake of the barbarian conspiracy. At this time some units were transferred to the Saxon Shore from the continent, including the *milites Tungrecani*, demoted from the field army after proclaiming the unsuccessful usurper Procopius in 365, and subsequently sent to Dover. Other units moved south from the northern frontier, including the *numerus Exploratum*, which was probably transferred from Hadrian's Wall to *Portus Adurni*.

The size and composition of the military force at each of the Shore Forts is almost entirely conjectural. Lewin, writing in the 1860s, suggested that the garrison of Bradwell may have numbered between 500 and 1000, which is to say a full strength auxiliary *millenaria* regiment. More recently, James has argued that for certain of the northern frontier forts the garrison may have numbered no more than 100 men.[31] If a similar situation prevailed at any of the Shore Forts, then the troops must be seen as little more than a 'caretaker' garrison, and certainly not a potent military force capable of opposing pirate landings. The absence of good evidence from the fort interiors, particularly relating to internal buildings, however, renders further speculation fruitless at the present time.

Beyond the defences: *vici* and extra-mural activity

Settlement was not confined to the area within the Shore Fort defences. A great many Roman forts in Britain – particularly those after the first century – were accompanied by an extra-mural settlement or *vicus*, positioned immediately outside the defensive walls. Such *vici* varied in scale and sophistication: some of those that grew up outside legionary fortresses ultimately attained the status of a city. Most were much more modest, and were centres for small-scale industry and trade in goods on a limited basis. Some consisted of only a cluster of houses beyond the fort gate, but typical elements of more developed *vici* included a bathhouse, *mansio*, temples and cemetery, alongside a network of houses and streets.[32] Agricultural activity, quite probably to support the population of the fort and its *vicus* is also often attested in the form of field systems, as at the northern frontier installations of Housesteads and Newton Kyme.

In recent years it has become increasingly apparent that *vici* were associated with many of the Shore Forts, particularly as the result of aerial photography, field-walking, and geophysical survey. The most extensive extra-mural settlement known thus far is at Brancaster. Here aerial photographs have revealed a complex series of enclosures and associated trackways to the east, west and south of the fort, the western area of which has since been excavated in advance of building development (**2, 70**).[33] Although plough erosion has removed many suspected occupation horizons, some traces of light, post-built structures have been found. This evidence, combined with abundant domestic rubbish in the dividing ditches, has led to the interpretation of the enclosures as having been house plots rather than stock pens. The regular arrangement of the *vicus* strongly suggests that the settlement was deliberately planned.

The coin series from the western part of the Brancaster *vicus* and the presence of much Antonine samian pottery indicates that occupation began during the later second century. The existence of a rigorously planned settlement at this date strongly suggests the presence of an earlier installation on the site of the Shore Fort. During the second half of the third century a very large 'quarry ditch' was dug, for unexplained reasons, parallel to the fort's west wall. This had the effect of severing the

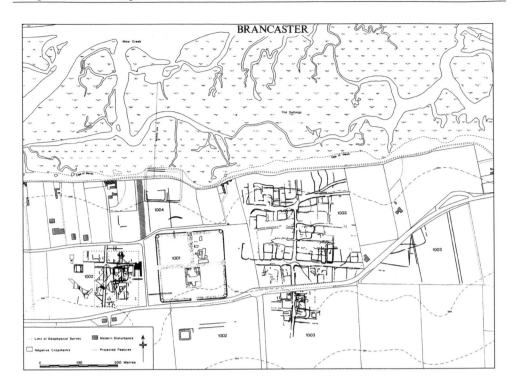

70   *The fort and* vicus *at Brancaster.* From Hinchliffe & Green (1985, Fig. 2).
Courtesy Norfolk Museums and Archaeology Service

western part of the *vicus* from the fort, and seems to have led to its demise. There is
a possibility that the settlement lying beyond the Shore Fort's east gate continued well
into the fourth century. As yet, however, this area has not been excavated, and only
greater investigation will tell.

At Burgh Castle, evidence is emerging for another sizeable *vicus* (**71, 72 & 73**).
Aerial photographs have revealed a large number of hidden features to the east, north
and south of the Shore Fort, some of which lie as far as 750m from the walls of the
fort. Although none of these cropmark complexes has been excavated, a Roman date
for most, if not all, is probable. No cropmarks are evident in the fields that immediately surround the fort, but investigations in the churchyard 250m to the north have
shown the Roman features to be obscured by over 1m of wind-blown overburden.[34]
Here, aerial photographs did not show Roman features, but excavations uncovered
a complex of late third- and fourth-century ditches, which were probably the boundaries of agricultural fields. Traces of one possible structure (perhaps a barn or shed)
were found, but it was thought that any houses were likely to have been closer to the
fort itself. Fieldwalking adjacent to the fort walls has certainly produced a large
number of finds, most of which are Roman in date, and which largely comprise
coins, pottery, and a little metalwork. The most curious of the metalwork finds was
a lead pattern for making brooch moulds. This item would normally be thought of

as continental, as military in character, and of early to mid-third-century date. Its significance, in particular its date, awaits explanation. Over 1000 coins were recovered: those analysed dated from 259/75 to 388/402, with the majority being of the mid-fourth century.[35] The extra-mural activity was thus contemporary with the occupation of the fort. Some concentrations of finds were encountered, which included domestic refuse and some building material: these may have been the sites of dwellings.

There are significant indications of extra-mural activity around other Shore Forts on the East Anglian and east Kent coast, although here the evidence is based on less intensive surveys. Aerial photographic evidence is lacking, and the picture is rather less coherent than for Brancaster and Burgh Castle. At Caister our knowledge is derived from antiquarian finds, and from limited modern excavations prior to building development.[36] Although there are sparse finds of material of the first and second centuries, there is no definite evidence for a pre-fort settlement. Most activity was contemporary with the Shore Fort, and much appears to have been to the south, south-east and west of the defences, in particular between the fort and the probable Roman shoreline. A cambered roadway with a metalled surface led from the fort's south gate in the direction of the 'harbour': a 'paved road' was suggested to have led westwards from the roadway, but the evidence on which this latter feature was proposed is not known. A pottery kiln was discovered some 350m distant from the fort gate in 1851, and a second lies a short distance to the north of the supposed 'paved road'. East of the fort was a second bay,

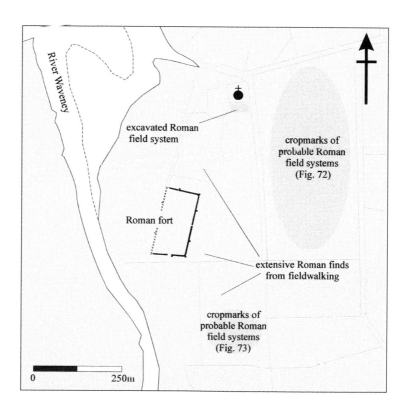

71   *Elements of the* vicus *at Burgh Castle*

72 *Aerial photograph of cropmarks to the east of Burgh Castle. Many of the ditches and trackways probably relate to the Roman fort (top left of the photograph), with which they are aligned. The churchyard, where Roman field systems have been excavated, can be seen in the right of the photograph.* Photo by Derek A. Edwards. Copyright Aerial Archaeology Publications

73 *Aerial photograph of cropmarks of probable Roman field systems to the south-east of Burgh Castle. The walls of the Roman fort appear in the extreme top left of the photograph.* Photo by Eileen A. Horne. Copyright Aerial Archaeology Publications

where trenches have revealed traces of timber foundations, pits and other domestic occupation debris. Also to the south-east, excavations have uncovered a number of Roman features, predominantly boundary ditches.[37] Traces of two ephemeral timber structures were detected, but there was little to indicate domestic habitation. The environmental evidence, which included much cattle bone and charred grain, suggested that this particular area was devoted to agricultural activity, though whether for production, processing or storage could not be established. Activity to the west of the fort was more limited, confined to an area within 100m of the fort walls. Small-scale excavations here revealed multiple phases of ditches and gullies, as well as clay-lined pits and posthole groups. Cropmarks suggest the line of a road running west-south-west from the fort, with a possible branch leading north-west. No activity has been detected in this area, suggesting that the settlement was focused on the area between fort and coast. One possible element lay elsewhere: a cremation cemetery approximately 350m to the north-east.

Only a small part of the extra-mural area at Bradwell has been excavated. Some investigations have taken place in an area 150m to the north of the fort, where shallow gullies – either land divisions or for drainage – have been found.[38] A number of these gullies are aligned north-west/south-east or north-east/south-west, and several cross at right angles. As such, they share the alignment of the Shore Fort defences, which suggests that the landscape had been deliberately, and regularly, divided up – a process that probably took place at the time of the settlement's inception. There were few finds from the excavations, and no specifically military items were discovered. For this reason it was proposed that domestic occupation would have been situated elsewhere, on areas of better-drained land. A recent field-walking survey appears to confirm this theory. The spread of Roman pottery and building material extends over some 3ha (7.5 acres), a large concentration of material to the south of the fort probably marking the main area of activity. In two locations, to the west and south-west of the fort, a detailed geophysical survey detected magnetic anomalies characteristic of pits and ditches, which appear to be part of a complex of irregularly shaped enclosures.[39]

The pottery recovered during both the excavations and the fieldwalking exercise indicated that the extra-mural occupation was contemporary with the lifetime of the fort (i.e. from the mid- or late third century to the early fifth). The recovery of Roman tile from the area to the south of the fort suggests that some substantial buildings existed.

Extra-mural activity is known to the west, north and south of the fort at Reculver (**74**). Early discoveries were reported by the Rev. J. Battely in the early eighteenth century, who noticed 'foundations of great bulk' and 'cisterns' (probably wells) to the north of the fort, in an area now lost to coastal erosion.[40] The foundations he discovered probably related to a bath block or other high-status dwelling associated with the fort. To the west, in an area also now destroyed by the sea, more recent excavations along the line of the Canterbury road (which entered the fort at the west gate) encountered a series of wells, rubbish pits, and hearths (one of which was used for smelting). No masonry structures were present in this area, but a settlement of huts was postulated.[41] Pottery and coins indicated that the wells had been in use over a lengthy period, and that some pre-dated the Shore Fort, containing material of late

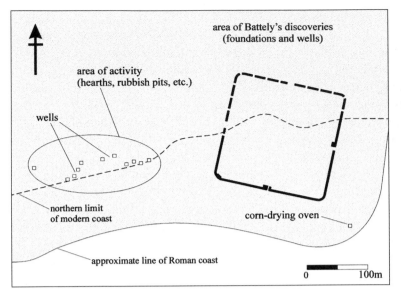

74 *Elements of the* vicus *at Reculver.* Based in part on Philp (1959, Fig. 1)

second-century date in their fill. Others remained open into the fourth century. The smelting hearth was also used in the late second century, and was overlain by the metalling of the Roman road leading to the fort. To the south-east of the defences a large corn-drying oven was discovered; at a later date in the Roman period the original drying chamber was converted for use as a furnace pit.[42]

Aerial photographs and past excavations suggest that there was extensive Roman settlement at Richborough, particularly to the south and west of the area now occupied by the Shore Fort. The amphitheatre lay over 500m south of the fort (and of the site of the monumental arch that formed the focus of the earlier Roman settlement), and so it must be assumed that the area of occupation was considerable. Two temples were located to the east of the amphitheatre, while another building, a cemetery, and traces of gravelled roads are present in the area between the temples and the fort. Streets are also known, branching from Watling Street, which led westwards from Richborough to Canterbury. This western area was excavated by Dowker during the 1880s, the work revealing wall foundations at several locations.[43]

The major question regarding the wider settlement at Richborough is not whether it existed, but at what date it did so, and in what form. It would be reasonable to expect extensive occupation during the first, second and early third centuries, much of it connected with the civilian port. Little dating evidence of any value arose from any of the investigations of the extra-mural area (most of which took place in the nineteenth century), and so the size and character of any *vicus* associated with the Shore Fort phase at Richborough is entirely unknown. The impact of the re-establishment of military control at Richborough during the mid- to late third century on settlement in the locality – whether a positive or negative influence – cannot be established with the existing data, and must await future investigation.

Unsurprisingly, practically nothing is known of settlement immediately around Walton Castle. Roman occupation in the Felixstowe district is itself fairly poorly understood, though the evidence combines to suggest that settlement began during the early Roman period, and that the occupied area was extensive. There appear to be several foci, including one around Felixstowe church which includes material that definitely pre-dates the establishment of the Shore Fort.[44] An area along the present cliff-top (Brackenbury Battery), 500m from the site of the fort, revealed ditches, pits and post holes of the Roman period, together with large quantities of tile. The pottery, however, spanned the second to the fourth centuries, and the relationship of this settlement area to the Shore Fort has not been established.[45]

When we turn our examination to the Shore Forts on the south coast, the situation appears markedly different. At none of the installations is there evidence of a *vicus*, or indeed of any significant Roman activity beyond the defences. For Dover and Lympne this conclusion must be tentative. There is no doubt that the construction of the Dover Shore Fort led to the destruction of much of the *vicus* of the *classis Britannica* fort, but the extra-mural zone of the late Roman installation has not been investigated to the same extent as the area within the defences. A similar lack of excavation at Lympne, combined with the destructive landslipping, also makes it unlikely that any activity beyond the fort walls would have been detected. A settlement 1km to the north-east at Shepway Cross has been suggested to have some connection with the Shore Fort,[46] but the finds indicate occupation spanning the first to fifth centuries, and the site is probably unrelated to the installation.

The negative evidence from both Pevensey and Portchester is rather more compelling. Both lay at the end of promontories, and are areas that were extensively developed for housing during the twentieth century. However, there are no reports of Roman features coming to light during any of the building works. At Pevensey, the areas beyond both the east and west gates have been partly excavated, but while medieval finds are abundant, Roman activity is barely attested.[47]

For the east coast forts, therefore, but not for those from Dover westwards, there is a growing body of evidence for activity beyond the fort walls. Whether in every case there can be considered to have been a *vicus* – that is to say an actual settlement, as opposed to simply 'activity' without habitation – has not yet been established, though the former alternative seems probable. The picture is in all cases incomplete, and it is clear that many elements have not yet been detected, in particular the mortuary areas. It is to be hoped that more details will become known in the future. At two of the forts, namely Brancaster and Burgh Castle, sufficient evidence has been found for there having been a planned division of the landscape, and thus a deliberate organisation of the settlement. Hints of the same process having occurred can be found at Bradwell. The arrangement of any settlement or activity around the other forts is less clearly established. However, the finds from these sites – which point to a combination of domestic habitation, small-scale industry and agriculture – seem to suggest that all were of similar character. The impression is of relatively humble settlements; certainly there do not seem to be any stone dwellings, as there were outside forts such as Vindolanda and Housesteads. Large structures (such as bathhouses or *mansio*) are in most cases lacking, though bath blocks were encompassed by the defences at certain of the forts.

From the present evidence it appears that much extra-mural activity is concurrent with the lifetime of the Shore Forts, with the majority of finds being of late Roman character. The forts at Caister, Burgh Castle and Bradwell in particular can be viewed as having stimulated new settlement in previously unoccupied areas. The major exception is Brancaster, where the settlement pre-dated the Shore Fort phase by several decades. Walton Castle also seems to have been built in a locality where Roman occupation was already established, and thus its impact on the human geography of the area would perhaps have been somewhat different. The activity to the west of Reculver fort also seems to have begun during the late second century; the significance of this (admittedly small-scale) occupation prior to the building of the Shore Fort awaits explanation. It may become clearer when the evidence from the interior of the fort is published in detail.

The apparent difference between the east and south coast forts requires some explanation. It is perhaps more illusory than real; future excavations may prove this to be so, although the situation at Lympne may never be known. However, the fact that the four Shore Forts from Dover westwards have failed to produce conclusive evidence for a *vicus*, while all those on the east coast have done so, may perhaps be more than merely coincidental. If it is a genuine difference, we must consider why this may be so. The most obvious solution is that the population lived entirely within the forts: certainly there is evidence for civilians and soldiers having lived within the defences as Portchester. In such a scenario, industrial activity and trade would also be undertaken within the fort; once again there is evidence for small-scale industry and butchery having taken place within the walls of Portchester. All this, however, still leaves open the central question as to why some or all of the southern forts (built in locations where there does not appear to have been existing occupation at the time of construction) failed to stimulate settlement beyond the defences.

The character of the occupation

Excavated material from the Shore Fort interiors, particularly in the form of small finds, provides an image of life within the forts and of the character of the occupation. The discussion that follows draws mostly from the more extensively published data concerning the eastern forts of Caister, Burgh Castle and Richborough, with Portchester alone representing those on the south coast. Investigations of the Brancaster *vicus* have also yielded a great number of finds, many of which were also doubtless derived from the fort itself, having been deposited as rubbish beyond the defences. What follows is inevitably something of a generalised view, but the basic character of many of the sites can be seen to have been similar. The differences lie in the details, especially in the commercial interactions of the sites with the wider Roman world. These correspond to local and regional patterns of supply, and the differing economic arrangements are once again particularly notable between those installations in East Anglia and east Kent, and those on the south coast.

Soldier and civilian

Military artefacts are reasonably well attested, though they are not as abundant as might be expected from supposed army bases (**75**). In general terms it can be said that they are sufficient to demonstrate some form of military presence, but the assemblage is far from overwhelming. Caister is a particularly interesting example in this respect, for here most military objects that could be assigned a date were of late second- and third-century age; there was no unequivocally fourth-century military material, despite certain occupation during this period.

Military finds from the Shore Forts include weapons, in the form of spearheads, sword and dagger fragments and missile heads (arrowheads and ballista bolts). Protective equipment is also represented: the pieces of a near-complete late Roman helmet were recovered from Burgh Castle,[48] and other fragments have been found at Caister, Richborough and Portchester. Shield bosses and, very occasionally, pieces of armour, for example *lorica Squamata* (scale armour) from Brancaster, also attest to the presence of soldiers. Although not specifically military objects, items relating to horses have been found that may have belonged to cavalry units stationed at the forts; these include harness fittings, spurs and horseshoes.

Items of military or official dress are rather more common finds, most notably metal strap- and belt-end fittings. Crossbow brooches, an essential piece of late Roman dress, are also well represented. Some are of definitely military type, but others could have been worn either by soldiers or by a civilian official. The status and value of the military objects recovered from the forts varies widely. Many, for instance a number of leaded bronze crossbow brooches from Caister, were items that would have belonged to the common soldier. Other jewellery was of higher quality. One of the most spectacular finds was a gold signet ring from Brancaster, which is suggested to have belonged to the commander of *cohors I Aquitanorum* during that unit's residency at the fort during the third century. It would have been used as a seal for documents and as authority for orders, and this ring may have represented a serious loss to its owner.[49]

Until recent times it was traditionally held that the interiors of Romano-British forts were exclusively occupied by the soldiers. *Vici* were seen as having been occupied by civilians, and in particular by the families and servants of soldiers garrisoned within the fort, together with the 'service industry' required to support such a population. Only during the late Roman period was it suggested that there was a change towards a more integrated community of soldiers and their families living within the fort defences. This perception is now changing. Excavations, for example at South Shields, have demonstrated that women and children lived inside the forts during the early as well as the late Roman period.[50] The idea of a rigid division between a 'military' and a 'civilian' zone within and outside the fort respectively is both over-simplistic, and quite probably based on incorrect assumptions.[51] The real situation is likely to have been of a far more complex mingling of soldier and civilian, male and female, both inside and beyond the walls of the forts.

The artefactual evidence from the Shore Fort interiors lends support to this impression. At Caister, hairpins were the commonest identifiable type of small find from the excavations. Personal jewellery, including finger rings, brooches, beads and

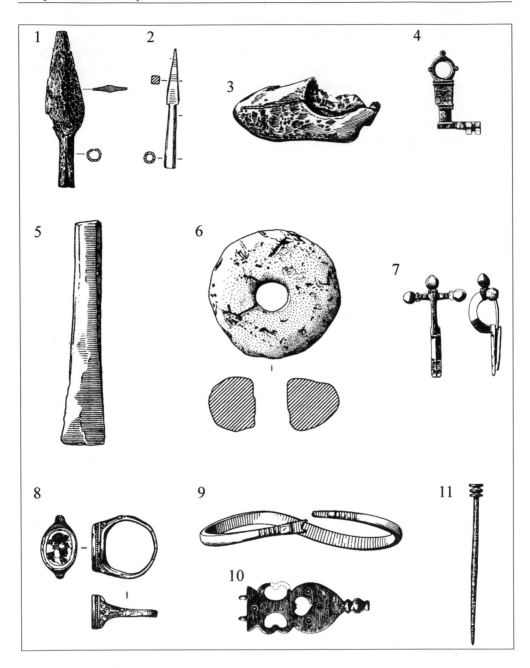

75   *Finds of late Roman date from the Shore Forts. 1. Iron spearhead (Portchester); 2. Iron
     ballista bolt or arrowhead (Brancaster); 3. Child's leather shoe (Portchester); 4. Bronze key
     for slide lock (Richborough); 5. Iron chisel (Caister); 6. Clay loomweight (Caister); 7. Brass
     crossbow brooch (Caister); 8. Gold ring with cornelian gemstone intaglio depicting an
     emperor. Possibly a commander's signet ring (Brancaster); 9. Copper alloy bracelet
     (Brancaster); 10. Bronze belt strap-end, shaped in the form of an amphora (Richborough);
     11. Bone hairpin (Portchester). Nos. 1-7 & 11 at scale 1:3; Nos. 8, 9 & 10 at scale 2:3*

bracelets, although not exclusively feminine articles, also seem to indicate the presence of women, particularly as many of the rings and bracelets seem too small to have been worn by men. Such items have been reported from most of the Shore Forts, including those that have been only poorly, or partially excavated, for example Bradwell. One of the most interesting sets of evidence came from the excavated wells at Portchester. These yielded a sizeable collection of preserved leatherwork, amongst which were a significant number of shoes, identified as belonging to women on the basis of their size, decoration and design. Articles pertaining to spinning and weaving (see below) also argue persuasively for the presence of women.

Evidence of a different nature comes in the form of infant burials within the fort perimeters. Five such inhumations have been encountered at Reculver, beneath the third-century barracks to the east and west of the *principia*. The bones of at least 27 infants were recovered during the excavations at Portchester, including 13 that had been interred in pits. At the latter fort, the context of the bones suggests that infant interments were taking place from around 300 onwards, with a particular preponderance between 325 and 345. Infant bones were discovered in disturbed contexts at Caister, but no actual burials. Parallels for infant burials in forts (particularly beneath barrack buildings) can be found on the northern frontier, for example at South Shields and Malton, but are more common on civilian sites.[52] An explanation for these burials is difficult, but they would seem to imply resident women 'disposing of dead infants with little ceremony in convenient places around the living site'.[53]

These were not the only burials within the precincts of the defences. At Richborough, an adult male and female, together with a child, were crudely, and probably rather hurriedly, interred during the mid-fourth century in the area once occupied by the earth fort ditch.[54] Most deceased inhabitants of the forts, however, were likely to have been buried with greater ceremony and dignity in mortuary areas beyond the defences. Nevertheless, the discovery of a female skeleton at the base of one of the wells in the extra-mural area of Reculver once again indicates that not all died under normal circumstances, or found conventional resting places.[55] The human crises which precipitated this, and the Richborough burials, are too distant in time for explanation

Other more mundane finds attest to everyday life within the forts. Domestic and household items are prominent, ranging from spoons, candlesticks, toilet implements and razors to styli, the latter showing that at least part of the population was literate. Keys indicate personal privacy, and imply that some items were considered worthy of protection. Dice and gaming counters represent part of the recreational aspect of life. Religious artefacts were mostly pagan, but there are rare examples of Christian finds, such as a ring from Richborough inscribed with the *chi-rho* symbol.

Industry

A variety of industrial activities took place both within the Shore Fort defences, and in their extra-mural areas. Metalworking is widely attested, for example at Portchester, where the evidence takes the form of iron slag, copper ore, lead trimmings and a crucible. Amongst the finds from Caister was a smith's punch and several other possible hot metal-working tools, along with others that could have been used in carpentry. Finds from the Brancaster *vicus* illustrate the wide range of occupations, including woodworking awls, a stonemason's chisel, and a sickle and cattle goad, implying agriculture.

Spinning and weaving, already noted above as likely evidence for the presence of women, are attested at many of the forts by items such as spindlewhorls and loomweights. Other production was also being undertaken. The pottery kiln just beyond the fort walls at Caister indicates that small-scale domestic pottery manufacture occurred here, and suggests that some of the grey ware mortaria found within the fort were made on the site. Manufacture of coarseware pottery in and around Roman forts is by no means unparalleled, one example being 'Housesteads ware', produced on the northern frontier and present in the forts at Housesteads, Chesterholm and Birdoswald.

Bone and antler working seems to have been another significant activity, particularly at Burgh Castle, which has yielded an unusually high volume of antler for a Roman site. The large quantities of cut and sawn antler at both Portchester and Caister also provide evidence for similar work. At Portchester, the very large number of bone pins (many found in a single location) has led to the suggestion that these were being locally made. At Caister, uncut pieces of shale imported from Dorset also imply that this material was being worked, albeit on very minor scale. Many of these products may have been intended for export, but the manufacture of these craft goods would have been an ancillary activity, likely to occur on any site where the materials were directly to hand.

Animal butchery and meat-processing on a large scale is also attested. Much of the slaughter took place within the forts themselves: the large volume of animal bones recovered from 'Building 1' at Caister, in particular from the rooms on the west range, strongly suggest that butchery was carried out at this location. Within the adjacent 'Building 2' a series of small 'rooms' lined with waterproof *opus signinum* plaster might have served as tannery tanks. The large numbers of animal bones recorded on other fort sites (Brancaster, Burgh Castle, Bradwell, Richborough and Portchester) also indicate that butchery was taking place, although most of the finds are derived from rubbish deposits, and thus the location of the slaughter has not been established. Cattle were the most common animals, as is the case on most late Roman military sites, with sheep and pigs also represented.

The requirements of the fort and *vicus* population would have been considerable, and many of the animals killed must have been intended for consumption on the site. This would certainly appear to be the case at Portchester, where all parts of the animal skeletons were represented in the bone assemblages. The situation at Brancaster, Caister and Burgh Castle may have been different, as there was a bias among the bone finds towards the non-meat-bearing bones. The evidence of the animal bones from Caister, particularly those from 'Building 1', implies that while slaughtering took place at this location, the prime joints were going elsewhere. The high incidence of metapodials at Burgh Castle is notable, and implies a similar scenario.[56] None of these three forts has been completely excavated, and it may be that the investigated areas are biased towards butchery, with meat being consumed elsewhere on the sites, and the debris disposed of in another location.

A plausible alternative, however, is that the East Anglian forts served as large-scale meat processing centres. The Roman army had a vast requirement for meat, and for other animal products such as hides and gut.[57] Alongside meat production, therefore, we might well envisage tanning, although hides could equally have been shipped 'green'. Animals could have been assembled at the forts for slaughter and processing, before onward trans-shipment. The northern British forts would have been one of the likely destinations for the products, doubtless with the installation at South Shields playing a major role. Another plausible destination would have been the Lower Rhine, as illustrated by Julian's re-opening of a supply route in 359. The coastal location of the Shore Forts made them ideally placed for such a task, acting as assembly points for livestock reared in their hinterlands.

The fen-edge sites of the Fenlands have been proposed as one possible area of production to meet military requirements, although whether those closest to the Shore Forts constituted an 'imperial estate' is far from clear.[58] Smoking or salting was necessary for the preservation of meat, and here again many of the eastern Shore Forts would have been well placed. The incidence of 'red hills', relating to salterns, is particularly notable around Bradwell, and the numerous industrial sites on the Fenlands could also have been producing salt. Animals were probably driven to the forts on the hoof; indeed, the conveyance of beasts over long distances to supply the army was specifically an official activity.[59] Cunliffe has raised the possibility that at Portchester animals may have been quartered within the fort for periods of some length, pointing out that the excavated area had at times been occupied by an open, gravelled surface, ideal for the coralling of livestock.

The evidence of the animal bones also points to a degree of hunting, adding variety to the diet of the forts' inhabitants. Hare and deer were hunted, while ducks, geese and a variety of waterfowl are also represented. Fishing is also attested by rare items such as fish hooks, netting needles and lead net weights. Large quantities of oyster and other mollusc shells were recovered from several of the forts, attesting to a considerable oyster-dredging industry in some locations. The Great Estuary seems to have been a particularly rich resource in this respect.

External contacts

The material culture from the Shore Forts demonstrates widespread contacts with the broader Roman world. The fact that this was occurring from the outset can be observed at Bradwell, where as we have seen, some of the stone used in the construction of the defences was procured from quarries situated at considerable distances from the fort. Many longer-term contacts are documented by the pottery, a great deal of which would have arrived on the site as part of cargoes moving along the British coast. Some of the more unusual or rare pottery may have been brought in amongst the personal possessions of the forts' inhabitants: not all can therefore necessarily be taken as a direct indication of trade. During the initial phases of occupation at Brancaster and Caister there is a reliance on samian fineware pottery from eastern and central Gaul. With the demise of the samian industry, a process that had begun in the later second century and continued apace during the first decades of the third century,

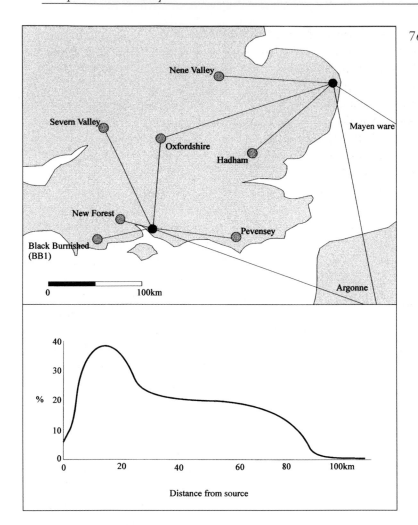

76 *Pottery supply to the sites at Caister and Portchester. The graph shows the percentage of pottery supplied to Portchester from production sources at varying distances from the fort.* Based in part on Cunliffe (1976, Fig. 162)

continental imports to Britain declined. Even during the late Roman period, however, sites such as Caister still received a limited quantity of goods from beyond the province. Here, later third- and fourth-century Gallic imports are represented by Argonne ware and a few vessels of *céramique a l'éponge*, with Mayen wares from Germany also present. Amphora fragments, though rare, demonstrate the wide range of sources from which goods arrived; wine from north Gaul, olive oil from Baetica (southern Spain), fish products or olive oil from North Africa, and wine from Egypt.

Most of the late pottery, however, even the fine wares, was from British production sources. The Shore Forts reflect a pattern of supply typical of other contemporary sites in the same region, the products present being greatly determined by which pottery industry's economic catchment they fell within. At the three East Anglian forts for which there are detailed data (Brancaster, Caister and Burgh Castle), the pottery assemblages all indicate the same sources (**76**). The Nene Valley industries were the major supplier of fine wares, and also of mortaria, supplemented by the Oxfordshire and Much Hadham (Essex) potteries, with a small amount of material from the prolific BB1 ('black burnished ware') industry based around Poole, Dorset. Trading links with local kilns, most probably in Norfolk, accounted for many of the coarsewares; some of the grey mortaria may even have been produced at the forts themselves, for example by kilns such as the one outside the walls of Caister. Portchester, unsurprisingly, yielded an assemblage far more typical of other Roman sites on the south coast. Virtually all has been shown to have been brought from distances less than 90km (60 miles), although imported Argonne wares were once again present in small quantities. The New Forest potteries made the greatest single contribution, with BB1, Alice Holt (Farnham) and Oxfordshire products also represented. Many of the coarsewares were probably made at sites 8-24km (5-15 miles) from the fort.

Other items recovered from the forts also attest to long-distance trade. Quern fragments of Niedermendig lava from the Eifel region of Germany are common finds on the East Anglian sites, and may have been imported alongside other commodities, notably Mayen pottery. Quernstones of other stone types attest to supply from a variety of sources in south-east and eastern England. Very little of the jewellery found at the forts was likely to have been produced on the site itself; beads and other items demonstrate links with the jet industry at Whitby, active during the third and fourth centuries, while bracelets of shale have an origin in Dorset. The latter products probably arrived by sea alongside the limited quantities of BB1 pottery.

The history of occupation

An historical framework of the Shore Forts' occupation using the present data can, for the most part, be understood only in general terms. Where excavation has taken place within the interiors, however, the findings have made interesting reading. The Portchester excavations have yielded the only detailed stratigraphic evidence published to-date, and the excavator postulated the following sequence:

285-290	Construction phase, followed by initial occupation of very slight character
290-300	Abandonment
300-325	Occupation
325	Tidying up of the site
325-345	Occupation
345	Reorganisation of the interior (remetalling of roads, rebuilding of structures)
345-364	'Ordered' occupation
364-378	Intensive 'disordered' occupation
378-400+	Continued 'disordered' occupation

A similar situation can be seen at Reculver, where the building of the fort defences and the *principia*, probably around the 220s, may have been followed shortly after by a period of inactivity or even complete abandonment. Renewed building work during the second half of the third century, notably the creation of two barrack buildings and a small bath block, together with modification of other structures, signify a revival of activity on the site, perhaps accompanying the creation of the new group of Shore Forts. A decline in the standard of the occupation is evident by 300; the *principia* was in ruins by this date, and both barracks had been destroyed and not replaced. The *via quintana*, the road to the south of the *principia*, lay buried beneath layers of domestic rubbish.[60] A similar situation may also have occurred at Dover, where organised, tidy occupation up to the late fourth century was followed by a situation in which rubbish was dumped onto the Shore Fort rampart.

Both these instances provide evidence that the occupation of these two sites at least was neither of a constant intensity, nor of consistent character. It is interesting to discover that at times the interiors were hardly a model of order, cleanliness and efficiency. The lack of stratigraphic sequences from the remaining forts renders their history much less certain, and here the only approach is to examine patterns of coin loss at each site (**77**). The Shore Forts have all yielded coins, mostly in the order of hundreds. The excavations at Richborough produced a staggering 56,000 coins, by a large margin the greatest number produced by any Romano-British site. Coin series for Reculver and Dover still await publication.

In his 1968 analysis of the coins from Richborough, Richard Reece interpreted the coin loss pattern in a way that fitted well with the supposed history of the site.[61] Crucially, the number of coins 'lost' during each period was directly equated to the intensity of occupation (i.e. the larger number of people occupying the fort, the greater the number of coins being dropped, lost or mislaid). Coin loss of issues minted in the 260s and 270s rose sharply after the site was refortified, first with earth defences and then with the stone Shore Fort. The collapse of the Allectan regime in 296 seemed to herald a period of low coin loss, which was equated to a desertion of the site, much as White had supposed when he outlined the installations as a Carausian and Allectan defensive scheme. Another peak in coin loss followed around the mid-part of the fourth century, perhaps when the forts were revitalised by the visit of Constans to the province, the site continuing in operation until the early fifth century.

More recent research on Romano-British coinage, not least by Reece himself, has demonstrated that the data cannot be interpreted in such uncritical fashion.[62] The mechanisms influencing coin loss are extremely complex, and even now are only partially understood. They are now known to be affected by a host of factors, including (to list only a few) the amount of currency in production or circulation and the quantity of coinage reaching a given site at any particular date. Hoarding, that is to say the retention of coinage, often during times of economic crisis (e.g. a period of inflation), also has great potential to distort the picture of normal, 'background' losses on a site. Study now shows that the coin losses at Richborough, and indeed the other Shore Forts, broadly compare to the general pattern of losses from other Romano-British sites. Most exhibit a peak during the period of the Gallic Empire, and again in the period 330-48, with a low loss rate for coins that were minted during the late third and early fourth century. Seen in this context the Richborough finds are unremarkable; the losses of coins of the 260s and 270s are still higher than might be expected, but those of the mid-fourth century are only marginally above the norm.

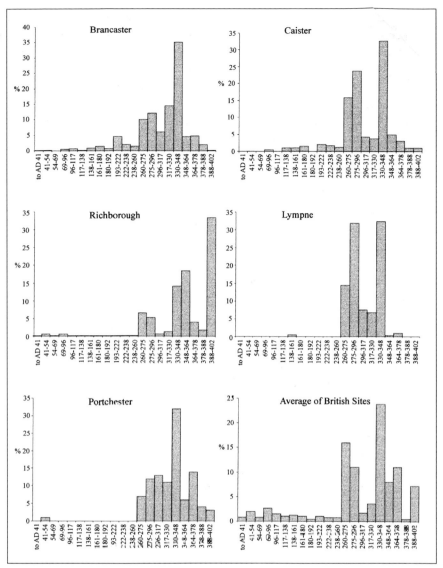

77 *Coin-loss histograms from the Shore Forts*

Coin series, therefore, cannot in themselves imply the density of occupation, and are too crude a tool to allow understanding of whether habitation of a given site was continuous. Despite these criticisms, they remain a useful tool for establishing the approximate duration of the activity on the sites. The absence of pre-Shore Fort activity at sites such as Lympne and Portchester contrasts markedly with Brancaster, Caister and Richborough, where prior occupation is indicated by significant losses of coins minted before 259. The end of the occupation is a subject that will be addressed in the final chapter. The sheer numbers of coins found (particularly at Richborough) are in themselves revealing, for in this respect the Shore Forts resemble far more the towns of southern Britain than the coin-poor forts of Hadrian's Wall.

The character of the sites

From the preceding discussion, what can be said of the character of the occupation? Cunliffe described Portchester in the following way:

> As to the general quality of life, the small finds offer some indications. The silver ring and the gemstone were evidently of some value; locks and keys imply personal privacy, while the number of styli represent a high level of literacy. Beyond this it is difficult to go, except to say that buildings were insubstantial, living conditions were sometimes squalid, and the site was infested with cats.[63]

In many ways this statement sums up the other Shore Forts, or at least those for which there is reasonable evidence. The impression gained is one of contrasts. The occupants were both male and female, of high and low status, and the activities taking place within the defences were of military and domestic character. Trade links with the wider empire were extensive, although unremarkable. Domestic industrial activity was common, and at several of the sites the extent of animal processing on a major scale should not be underestimated.

Many of the forts may not have been continuously garrisoned, and at times the occupation was neither particularly intensive nor orderly. The idea of organised, 'clean' military occupation, as opposed to squalid civilian activity is however a cliché, and one that is probably best avoided. The impression of disorder within the forts is particularly strong during the fourth century. By this date the substantial internal buildings that had been present at Caister and Reculver are known to have been demolished, or, at the very least, were in serious disrepair, and there is little evidence of any structures built to replace them. For much of the time the state of the interiors does indeed seem rather squalid. Rubbish was disposed of in pits within the forts, or directly tipped onto the rampart behind the wall – at times the rubbish spilt over and covered the internal roads of the fort, as at Reculver. Gnaw marks on some of the butchered animal bones indicate that dogs scavenged amongst the refuse. Some of the industrial activity on the sites – above all the tanning of hides – could have made the living environment particularly unpleasant.

All this quite possibly places too much emphasis on the one extreme. As can be shown for some of the better-understood forts such as Reculver and Portchester, lengthy periods of much more orderly occupation were interspersed with less tidy phases of activity. It must also be reiterated that we only have good evidence from a few of the fort interiors to support this kind of picture. It should be said, however, that this somewhat more chaotic view of the occupation does not differ in any major sense from other contemporary military sites in Britain. This is particularly true during the last years of Roman rule in the province. Thus, while this portrayal is not quite what one might expect of the 'Roman War Machine', it is perhaps a truer reflection of what these, and many other installations of the late Empire, might well have resembled.

8 The closing years

The end of Roman Britain has traditionally been assigned to AD 410, when the supposed communication of the western emperor Honorius to the Britons instructed them to look to their own defence (the so-called 'Rescript of Honorius'). The passing of Roman Britain was, in reality, a far more complex affair. At present, the vision of the last years of Roman Britain very much depends on one's individual point of view. The ending is seen by some scholars as a gradual process, with elements of continuity of Roman life extending for some period into the fifth century. Others, however, envisage a sudden and total collapse of the Romanised way of life; within a generation or so of 410, the towns, villas and industries are argued to have entirely vanished. In this latter scenario the end is often seen as 'nasty, brutish and short'.[1]

In whatever manner the decline and fall of Roman Britain actually came about, there is a body of evidence to suggest that some of the Shore Forts, alongside other elements of the military coastal network, were not held long into the fifth century. The demise of some of these installations preceded the end of Roman rule in Britain, often by several decades. The fort at Lympne was one site that would seem to have been abandoned exceptionally early. The latest coin yet recovered from the site *may* be an issue of Gratian (367-83), but the coin series as a whole suggests that large-scale occupation ended shortly after 348. The same conclusion is supported by the pottery assemblage, in which wares of the second half of the fourth century are markedly absent.[2] The reason why Lympne was given up at this early date is unclear, but it is notable that the abandonment appears to have been total; there is no trace of any residual civilian occupation after the site ceased to be garrisoned, as has been proven or postulated for other forts in Britain. The decommissioning of Lympne may have been only part of a wider military reorganisation, a rationalisation of coastal bases set against a background of declining army numbers. Alternatively, the land-slipping that would later destroy the fort may already have been in evidence, rendering the site unusable.

Other Shore Forts may also have been abandoned shortly after the middle of the fourth century. The coin evidence from Reculver suggests that the garrison was withdrawn at about 360.[3] However, some caution must be exercised if relying on coin evidence alone, as the operation of the *annona militaris* (the system of paying troops in kind rather than in money) may reduce the number of coins in use at a site, and thus disguise the presence of a garrison. The *annona* could well have been in operation since the later third century, but its practice may have become more widespread from the mid-fourth century onwards. One historical reference suggesting this may have been the case is a rescript of Valentinian of 365, which refers to cash payments only being made for three months in every year. Nevertheless, the absence of any late coins from

Reculver is notable. The evidence of the coins, as well as other archaeological material from Burgh Castle and Caister would be consistent with another early abandonment, probably around 380. This date could be revised by ten years either way, but would still place the decommissioning of the forts well before the close of the century. A late Roman glass hoard from Burgh Castle, once thought to be indicative of activity on the site during the early fifth century, has now been re-dated to the late fourth century.[4]

Beyond the Saxon Shore other installations fell out of use during the same period. The Shadwell signal station was abandoned soon after 360 – the fact that this is the same as the suggested date for the end of the occupation at Reculver may be more than just coincidental. The last-dated coin from Brough-on-Humber is of Magnus Maximus (383-8), and the absence of Crambeck pottery from the uppermost Roman layers suggests that activity did indeed end around this date. The Yorkshire signal stations had also ceased to operate by the end of the century, their lifetime having spanned only 20 years or so. The installation at Goldsborough quite possibly met with a violent end, for here the skeleton of a man was found lying face down across a hearth, his hand twisted behind him as if he had been stabbed in the back. Another man lay at his feet, sprawled across the skeleton of a large dog.[5] The signal stations do not feature in the *Notitia Dignitatum*, and their omission may owe much to the fact that they had been decommissioned or destroyed before the document came to be compiled. However, in a situation where Lympne was certainly out of use by 400, and so too probably Reculver, Caister and Burgh Castle, the listings for garrisons at these sites in the *Notitia* await a different explanation.

Several of the Shore Forts continued to be inhabited until at least the early fifth century. The 'disorderly' occupation described by Cunliffe at Portchester lasted into the period beyond 400, though it is uncertain for how long. Early Saxon activity has been detected on the site, but the evidence does not preclude there having been a break in habitation during the early decades of the fifth century. Whether the last Roman occupation was that of a formal garrison, of a militia, or only of a civilian population, remains to be established.

Several other Shore Forts share both a broadly similar date to that of Portchester, and the same questions about the character of the last occupation. Tiles stamped HON AUG ANDRIA, found during early excavations at Pevensey, were once presumed to be evidence of a reconstruction of the fort during the reign of the western emperor Honorius (395-423). These have since been proved to be forgeries, quite possibly planted on the site by Charles Dawson, the likely perpetrator of the Piltdown Man fake and other Sussex hoaxes of the early twentieth century.[6] Nevertheless, the few coins from the site do indicate that occupation continued at least until AD 400, although the likelihood that the defences were renovated at such a late date now seems remote. The coin series from Brancaster (from the *vicus* excavations, supplemented by surface finds from the interior and elsewhere on the site) includes a significant proportion of issues of Theodosius I (379-95). Two other late coins have been found, one of Magnus Maximus, and the other of Arcadius (395-423).[7] The few reported coins from the nineteenth-century excavations at Bradwell tell much the same story, with issues of Arcadius and Honorius recorded. Activity in the extra-mural area to the north also lasted into the early fifth century. At Dover, dumping of rubbish onto the fort rampart continued until at least 402, and it has been suggested that occupation of the site continued long after this date. Once again, however, the date at which a military garrison gave way to civilian habitation has yet to be demonstrated.

Richborough is widely thought to have been one of the last sites to be garrisoned in force by the Roman army in Britain. Use of the installation is documented in the year 368, for it is here that count Theodosius landed his troops during the barbarian conspiracy. Probably by the late fourth century the fort became the base of *Legio II Augusta*, which is listed at this location in the *Notitia*. The Richborough coin series goes down to 402, and one of the most remarkable aspects of the archaeology of the site is the vast number of bronze coins issued between 395 and 402. Some 20,000 were found, uniformly distributed in the latest Roman deposits and the topsoil; these account for 45% of all coins recovered from Richborough, and comprise a greater number of such issues than from excavations of all other British sites combined. The cause of such a large (and presumably deliberate) discard of coins represents an enigma. True, they were base issues and even taken together they were not worth a great deal, but the reason why so many were present at Richborough still needs to be addressed. It seems plausible that the fort operated in some fiscal capacity during the first years of the fifth century, either as a collection or distribution centre, but this does nothing to explain why discarding of coins took place on such a massive scale.[8] Unfortunately, excavation has once again failed to shed a great deal of light on the character of occupation during the final years of the fort, and the cause remains a mystery. However, a small Christian church has been identified in the north-west corner of the defences, revealing a different aspect of the fort's final years. The structure was of timber, and all that now remains visible is the hexagonal baptismal font, which was probably located in a side chapel of the main building (**78**). Late Roman churches comparable with this one have been discovered within Roman forts in Germany and Switzerland. The

78 The Christian baptismal font, Richborough

precise date of the church cannot now be established, but it must be of the late fourth or early fifth century. The intensity of occupation within the fort during this final period is not known, but the evidence of the coins and the church indicates activity of both an official, and a religious nature.

In the absence of deposits within the Shore Forts dating to the early fifth century, it is difficult to suggest when 'Roman' occupation ended and 'sub-Roman' habitation began. Any attempt to distinguish between the two may be meaningless, because the sparse evidence for the period suggests that the passing of the installations was gradual. There are no late destruction layers from within the forts that might imply a violent demise. During the sub-Roman period at least some of the installations continued to find use: occupation within the walls at Dover, for example, is said to have extended at least into the sixth century. Several sites continued to have military associations during the fifth century, though they would have been concerned with local defence, rather than as part of any wider-ranging coastal scheme. One such fort was Portchester, where the presence of early Saxon sunken-floored huts has led to suggestions of barbarian mercenary troops occupying the defences. The use of Pevensey by the Britons as a fortress, or perhaps more accurately as a refuge, also continued well into the fifth century. Ultimately, however, it offered no sanctuary, for as the Anglo-Saxon Chronicle recorded in AD 491, the chieftains Aelle and Cissa 'besieged *Andredadceaster* [a corruption of *Anderitum*] and slew everyone who lived there.' During the early fifth century the inhabitants had, rather inexplicably, built a causeway across the ditch that in Roman times had cut off the west gate from the mainland. This causeway may have done much to render the fort indefensible.

The post-Roman history of many of the monuments was long and varied, though Brancaster and Lympne appear to have found little use, while the fort at Dover passed out of knowledge at an early stage. Portchester continued to be a focus for settlement throughout much, if not the entire Saxon period, while other sites, notably those on the east coast, provided the location for early Christian mission stations.[9] The chapel at Bradwell survives as a lasting testament to this episode. From Norman times onwards the defences of many of the forts were revived, the Roman perimeters forming the baileys of 'hermit crab' castles, as at Portchester, Pevensey, Burgh Castle and Walton Castle (**colour plate 25**). In every period, and particularly during the Post Medieval era, each site was used as a 'quarry' of stone for new building work, a process that has done much to reduce the defences to their present ruinous state. The longest-lived of all the forts was Portchester, which became a late medieval royal palace and continued in military or official use until the nineteenth century, its last roles including barracks, stores base and prisoner of war camp. Only in 1819 was the site finally closed, and left to lapse into ruin. With the passing of Roman Britain, however, this particular book reaches its conclusion. The later history of the Shore Forts is one which must await another telling.

References

1 The monuments

1 Rose (1985).
2 Blomefield (1805, X, 298).
3 Lee-Warner (1851).
4 St Joseph (1936).
5 Edwards & Green (1977).
6 Hinchliffe & Green (1985).
7 Darling & Gurney (1993).
8 The excavations by Charles Green (1951-5) have now been published by Darling & Gurney (1993); Slightly later investigations were conducted by Ellison (1965; 1969).
9 The fort has been investigated on several occasions since the mid-nineteenth century. The two major excavations are those of Harrod (1859) and Green (Johnson 1983a). Various short accounts can also be found, most relating to discoveries made during the restoration of the site by the Ministry of Works, for example Bushe-Fox (1932a) and Morris (1947). Recent investigations have examined the extra-mural aspects of the fort (Gurney unpublished; Wallis 1998).
10 Summarised by Fox (1911) and Fairclough & Plunkett (2000).
11 S.A.L. Minutes Vol. 1, 72-3.
12 Kirby (1735); 2nd edition published by Canning (1764).
13 Wall (1937).
14 Errington MS, reported in Fairclough & Plunkett (2000, 424).
15 'Roman Britain in 1994', *Britannia* 26 (1995), 357.
16 Hagar (1987).
17 Allen & Fulford (1999).
18 Camden (1637, 443).
19 See for example Cromwell Mortimer's writings on *Othona* (Walford 1812, 145-50).
20 Lewin (1967). For descriptions of the fort and chapel see Pugh (1963) and RCHME (1923).
21 Reproduced in Pugh (1963).
22 Lavender (2000); Wardill (2000).
23 The extensive post-war excavations await detailed publication. They have been periodically reported in *The Journal of Roman Studies* (volumes for 1960-9), *Archaeologia Cantiana* and *Kent Archaeological Review*. A few short articles exist (Philp 1957; 1958; 1959; 1969) and the site is briefly summarised up to 1990 in Philp (1996). Earlier works such as Dowker (1878) are also informative.

24 The major reports, published by the Society of Antiquaries of London, are Bushe-Fox (1926; 1928; 1932b; 1949) and Cunliffe (1968). Earlier investigations include Rolfe (1843), Roach-Smith (1850) and Dowker (1889).
25 The construction of the fort, including these errors, is discussed by Johnson (1970).
26 Philp (1981).
27 Philp (1989).
28 Wilkinson (1994).
29 Note in *Journal of Roman Studies* 34 (1944), 85.
30 Hutchinson *et al.* (1985, Fig. 12).
31 Philp (1982, Site 6).
32 Salzman (1907; 1908). On the later excavations see Lyne (unpublished).
33 Cunliffe (1975; 1976; 1977); Cunliffe & Munby (1985); Cunliffe & Garratt (1994); For a general narrative on the site see Munby (1990).

2 The Roman Empire in the third century

1 Birley (1971).
2 *Dio Cass.* lxxv, 5, 4.4.
3 A catalogue of this unhappy procession is given by Wood (1999). On the third-century crisis see Watson (1999).
4 RIC Postumus 30, 76, 214; Nemesianus, *Cynegetica*, 65-75.
5 The episode is admirably discussed in detail by Casey (1994).
6 *Pan. Lat.* x(ii); viii(v); vi(vii). Translations of these texts can be found in Casey (1994).
7 Aurelius Victor, *De Caesaribus*, xxxix; Eutropius, *Breviarum ab urbe condita*, ix.
8 Casey (1994, 93); Salway (1993, 206).

3 The development of a coastal system

1 Fox (1911, 304). On medieval Dunwich see Rigold (1961; 1974).
2 White (1961, 51) lists seven further possible signal stations and notes that other coastal sites, for example towns, could have served as watch points.
3 White (1961, 11 & ff. 82-4).
4 *Digest* 36.1.48.
5 See Philp (1981, Table B).
6 Brulet (1989, 62-72).
7 Cunliffe (1968, 255-6); Philp (1996, 4).
8 Philp (1981).
9 Ptolemy, *Geog.* Books I-VIII. Philp (1981, 99-100); Rivet & Smith (1979, 341).
10 Mann (1989, 2).
11 Cleere & Crossley (1985).
12 Cleere (1974; 1976).

13 Lemmon & Hill (1966).

14 Brodribb (1969; 1980).

15 Philp (1981, 113-4).

16 Peacock (1977).

17 See Philp (1981b, 45-6).

18 Arnold & Davies (2000); Nash-Williams (1969).

19 Wacher (1995, 398).

20 Wacher (1995, 394-98).

21 Bidwell & Speak 1994; Dore & Gillam (1979); see also reports in *Britannia* (1985, 268; 1986, 347; 1987, 315).

22 Darling & Gurney (1993, 10-11 & 15); Ellison (1962 Fig. 4a).

23 Birley (1981, 173-6); Mann (1977); Richmond (1961).

24 Philp (1981, 13).

25 St Joseph (1936, 451).

26 Casey (1994, 124).

27 Wacher (1969).

28 Whitwell (1970, 50-53 & 136).

29 Harrison & Flight (1968); Harrison (1970).

30 Philp (1981, 98-99).

31 *CIL*, XII, 686.

32 Johnson (1983b, 117).

33 Morris (1947, 68).

34 Esmonde Cleary (1994, 357).

35 Casey (1994, 122); Lewin (1867).

36 Bushe-Fox (1949, 65); Cunliffe (1968, 244).

37 Johnson (1970, 245).

38 Wilkinson (1994, 70).

39 Wilkinson (1994, 72-3).

40 Reece (in Cunliffe 1980, 260-64); Casey (1994, 123); Roach Smith (1852, 32).

41 Bushe-Fox (1932a).

42 Lyne (unpublished).

43 Fulford & Tyers (1995).

44 Cunliffe (1975, 60).

45 Gathercole & Cotton (1958).

46 King (1989; 1990).

47 Rigold (1969b).

48 Young (1983).

49 Wacher (1995, 255-71).

50 Johnson (1975).

51 Ward (1901); Webster (1981).

52 Brulet (1989); Johnson (1976; 1983b); Johnston (1977).

53 For a review of the building of the Gallic town walls see Johnson (1983b).

4 Building the Shore Forts

1 Johnson (1983a).
2 Vitruvius, *On Architecture*, I.v.1.
3 This subject is extensively discussed elsewhere, principally by Cunliffe (1968) and Johnson (1976; 1989).
4 Adam (1994, 143); Sear (1982, 77).
5 Butler (1959).
6 Wilkinson (1994, 72).
7 Salzman (1907).
8 Cunliffe (1968, 419-22); Johnson (1976, Chapter 6).
9 von Petrikovits (1971, 273).
10 Laurence & Wallace-Hadrill (1997).
11 Wilson (1980, 74).
12 Johnson (1989, 43).
13 For discussion, ancient plans and models see Gros (1985; 1996) and Haselberger (1997).
14 The calculations, and the detail of how they were produced, are given in full in Pearson (1999b; 2002b).
15 Bennett (1990). The figure for Hadrian's Wall excludes estimates for the turf wall at the western end, and the nearby forts added after its initial construction.
16 Cotterill (1993, 236).
17 For a discussion see Hanson (1978).
18 Allen & Fulford (1999) have considered the provenance of the building stones in the Shore Forts of the eastern coast. Subsequent studies by Pearson (1999b; 2002; 2002b) reached similar conclusions (albeit with a few minor differences) and also extended the study to the south coast forts.
19 Blagg (1984; 1990).
20 See for example George (1984) on the 'Roman cement' industry of the eighteenth and nineteenth centuries, where septarian cementstones were removed on a vast scale from the Kent, Essex and Suffolk coasts.
21 Fowles (1991, 48-9).
22 Peacock (1977); Philp (1981, 45-6).
23 Fulford, Champion & Long (1997, 166).
24 Worssam & Tatton-Brown (1993).
25 Hillam & Morgan (1986, 83-4); Sheldon & Tyers (1983, 358).
26 Marsden (1994, 83 & 88).
27 Duncan-Jones (1974, 366-9).
28 Fulford & Hodder (1975); Millett (1979).
29 Blackfriars I: Marsden (1994); Worssam & Tatton-Brown (1993). Barlands Farm vessel: Nayling *et al.* (1994, 599).
30 Marsden (1994, 89).
31 Kendall (1996, 144).
32 Casson (1971) discusses the practicalities of ancient sailing in the Mediterranean, whilst historic seafaring in northern European waters is addressed by Marsden

(1994, 73) and McGrail (1987, 225-7). Garnsey (1983, 59) describes the famines in Rome when the grain fleets were delayed by unfavourable winds.

33 Caesar, *B. Gall.*, 4.21-4.22; 5.1-5.2; 5.8.

34 The method used to calculate the labour demand is essentially the same as that developed by DeLaine (1997). The calculations for Pevensey and the Shore Forts as a whole are discussed in Pearson (1999a) and (1999b; 2002b) respectively.

35 Knight & Knight (1955); Pearson (1999a, 107).

36 Pearson (1999a).

37 Davies (1989, 64-65).

38 Tarruntenus Paturnus, *Digest*, 50.vi.7.

39 Taylor & Wilson (1961); Wilson (1969).

40 Holder (1982, 112).

41 Breeze (1984, 267).

42 Frere (1987, 173).

43 Breeze (1984); Duncan-Jones (1978).

44 Millett (1990, Table 8.5).

45 *Pan. Lat.* IV.xxi.2.

46 Gonzalez (1986).

47 Goldthwaite (1980).

48 Crickmore (1984); Frere (1984); Wacher (1995, Chapter 2).

49 Fulford (1984, 236); Wacher (1995, 198).

50 Williams (1993).

51 Butler (1959, Appendix 1).

52 Johnson (1983b, Chapter 5).

53 DeLaine (1997, 193).

54 Shirley (1996; 2000).

55 Edwards (1946).

56 Reece (1997, 22-24).

57 James (2001, 78-9).

58 See for example Southern & Dixon (1996, Chapter 5).

59 Tacitus, *Agricola*, 16.

5 The landscape setting

1 Milne (1990, 84).

2 Leland (1964, 60).

3 Camden (1637, 341-2).

4 Roach-Smith (1852, 39-45).

5 Burnham (1989).

6 Hawkes (1968).

7 See Long & Roberts (1997).

8 Mitchell (1977).

9 Akeroyd (1972); D'Olier (1972); Everard (1980).

10 Devoy (1979, Fig. 59). Calculation of the Highest Astronomical Tide during Roman times based on the height of contemporary quays, breakwaters and buried land surfaces produce a similar figure for sea-level (Waddelove & Waddelove 1990).

11 Milne (1985, 84-86 & Fig. 50).

12 Devoy (1979).

13 Greensmith & Tucker (1971).

14 Tooley & Switsur (1988).

15 May (1966).

16 Clayton (1989).

17 May (1966, 16); So (1966, 481-88).

18 Green (1961).

19 Boswell (1928, 59); George (1984).

20 Waller, Burrin & Marlow (1988).

21 Applebaum (1972); Burnham (1989, 13).

22 Green & Hutchinson (1960); Salzman (1910).

23 Simmons (1978).

24 Hawkes (1968, 226-227).

25 Steers (1960).

26 Murphy & Funnell (1985).

27 I am grateful to Charlie Bristow for access to this information prior to its publication.

28 Press (1956).

29 Taylor (1827).

30 Arthurton *et al.* (1994, 86-8).

31 Darling & Gurney (1993, 3).

32 Clowes (1837, 521); Green & Hutchinson (1960, 116).

33 Fox (1911, 286-7). Nineteenth-century discoveries, *Norfolk Archaeology* 4 (1855), 314-15. On the church, Rose (1994).

34 BGS Sheet 208/225; Boswell (1928).

35 Cunliffe (1968, 271).

36 Burnham (1989).

37 Wilkinson & Murphy (1987; 1995).

38 Fawn (1990).

39 Greensmith & Tucker (1973, 200).

40 Robinson & Cloet (1953, 77).

41 Holmes (1981).

42 Hawkes (1968).

43 Goodsall (1981).

44 Worssam & Tatton Brown (1990).

45 Ogilvie (1968).

46 Philp, letter in *British Archaeology,* February 1999.

47 Rolfe (1843); Roach Smith (1850, 52-54).

48 Amos & Wheeler (1929); Burnham (1989); Philp (1981a); Wheeler (1929).

49 Rigold (1969a).

50 Shephard-Thorn (1988, 36).

51 Waddelove & Waddelove (1990, 259).

52 Rigold (1969a, 83-4, Site 12).

53 Cunliffe (1980b); Tooley & Switsur (1988). For a general work on Romney Marsh see Eddison (2000).

54 Needham (1988); Philp & Willson (1984).

55 Green (1968).

56 Eddison (2000); Philp (1982).

57 Cunliffe (1980; 1988).

58 Reeve (1995).

59 Hutchinson *et al.* (1985).

60 Jennings & Smyth (1987; 1990); Moffat (1986).

61 Dulley (1966, 26-28).

62 Dulley (1966, 33); Salzman (1910).

63 Cunliffe (1975, 4).

64 On the Roman coast see Cleere (1978); Fryer (1973).

65 Mann (1989); Stevens (1941).

66 Marsden (1994, 105-108).

67 Milne (1985, 98).

68 de Boe (1978); de Weerd (1990); Milne (1985, 97-98).

6 Strategy

1 Bidwell (1997, 42).

2 Ammianus Marcellinus, *Rerum Gestarum Libri*, xviii, 2, 3; Julian, *Letter to the Athenians*, 279-80; Zosimus, *New History*, iii, 5.

3 Bartholomew (1984).

4 See Frere (1987, 247).

5 Gildas, *De Excidio Britanniae*.

6 *ND. Occ.* xlii, 23.

7 Rivet & Smith (1979).

8 *ND. Occ.* xl.

9 Hind (1979, 322).

10 Bartholomew (1984, 185).

11 Camden (1637).

12 Esmonde Cleary (1989, 43).

13 For example Cunliffe (1975, 421)

14 Johnson (1976, Chapter 7).

15 Johnson (1976, 6-7).

16 Eutropius, *Breviarum ab urbe condita*, ix, 21.

17 *Pan. Lat.*, 17, 1.

18 Amm. Marc., xxviii.5; xxx.7.

19 Ambrosius, *Ep.* 40, 23.

20 *Pan. Lat.*, IV, XII.

21 Wood (1990).
22 Robertson (1988, 29-32).
23 Cotterill (1993). Calculations based on Green (1963, 103-13).
24 Cotterill (1993, 228).
25 White (1961). See in particular Chapters 2-4.
26 Cotterill (1993).
27 Milne (1990); Wood (1990); Cleere (1978); Fryer (1973).
28 Bidwell (1997, 43).

7 Occupation and economy

1 von Petrikovits (1971, 201-3 and Fig. 31).
2 Southern & Dixon (1996, 139-41).
3 Philp (1996).
4 *Journal of Roman Studies* (1962, 190; 1963, 191; 1969, 233).
5 *Journal of Roman Studies* (1967, 202).
6 Phase II stone building; Philp (1959, 102-3).
7 *Journal of Roman Studies* (1961, 191).
8 Edwards (1976).
9 St Joseph (1936, 450-1).
10 Ellison (1965, 55-6).
11 Darling & Gurney (1993).
12 Ellison (1969, 99)
13 Cunliffe (1968).
14 Roach Smith (1852).
15 Roach Smith (1852, 18).
16 Cunliffe (1976).
17 Salzman (1907).
18 Salzman (1908); Sands (1908).
19 Lyne (unpublished).
20 Wilkinson (1994, 76-7). Multiple phases of huts, 'Roman Britain in 1974, *Britannia* 6 (1975), 283; 'Roman Britain in 1975', *Britannia* 7 (1976), 376.
21 *Current Archaeology* 38 (1973), 87.
22 *Britannia* (1979, 401).
23 Lewin (1867, 444); Wardill (2000).
24 Cotterill (1993, 234-5).
25 Mann (1989, 2).
26 Holder (1982).
27 Frere (1987, 329-30).
28 Holder (1982, 105).
29 Fulford (1996, 24-25).
30 *ND. Occ.* xlii, 23; xli, 17.
31 Lewin (1867); James (1984).

32 Sommer (1984).

33 Edwards & Green (1977); Hinchliffe & Green (1985).

34 Aerial photographs, Horne (1977, 17-18); Edwards (1983, 39-40). Church Loke excavations, Wallis (1998).

35 Gurney (1995).

36 The findings are summarised in Darling & Gurney (1993).

37 Albone (2001).

38 Medlycott (1994).

39 Lavender (2000); Wardill (2000).

40 Battely, *Antiquitates Rutupinae* (published posthumously 1711); translated version, *The Antiquities of Richborough and Reculver* (1774).

41 Philp (1957; 1958; 1959).

42 Philp (1996, 11).

43 Dowker (1889).

44 Fairclough & Plunkett (2000, 446-7).

45 'Roman Britain in 1994', *Britannia* 26 (1995), 357.

46 Kent Sites and Monuments Record No. 15810.

47 E.g. Barber (1999); Dulley (1967).

48 Johnson (1980).

49 Hinchliffe & Green (1985, Appendix IV, 194-5).

50 Bidwell (1997, Chapter 4).

51 James (2001, 82-4).

52 Bidwell (1997, 64-5).

53 Cunliffe (1976, 427).

54 Cunliffe (1968, 36).

55 Philp (1958, 164).

56 Brancaster, R. Jones in Hinchliffe & Green (1985); Caister, Darling & Gurney (1993, Chapter 8); Burgh Castle, Grant in Johnson (1983a).

57 See Breeze (1984).

58 Salway (1970, 13-14).

59 Jones (1964, 845).

60 Philp (1969).

61 'Summary of the Roman Coins from Richborough', in Cunliffe (1968).

62 See Reece (1987); Casey & Reece (1988).

63 Cunliffe (1976, 427).

8 The closing years

1 Esmonde Cleary (1989); Reece (1980). The quote is derived from Thomas Hobbes' *Leviathan* (1651, Pt. 1, Chapter 13).

2 Reece in Cunliffe (1980a).

3 Philp (1969).

4 H. Cool (pers. comm. in Darling & Gurney 1993, 251).

5 Wilson (1996, 265).

6 Peacock (1973).

7 Hinchliffe & Green (1985, Appendix IV and Table 30); St Joseph (1936).

8 Reece (1981).

9 Rigold (1977).

Bibliography

Adam, J.P., 1994. *Roman Building: Materials and Techniques*. London.

Akeroyd, A.V., 1972. 'Archaeological and historical evidence for subsidence in southern Britain', *Philosophical Transactions of the Royal Society of London A* 272, 151-69.

Albone, J., 2001. *Archaeological evaluation at land south of Norwich Road, Caister-on-Sea, Norfolk*. APS Report No. 031/01

Allen, J.R.L. & Fulford, M., 1999. 'Fort Building and Military Supply along Britain's Eastern Channel and North Sea Coasts: the later Second and Third Centuries', *Britannia* 30, 163-84.

Amos, E.G.J. & Wheeler, R.E.M., 1929. 'The Saxon-Shore Fortress at Dover', *Archaeological Journal* 86, 47-58.

Applebaum, S., 1972. 'Roman Britain', in Finberg, H.P.R. (ed.), *The Agrarian history of England and Wales*, 3-282. Cambridge.

Arnold, C.J. & Davies, J.L., 2000. *Roman and Early Medieval Wales*. Stroud.

Arthurton, R.S., Booth, S.J., Morigi, A.N., Abbott, M.A.W. & Wood, C.J., 1994. *Geology of the country around Great Yarmouth*. Memoir of the Geological Survey Sheet 162 (England and Wales). London.

Barber, L., 1999. 'Land adjacent to the Old Farmhouse, Pevensey, East Sussex', *Sussex Archaeological Collections* 137, 91-120.

Barford, P. unpublished. Bradwell, Essex: The Roman Shore Fort and Saxon Monastery and Church.

Bartholomew, P., 1984. 'Fourth-Century Saxons', *Britannia* 15, 169-85.

Bennett, J., 1990. *The Setting, Development and Function of the Hadrianic Frontier in Britain*. Ph.D. Thesis, University of Newcastle.

Bidwell, P., 1997. *Roman Forts in Britain*. London.

Bidwell, P. & Speak, S., 1994. *Excavations at South Shields Roman Fort, Volume 1*. The Society of Antiquaries of Newcastle upon Tyne Monograph Series No. 4.

Birley, A., 1971. *Septimius Severus: the African Emperor*. London.

Birley, A.R., 1981. *The Fasti of Roman Britain*. Oxford.

Blagg, T.F.C., 1984. 'Roman Architectural Ornament in Kent', *Archaeologia Cantiana* 100, 65-89.

Blagg, T.F.C., 1990. 'Building Stone in Roman Britain', in Parsons, D. (ed.), *Stone: Quarrying and Building in England AD43-1525*, 33-50. Chichester.

Blomefield, F., 1805. *An Essay towards a topographical history of the County of Norfolk*. London.

Boswell, P.G.H., 1928. *The Geology of the Country around Woodbridge, Felixstowe and Orford*. Memoir of the Geological Survey Sheets 208 and 225 (England and Wales). London.

Breeze, D.J., 1984. 'Demand and Supply on the Northern Frontier', in Miket, R. & Burgess, C. (eds), *Between and beyond the Walls: essays in honour of George Jobey*, 265-76. Edinburgh.

Brodribb, G., 1969. 'Stamped tiles of the "Classis Britannica"', *Sussex Archaeological Collections* 107, 102-25.

Brodribb, G., 1980. A further survey of stamped tiles of the Classis Britannica, *Sussex Archaeological Collections* 118, 183-96.

Brooks, N., 1988. 'Romney Marsh in the Early Middle Ages', in Eddison, J. & Green, C. (eds), *Romney Marsh: Evolution, Occupation, Reclamation*. Oxford University Committee for Archaeology Monograph No. 24, 90-104. Oxford.

Brulet, R., 1989. 'The Continental Litus Saxonicum', in Maxfield, V. (ed.), *The Saxon Shore: a handbook*, 45-77. Exeter.

Burnham, C.P., 1989. 'The coast of south-east England in Roman times', in Maxfield, V. (ed.), *The Saxon Shore: a handbook*, 12-17. Exeter.

Bushe-Fox, J.P., 1926. *First Report on the Excavation of the Roman Fort at Richborough, Kent.* Report of the Research Committee of the Society of Antiquaries of London VI.

Bushe-Fox, J.P., 1928. *Second Report on the Excavation of the Roman Fort at Richborough, Kent.* Report of the Research Committee of the Society of Antiquaries of London VII.

Bushe-Fox, J.P., 1932a. 'Some notes on Roman coastal defences', *Journal of Roman Studies* 22, 60-72.

Bushe-Fox, J.P., 1932b. *Third Report on the Excavation of the Roman Fort at Richborough, Kent.* Report of the Research Committee of the Society of Antiquaries of London X.

Bushe-Fox, J.P., 1949. *Fourth Report on the Excavation of the Roman Fort at Richborough, Kent.* Research Report of the Society of Antiquaries of London XVI.

Butler, R.M., 1959. 'Late Roman town walls in Gaul', *Archaeological Journal* 116, 25-50.

Camden, W., 1637. *Britannia.* London.

Canning, R., 1764. *The Suffolk Traveller; or, a Journey through Suffolk.* Woodbridge.

Casey, P.J., 1994. *Carausius and Allectus: The British Usurpers.* London.

Casey, P.J. & Reece, R., 1988. *Coins and the archaeologist.* London.

Casson, L., 1971. *Ships and Seamanship in the Ancient World.* Princeton, New Jersey.

Clayton, K.M., 1989. 'Sediment input from the Norfolk Cliffs, Eastern England – a century of coast protection and its effect', *Journal of Coastal Research* 5, 433-42.

Cleere, H., 1974. 'The Roman Iron Industry of the Weald and its connections with the Classis Britannica', *Archaeological Journal* 31, 171-99.

Cleere, H., 1978. 'Roman harbours in Britain south of Hadrian's Wall', in du Plat Taylor, J. & Cleere, H. (eds), *Roman Shipping and Trade: Britain and the Rhine Provinces.* CBA Research Report No. 24, 36-40.

Cleere, H. & Crossley, D., 1985. *The Iron Industry of the Weald.* Leicester.

Clowes, T., 1837. 'Caister, next Yarmouth', *Gents Magazine* New Series 8 (2), 518-21.

Cotterill, J., 1993. 'Saxon raiding and the role of the late Roman coastal forts of Britain', *Britannia* 24, 227-41.

Crickmore, J., 1984. *Romano-British Urban Defences.* BAR British Series No. 126.

Cunliffe, B., 1968. *Fifth Report on the Excavations of the Roman Fort at Richborough, Kent.* Research Report of the Society of Antiquaries of London XXIII.

Cunliffe, B., 1975. *Excavations at Portchester Castle I: Roman.* Research Report of the Society of Antiquaries of London XXXII.

Cunliffe, B., 1976. *Excavations at Portchester Castle II: Saxon.* Research Report of the Society of Antiquaries of London, XXXIII.

Cunliffe, B., 1980a. 'Excavations at the Roman Fort at Lympne, Kent 1976-78', *Britannia* 11, 227-88

Cunliffe, B., 1980b. 'The evolution of Romney Marsh: a preliminary statement', in Thompson, F.H. (ed.), *Archaeology and Coastal Change*, 37-55. London.

Cunliffe, B., 1988. Romney Marsh in the Roman Period, in Eddison, J. & Green, C. (eds), *Romney Marsh: Evolution, Occupation, Reclamation.* Oxford University Committee for Archaeology Monograph No. 24, 83-7. Oxford.

Cunliffe, B. & Garratt, B., 1994. *Excavations at Portchester Castle V: Post-medieval 1609-1819.* Research Report of the Society of Antiquaries of London LII.

Cunliffe, B. & Munby, J., 1985. *Excavations at Portchester Castle IV: Medieval, the inner bailey.* Research Report of the Society of Antiquaries of London XLIII.

Darling, M.J. & Gurney, D., 1993. *Caistor-on-Sea: Excavations by Charles Green 1951-55.* East Anglian Archaeology No. **60**.

Davies, R.W., 1989. *Service in the Roman Army.* Edinburgh.

De Boe, G., 1978. 'Roman boats from a small river harbour at Pommeroeul, Belgium', in Du Plat Taylor, J. & Cleere, H. (eds), *Roman Shipping and Trade: Britain and the Rhine Provinces.* CBA Research Report No. **24**, 22-31.

DeLaine, J., 1997. *The Baths of Caracalla: A study of the design, construction and economics of large-scale building projects in imperial Rome.* Portsmouth, R.I.

Devoy, 1979. 'Flandrian sea level changes and vegetational history of the lower Thames Estuary', *Philosophical Transactions of the Royal Society of London B* **285,** 355-407.

de Weerd, M.D., 1990. 'Barges of the Zwammerdam type and their building procedures', in McGrail, S. (ed.), *Maritime Celts, Frisians and Saxons.* CBA Research Report No. **71**, 75-6.

D'Olier, B., 1972. 'Subsidence and sea-level rise in the Thames estuary', *Philosophical Transactions of the Royal Society of London A* 272, 121-30

Dore, J.N. & Gillam, J.P., 1979. *The Roman Fort at South Shields*. Newcastle.

Dowker, G., 1878. 'The Roman Castrum at Reculver', *Archaeologia Cantiana* 12, 1-13.

Dowker, G., 1889. 'Excavations at Richborough in 1887', *Archaeologia Cantiana* 18, 6-15.

Dulley, A.J.F., 1966. 'The Level and Port of Pevensey in the Middle Ages', *Sussex Arch. Collections* 104, 26-46.

Dulley, A.J.F., 1967. 'Excavations at Pevensey, Sussex, 1962-6', *Medieval Archaeology* 11, 209-32.

Duncan-Jones, R., 1974. *The economy of the Roman Empire: quantitative studies*. London.

Duncan-Jones, R., 1978. 'Pay and Numbers in Diocletian's Army', *Chiron* 8, 173-93.

Eddison, J & Green, C. (eds). 1988. *Romney Marsh: Evolution, Occupation, Reclamation*. Oxford University Committee for Archaeology Monograph No. 24. Oxford.

Eddison, J. (ed.). 1995. *Romney Marsh, The Debatable Ground*. Oxford University Committee for Archaeology Monograph No. 41, 83-7. Oxford.

Eddison, J., 2000. *Romney Marsh: survival on a frontier*. Stroud.

Edwards, D., 1976. 'The Air Photographs Collection of the Norfolk Archaeological Unit', in Wade-Martins, P. (ed.), *East Anglian Archaeology*, 251-58. Dereham.

Edwards, D.A., 1983. 'Aerial Reconnaissance in 1981', *Aerial Archaeology* 7, 33-42.

Edwards, D.A. & Green, C.J.D., 1977. 'The Saxon Shore Fort and settlement at Brancaster, Norfolk', in Johnston, D.E. (ed.), *The Saxon Shore*. CBA Research Report No. 18, 21-9.

Edwards, J.G., 1946. 'Edward I's castle-building in Wales', *Proceedings of the British Academy* 32, 15-81.

Ellison, J.A., 1965. 'Excavations at Caister-on-Sea, 1961-2', *Norfolk Archaeology* 33, 95-103.

Ellison, J.A., 1969. 'Excavations at Caister-on-Sea, 1962-63', *Norfolk Archaeology* 34, 45-73.

Errington, J., MS 1969. *Report of a survey carried out at site of Walton Castle*. Ipswich Museum Parish Files.

Esmonde Cleary, A.S., 1989. *The Ending of Roman Britain*. London.

Everard, C.E., 1980. 'On Sea Level Changes', in Thompson, F.H. (ed.), *Archaeology and Coastal Change*, 1-23. London.

Fairclough, J. & Plunkett, S.J., 2000. 'Drawings of Walton Castle and other monuments in Walton and Felixstowe', *Proceedings of the Suffolk Institute of Archaeology* 39 (4), 419-35.

Fawn, A.J., Evans, K.A., Davies, G.M.R. & McMaster, I., 1990. *The Red Hills of Essex: Salt making in Antiquity*. Colchester.

Fowles, J., 1991. *A Short History of Lyme Regis*. Stanbridge.

Fox, G.E., 1911. 'Romano-British Suffolk', in Page, W. (ed.), *The Victoria History of the Counties of England: A History of Suffolk, Vol. 1*, 279-320. London.

Frere, S.S., 1984. 'British Urban Defences in Earthwork', *Britannia* 15, 63-74.

Frere, S.S., 1987. *Britannia: a history of Roman Britain*. London.

Fryer, J., 1973. 'The harbour installations of Roman Britain', in Blackman, D.J. (ed.), *Marine archaeology*, 261-73. Bristol.

Fulford, M.G., 1984. *Silchester: Excavations on the defences 1974-80* Britannia Monograph Series No. 5. London.

Fulford, M.G., 1996. *The Second Augustan Legion in the west of Britain*. Cardiff.

Fulford, M.G., Champion, T. & Long, A., 1997. *England's Coastal Heritage: A survey for English Heritage and the RCHME*. English Heritage Archaeological Report No. 15.

Fulford, M.G. & Hodder, I.R., 1975. 'A regression Analysis of some Late Romano-British Pottery: a case study', *Oxeniensia* 39, 26-33.

Fulford, M.G. & Tyers, I., 1995. 'The date of Pevensey and the defence of an "Imperium Britanniarum"', *Antiquity* 69, 1009-14.

Garnsey, P., 1983. 'Famine in Rome', in Garnsey, P. & Whittaker, C.R. (eds), *Trade and Famine in Classical Antiquity*, 57-65. Cambridge.

Gathercole, P.W. & Cotton, M.A., 1958. *Excavations at Clausentum, Southampton*. Archaeological Reports 2. London.

George, W.H., 1984. 'A short account of the cement stone industry of the Isle of Sheppey, Kent', *Tertiary Research* 5 (4), 165-8.

Goldthwaite, R., 1980. *The Building of Renaissance Florence: an economic and social history*. Baltimore.

Gonzalez, J., 1986. 'The Lex Irnitana: a New Copy of the Flavian Municipal Law', *Journal of Roman Studies* **76**, 147-244.

Goodburn, R. & Bartholomew, P., 1976. *Aspects of the Notitia Dignitatum*. BAR Supplementary Series No. 15.

Goodsall, R.H., 1981. *The Kentish Stour*. Rochester.

Green, C., 1961. 'East Anglian Coast-line Levels Since Roman Times', *Antiquity* 35, 21-8.

Green, C., 1963. *Sutton Hoo*. London.

Green, C., 1988. 'Paleogeography of marine inlets of the Romney Marsh area', in Eddison, J. & Green, C. (eds), *Romney Marsh: Evolution, Occupation, Reclamation*. Oxford University Committee for Archaeology Monograph No. 24, 167-74. Oxford.

Green, C. & Hutchinson, J.N., 1960. 'Archaeological Evidence', in Lambert, J.M., Smith, J.N., Green, C.T. & Hutchinson, J.N. (eds), *The making of the Broads*. Memoir of the Royal Geographical Society No. 3.

Green, R.D., 1968. *Soils of Romney Marsh*. Soil Survey of Great Britain Bulletin 4. Harpenden.

Greensmith, J.T. & Tucker, E.V., 1971. 'The effects of late Pleistocene and Holocene sea-level changes in the vicinity of the river Crouch, east Essex', *Proceedings of the Geologists' Association* 82, 301-22.

Greensmith, J.T. & Tucker, E.V., 1973. 'Holocene transgressions and regressions on the Essex coast outer Thames estuary', *Geologie en Mijnbouw* 52, 193-202.

Gros, P., 1985. 'Le role de la scaenographia dans les projets architectraux du debut de l'empire romain', in *Le dessin d'architecture dans les societes antiques. Actes du Colloque de Strasbourg, 26-28 janvier 1984*. Leiden.

Gros, P., 1996. 'Les illustrations du De Architectura de Vitruve. Histoire d'un malentendu', in Nicolet, C. (ed.), *Les Litteratures techniques dans l'antiquite Romaine*, 19-44. Geneva.

Gurney, D., 1995. *Burgh Castle: The Extra-Mural Survey*. Dereham.

Hagar, J., 1987. 'A new plan for Walton Castle', *Archaeology Today* 8 (1), 22-25.

Hanson, W.S., 1978. 'The organisation of the Roman military timber supply', *Britannia* 9, 293-307.

Hanson, W.S., 1996. 'Forest clearance and the Roman army', *Britannia* 27, 354-57.

Harrison, A.C., 1970. 'Excavations in Rochester', *Archaeologia Cantiana* 85, 95-112.

Harrison, A.C. & Flight, C., 1968. 'The Roman and Medieval Defences of Rochester in the Light of Recent Excavations', *Archaeologia Cantiana* 83, 55-104.

Harrod, H., 1859. 'Notice of excavations made at Burgh Castle, Suffolk, in the years 1850 and 1855', *Norfolk Archaeology* 5, 146-60.

Haselberger, L., 1997. 'Architectural likenesses: models and plans of architecture in classical antiquity', *Journal of Roman Archaeology* 10, 77-94.

Hawkes, S.C., 1968. 'The physical geography of Richborough', in Cunliffe, B. (ed.), *Fifth Report on the Excavations of the Roman Fort at Richborough, Kent*, 224-30.

Hillam, J. & Morgan, R.A., 1986. 'Tree-ring analysis of the Roman timbers', in Miller, L., Schofield, J. & Rhodes, M. (eds), *The Roman Quay at St. Magnus House, London*, 74-86. London.

Hinchliffe, J. & Green, C.S., 1985. *Excavations at Brancaster, 1974 and 1977*. East Anglian Archaeology Report No. 23.

Hind, J.G.F., 1980. 'Litus Saxonicum – the meaning of Saxon Shore', in Hanson, W.S. & Keppie, L.J.F. (eds), *Roman Frontier Studies 1979: papers presented to the 12th International Congress of Roman Frontier Studies*, 317-25.

Holder, P.A., 1982. *The Roman Army in Britain*. London.

Holmes, S.C.A., 1981. *Geology of the country around Faversham* Memoir of the Geological Survey (England and Wales) Sheet 273.

Horne, E.A., 1977. 'Air Reconnaissance, 1975-1977', *Aerial Archaeology* 1, 16-20.

Hutchinson, J.N., Poole, C., Lambert, N. & Bromhead, E.N., 1985. 'Combined Archaeological and Geotechnical Investigations of the Roman Fort at Lympne, Kent', *Britannia* 16, 209-36.

James, S., 1984. 'Britain and the late Roman army', in Blagg, T.F.C. & King, A.C. (eds), *Military and civilian in Roman Britain: Cultural Relationships in a Frontier Province*. British Archaeological Report No. 136, 161-83.

James, S., 2001. 'Soldiers and civilians: identity and interaction in Roman Britain', in James, S. & Millett, M. (eds), *Britons and Romans: advancing an archaeological agenda*. CBA Research Report No. 125, 77-89.

Jennings, S. & Smyth, C., 1987. 'Coastal Sedimentation in East Sussex during the Holocene', *Progress in Oceanography* 18, 205-41.

Jennings, S. & Smyth, C., 1990. 'Holocene Evolution of the gravel coastline of East Sussex', *Proceedings of the Geologists' Association* 101(3), 213-24.

Johnson, A., 1975. 'A Roman Signal Tower at Shadwell, E.1., an interim note', *Transactions of the London and Middlesex Archaeological Society* 26, 278-80.

Johnson, J.S., 1970. 'The date of the construction of the Saxon Shore Fort at Richborough', *Britannia* 11, 240-8.

Johnson, S., 1976. *The Roman Forts of the Saxon Shore*. London.

Johnson, S., 1980. 'A Late Roman Helmet from Burgh Castle', *Britannia* 11, 303-12.

Johnson, S., 1983a. *Burgh Castle: excavations by Charles Green, 1958-61*. East Anglian Archaeology No. 20.

Johnson, S., 1983b. *Late Roman Fortifications*. London.

Johnson, S., 1989. 'The architecture of the Shore Forts', in Maxfield, V. (ed.), *The Saxon Shore*, 30-44. Exeter.

Johnston, D.E., 1977. *The Saxon Shore*. CBA Research Report No. 18.

Jones, A.H.M., 1964. *The Later Roman Empire, 284-602*. Oxford.

Kendal, R., 1996. 'Transport Logistics Associated with the Building of Hadrian's Wall', *Britannia* 27, 129 52.

King, A., 1989. 'Roman Bitterne in the third and fourth centuries', *Hampshire Field Club & Archaeological Society: Section Newsletters (Archaeology)* 11, 19-20.

King, A., 1990. 'Bitterne redating confirmed', *Hampshire Field Club & Archaeological Society: Section Newsletters (Archaeology)* 13, 29.

Kirby, J., 1735. *The Suffolk Traveller; or, a Journey through Suffolk*. Ipswich.

Knight, B.H. & Knight, R.G., 1955. *Builders' Materials*. London.

Laurence, R. & Wallace-Hadrill, A., 1997. *Domestic space in the Roman world: Pompeii and beyond*. Portsmouth, R.I.

Lavender, N.J., 2000. *Othona, Bradwell on Sea, Essex. Archaeological Survey: synthesis of results*. Chelmsford.

Lee Warner, R.J.L., 1851. 'Notices of the original structure of the Roman fortifications at Brancaster (The ancient Branodunum), Norfolk', in *Memoirs illustrative of the History and Antiquities of Norfolk and the City of Norwich*, 9-16. London.

Leland, J., 1907. *The itinerary of John Leland in or about the Years 1535-1543*. London.

Lemmon, C.H. & Hill, J.D., 1966. 'The Roman-British site at Bodiam', *Archaeologia Cantiana* 104, 86-102.

Lewin, T., 1867. 'On the Castra of the Littus Saxonicum, and particularly the Castrum of Othona', *Archaeologia* 41, 421-52.

Lyne, M., unpublished. *Excavations at Pevensey 1936-1964*.

Mann, J.C., 1977. 'The Reculver Inscription \ a note', in Johnston, D.E. (ed.), *The Saxon Shore*. CBA Research Report No. 18, 15.

Mann, J.C., 1989. 'The historical development of the Saxon Shore', in Maxfield, V. (ed.), *The Saxon Shore: a handbook*, 1-11. Exeter.

Marsden, P., 1994. *Ships of the Port of London: first to eleventh centuries AD*. English Heritage Archaeology Report No. 3.

May, V.J., 1966. *A preliminary study of recent coastal change and sea defences in South east England* Southampton Research Series in Geography 3. Southampton University.

McGrail, S., 1987. *The ancient boats of north-west Europe*. London.

Medlycott, M., 1994. 'The Othona Community site, Bradwell-on-Sea, Essex: the extra mural settlement', *Essex Archaeology and History* 25, 60-71.

Millett, M., 1979. 'The Dating of Farnham Pottery', *Britannia* 10, 121-38.

Millett, M., 1990. *The Romanisation of Britain*. Cambridge.

Milne, G., 1985. *The Port of Roman London*. London.

Milne, G., 1990. 'Maritime traffic between the Rhine and Roman Britain: a preliminary note', in McGrail, S. (ed.), *Maritime Celts, Frisians and Saxons*. CBA Research Report No. 71, 82-85.

Mitchell, G.F., 1977. 'Raised beaches and sea levels', in Shotton, F.W. (ed.), *British Quarternary Studies*, 169-86. Oxford.

Moffat, B., 1986. The environment of Battle Abbey estates (East Sussex) in medieval times; a re-evaluation using analysis of pollen and sediments, *Landscape History* 8, 77-89.

Morris, A.J., 1947. 'The Saxon Shore Fort at Burgh Castle', *Proceedings of the Suffolk Institute of Archaeology* 24, 100-120.

Munby, J.T., 1990. *Portchester Castle*. London.

Murphy, P. & Funnell, B.M., 1985. 'A preliminary study of the Holocene coastal sediments at Brancaster Marsh', in Hinchliffe, J. & Green, C.S. (eds), *Excavations at Brancaster 1974 and 1977*, 182-85.

Nash-Williams, 1969. *The Roman Frontier in Wales*. Cardiff.

Nayling, N., Maynard, D. & McGrail, S., 1994. 'Barlands Farm, Magor, Gwent: a Romano-Celtic boat', *Antiquity* 68, 596-603.

Needham, S., 1988. 'A group of Early Bronze Age axes from Lydd', in Eddison, J. & Green, C. (eds), *Romney Marsh: Evolution, Occupation, Reclamation*. Oxford University Committee for Archaeology Monograph No. 24, 77-82. Oxford.

Ogilvie, J.D., 1968. 'The Fleet Causeway', in Cunliffe, B. (ed.), *Fifth Report on the Excavations of the Roman Fort at Richborough, Kent*, 37-39.

Peacock, D.P.S., 1973. 'Forged brick-stamps from Pevensey', *Antiquity* 47, 138-40.

Peacock, D.P.S., 1977. 'Bricks and Tiles of the "Classis Britannica": Petrology and Origin', *Britannia* 8, 235-48.

Pearson, A.F., 1995. *Building Anderita: the construction of the Saxon Shore Fort at Pevensey*. M.A. Dissertation, University of Reading.

Pearson, A.F., 1999a. 'Building Anderita: late Roman coastal defences and the construction of the Saxon Shore Fort at Pevensey', *Oxford Journal of Archaeology* 18 (1), 95-117.

Pearson, A.F., 1999b. *The Saxon Shore Forts: an economic and contextual study*. Ph.D. Thesis, University of Reading.

Pearson, A.F. 2002a. 'Stone supply to the Saxon Shore Forts at Reculver', Richborough, Dover and Lympne. *Archaeologia Cantiana* 122.

Pearson, A.F. 2002b. *The construction of the Saxon Shore Forts*. BAR British Series.

Petrikovits, H. von, 1971. 'Fortifications in the North-western Roman Empire from the Third to the Fifth Centuries A.D', *Journal of Roman Studies* 61, 178-219.

Philp, B.J., 1957. 'Recent discoveries at Reculver', *Archaeologia Cantiana* 71, 167-81.

Philp, B.J., 1958. 'Discoveries at Reculver 1955-57', *Archaeologia Cantiana* 72, 160-66.

Philp, B.J., 1959. 'Reculver: Excavations on the Roman Fort in 1957', *Archaeologia Cantiana* 73, 96-115.

Philp, B.J., 1969. 'The Roman fort at Reculver', *Archaeological Journal* **126**, 223-25.

Philp, B.J., 1981a. *The Excavations of the Roman Forts of the Classis Britannica at Dover 1970-77*. Kent Monograph Series 3.

Philp, B.J., 1981b. 'Richborough, Reculver and Lympne: A reconsideration of three of Kent's late-Roman Shore-Forts', in Detsicas, A. (ed.), *Collectanea Historica: Essays in memory of Stuart Rigold*, 41-49. Maidstone.

Philp, B.J., 1982. 'Romney Marsh and the Roman Fort at Lympne', *Kent Archaeological Review* 68, 175-91.

Philp, B.J., 1989. *The Roman House with bacchic murals at Dover*. Dover Castle.

Philp, B.J., 1996. *The Roman fort at Reculver*. Dover.

Philp, B.J. & Willson, J., 1984. 'Roman site at Scotney Court, Lydd', *Kent Archaeological Review* 77, 156-61.

Press, M.H., 1956. 'The seven havens of Great Yarmouth and their bridges', *Edgar Allen News* 35, 272-74.

Pugh, R.B., 1963. *The Victoria History of the Counties of England: A History of Essex*. London.

RCHM(E), 1923. *An Inventory of the Historical Monuments in Essex (South East)*. London.

Reece, R., 1980. 'Town and Country; the end of Roman Britain', *World Archaeology* 12, 77-92.

Reece, R., 1981. 'The Roman Coins from Richborough - A Summary', *Bulletin of the Institute of Archaeology, University of London* 18, 49-71.

Reece, R., 1987. *Coinage in Roman Britain*. London.

Reece, R., 1997. *The future of Roman Military Archaeology*. The Tenth Annual Caerleon Lecture. Cardiff.

Reeve, A., 1995. 'Romney Marsh: the Field-Walking Evidence', in Eddison, J. (ed.), *Romney Marsh: The Debatable Ground*. Oxford University Committee for Archaeology Monograph No. 41, 78-91. Oxford.

Richmond, I.A., 1961. 'A new inscription from the Saxon Shore Fort at Reculver, Kent', *Antiquaries Journal* 41, 224-28.

Rigold, S.E., 1961. 'The Supposed See of Dunwich', *Journal of the British Archaeological Association* 114, 55-59.

Rigold, S.E., 1969a. 'The Roman Haven of Dover', *Archaeological Journal* 126, 78-100.

Rigold, S.E., 1969b. 'The earliest defences of Carisbrooke Castle', *Chateau Gaillard* 3, 128-38.

Rigold, S.E., 1974. 'The Site of 'Dummoc': further evidence', *Journal of the British Archaeological Association* 127, 97-102.

Rigold, S.E., 1977. 'Litus Romanum – the Saxon Shore as mission stations', in Johnston, D.E. (ed.), *The Saxon Shore*. CBA Research Report No. 18, 70-75.

Rivet, A.L.F. & Smith, C., 1979. *The Place Names of Roman Britain*. London.

Roach Smith, C., 1850. *The Antiquities of Richborough, Reculver and Lympne in Kent*. London.

Roach Smith, C., 1852. *Report on Excavations made on the site of the Roman Castrum at Lympne in Kent in 1850*. Lympne Castle, Kent.

Robertson, A.S., 1988. *Coins and the Archaeologist*. London.

Robinson, A.H.W. & Cloet, R.L., 1953. 'Coastal Evolution in Sandwich Bay', *Proceedings of the Geologists' Association* 64, 69-82.

Rolfe, W., 1843. *The History of Richborough Castle, near Sandwich, Kent*. Sandwich.

Rose, E.J., 1985. 'A note on the demolition of the walls of the Roman fort', in Hinchliffe, J. & Green, C.S. (eds), *Excavations at Brancaster 1974 and 1977*, 188-89.

Rose, E.J., 1994. 'The Church of Saint John the Baptist, Reedham, Norfolk: the re-use of Roman materials in a secondary context', *Journal of the British Archaeological Association* 147, 1-8.

St Joseph, J.K.S., 1936. 'The Roman Fort at Brancaster', *Antiquaries Journal* 16, 444-60.

Salway, P., 1970. 'The Roman Fenland', in Phillips, C.W. (ed.), *The Fenland in Roman Times*, 1-21. London.

Salway, P., 1993. *The Oxford Illustrated History of Roman Britain*. London.

Salzman, L.F., 1907. 'Excavations at Pevensey 1906-7', *Sussex Archaeological Collections* 51, 99-114.

Salzman, L.F., 1908. 'Excavations at Pevensey 1907-8', *Sussex Archaeological Collections* 52, 83-95.

Salzman, L.F., 1910. 'The Inning of the Pevensey Levels', *Sussex Archaeological Collections* 54, 32-60.

Sands, H., 1908. *Excavations at Pevensey Castle 1908*. London.

Sear, F., 1982. *Roman Architecture*. London.

Sheldon, H.L. & Tyers, I., 1983. 'Recent dendrochronological work in London and its implications', *The London Archaeologist* 4 (13), 355-61.

Shephard-Thorn, E.R., 1988. *Geology of the country around Ramsgate and Dover*. London.

Shirley, E.A.M., 1996. 'The Building of the Legionary Fortress at Inchtuthil', *Britannia* 27, 111-28.

Shirley, E.A.M., 2000. *The Construction of the Roman legionary fortress at Inchtuthil*. Oxford.

Simmons, B.B., 1978. 'Ancient coastlines around the Wash', *South Lincolnshire Archaeology* 1, 6-9.

So, L.C., 1966. 'Some coastal changes between Whitstable and Reculver, Kent', *Proceedings of the Geologists' Association* 77, 475-90.

Sommer, C.S., 1984. *The Military Vici in Roman Britain. Aspects of their Origins, their Location and Layout, Administration, Function and End*. BAR British Series No. 129.

Southern, P. & Dixon, K.R., 1996. *The Late Roman Army*. London.

Steers, J.A., 1960. *Scolt Head Island*. Cambridge.

Stevens, C.E., 1941. 'The British sections of the Notitia Dignitatum', *Archaeological Journal* 97, 125-54.

Taylor, M.V. & Wilson, D.R., 1961. 'Roman Britain in 1960', *Journal of Roman Studies* 51, 157-91.

Taylor, R.C., 1827. 'On the geology of East Norfolk; with remarks upon the hypothesis of Mr Robberds, respecting the former level of the German Ocean', *Philosophical Magazine* series 2, volume 1.

Tooley, M. & Switsur, R., 1988. 'Water level changes and sedimentation during the Flandrian Age in the Romney Marsh area', in Eddison, J. & Green, C. (eds), *Romney Marsh: Evolution, Occupation, Reclamation*. Oxford University Committee for Archaeology Monograph No. 24, 53-71. Oxford.

Wacher, J.S., 1969. *Excavations at Brough-on-Humber 1958-61* Research Report of the Research Committee of the Society of Antiquaries of London XXV.

Wacher, J.S., 1995. *The Towns of Roman Britain*. London.

Waddelove, A.C. & Waddelove, E., 1990. 'Archaeology and Research into sea level during the Roman era: towards a methodology based on Highest Astronomical Tide', *Britannia* 21, 253-66.

Walford, T, 1812. 'Observations on the Situation of Camulodunum', in a Letter from Thomas Walford, Esq. F.A.S. to Samuel Lysons, Esq. F.R.S. Director, *Archaeologia* 16, 145-50.

Wall, S.D., 1937. 'Historic Felixstowe. The Roman station', *Felixstowe Times*, 13 March 1937.

Waller, M., Burrin, P. & Marlow, A., 1988. 'Flandrian sedimentation and paleoenvironments in Pett Level, the Brede and lower Rother valleys and Walland Marsh', in Eddison, J. & Green, C. (eds), *Romney Marsh: Evolution, Occupation, Reclamation*. Oxford University Committee for Archaeology Monograph No. 24, 3-30. Oxford.

Wallis, H., 1998. 'Excavations at Church Loke, Burgh Castle, 1993-4', *Norfolk Archaeology* 43 (1), 62-78.

Ward, J., 1901. 'Cardiff Castle: its Roman origin', *Archaeologia* 57, 335-52.

Wardill, R., 2000. *Othona, Bradwell on Sea, Essex. Geophysical Survey Report*. Chelmsford.

Watson, A., 1999. *Aurelian and the third century*. London.

Webster, P., 1981. 'Cardiff Castle Excavations 1974-1981', *Morgannwg* 25, 201-11.

Wheeler, R.E.M., 1929. 'The Roman lighthouses at Dover', *Archaeological Journal* 86, 28-46.

Whitaker, W. & Dowker, G., 1885.' Excursion to Canterbury, Reculvers, Pegwell Bay and Richborough', *Proceedings of the Geologists' Association* 9, 168-77.

White, D.A., 1961. *Litus Saxonicum: the British Saxon Shore in scholarship and history*. Wisconsin.

Whitwell, J.B., 1970. *Roman Lincolnshire*. Lincoln.

Wilkinson, D.R.P., 1994. 'Excavations on the White Cliffs Experience site, Dover 1988-91', *Archaeoogia Cantiana* 114, 51-148.

Wilkinson, T.J. & Murphy, P., 1987. *The Hullbridge Basin Survey, Interim Report No.7*. Chelmsford.

Wilkinson, T.J. & Murphy, P.L., 1995. *The Archaeology of the Essex Coast, Volume I: The Hullbridge Survey* East Anglian Archaeology Report No. 71.

Williams, T., 1993. *The archaeology of Roman London, vol.3: public buildings in the south-west quarter of Roman London*. CBA Research Report No. 88.

Wilson, D.R., 1969. 'Roman Britain in 1968', *Journal of Roman Studies* 59, 198-234.

Wilson, R.J.A., 1980. *Roman forts*. London.

Wilson, R.J.A., 1996. *A guide to the Roman remains in Britain*. London.

Wood, I., 1990. 'The Channel from the fourth to the seventh centuries A.D', in McGrail, S. (ed.), *Maritime Celts, Frisians and Saxons*. CBA Research Report No. 71, 93-8.

Wood, M., 1999. *The Collapse and Recovery of the Roman Empire*. London.

Worssam, B.C. & Tatton-Brown, T., 1990. 'The Stone of the Reculver Columns and the Reculver Cross', in Parsons, D. (ed.), *Stone: Quarrying and Building in England AD43-1525*, 51-69. Chichester

Worssam, B.C. & Tatton-Brown, T., 1993. 'Kentish Rag and other Kent building stones', *Archaeologia Cantiana* 112, 93-126.

Young, C.J., 1983. 'The Lower Enclosure at Carisbrooke Castle, Isle of Wight', in Hartley, B.R. & Wacher, J.S. (eds), *Rome and Her Northern Provinces*, 290-301. Gloucester.

Index

Page numbers in **bold** denote illustrations